VoiceXML 2.0
Developer's Guide

Building Professional Voice-Enabled
Applications with JSP™, ASP, & ColdFusion®

About the Authors

Charul Shukla is a senior programmer at DreamTech Software India, Inc. He has an excellent track record designing and implementing large-scale applications for the latest environments. An expert in web-based development and voice-based applications, he is actively engaged in designing and developing solutions using VoiceXML and related technologies.

Avnish Dass and Vikas Gupta are the co-founders of DreamTech Software India, Inc. Avnish is a talented and seasoned programmer with 15 years of experience in systems and database programming. He has developed numerous security systems, anti-virus programs, wireless and communication technologies, and voice-based solutions. Vikas holds a B.E. in electronics, with postgraduate degrees in sales and marketing and in Publishing and Printing Studies. He is currently engaged in developing and designing new technologies for wireless and voice-based applications, e-learning, and other cutting-edge areas.

VoiceXML 2.0
Developer's Guide

Building Professional Voice-Enabled Applications with JSP™, ASP, & ColdFusion®

Dreamtech Software India, Inc.

McGraw-Hill/Osborne

New York   Chicago   San Francisco
Lisbon   London   Madrid   Mexico City
Milan   New Delhi   San Juan
Seoul   Singapore   Sydney   Toronto

McGraw-Hill/Osborne
2600 Tenth Street
Berkeley, California 94710
U.S.A.

To arrange bulk purchase discounts for sales promotions, premiums, or fund-raisers, please contact **McGraw-Hill**/Osborne at the above address. For information on translations or book distributors outside the U.S.A., please see the International Contact Information page immediately following the index of this book.

VoiceXML 2.0 Developer's Guide: Building Professional Voice-Enabled Applications with JSP™, ASP, & ColdFusion®

1234567890 FGR FGR 0198765432

ISBN 0-07-222458-4

Publisher	Brandon A. Nordin
Vice President & Associate Publisher	Scott Rogers
Editorial Director	Wendy Rinaldi
Senior Project Editor	Carolyn Welch
Acquisitions Coordinator	Tim Madrid
Technical Editor	DreamTech Software India, Inc.
Copy Editor	Ami Knox
Proofreader	Susie Elkind
Indexer	Claire Splan
Computer Designers	Elizabeth Jang, Jim Kussow
Illustrators	Michael Mueller, Jackie Sieben, Lyssa Wald
Series Design	Roberta Steele
Cover Series Design	Greg Scott
Cover Illustration	Eliot Bergman

This book was composed with Corel VENTURA™ Publisher.

To our parents, family and colleagues, and our beloved country, India, for providing an excellent environment in which to nurture and create world-class IT talent.

Contents at a Glance

Contents

Acknowledgments

We thank the following individuals: **Ankur Verma** and **Deepak Kumar Sharma** for their contributions in developing the content for this book and meticulously analyzing the technical aspects of the subject, and **V. K. Rajan** for perusing the text in detail and providing valuable suggestions for organizing the content.

We would also like to thank Brandon Nordin and Derek Stordahl of McGraw-Hill/ Osborne, our friends for many years. It was a pleasure working with them.

Special thanks go to Wendy Rinaldi, Timothy Madrid, Ami Knox, and the rest of the editorial team at McGraw-Hill/Osborne for their assistance in the production of this book.

Preface

Perhaps the most unread part of any book is the preface. However, this preface contains some very useful tidbits, and it might do you good not to skip it. Read on to find out what this book is all about and whether it's right for you.

Who Is This Book For?

This book targets professionals who want to develop voice-based applications using VoiceXML as well as those new to developing such applications. The schema of the book addresses both advanced as well as intermediate-level programmers.

What Is Special About This Book?

This book explains the techniques of developing VoiceXML-based voice applications in a manner notably different from that of other books on this topic. Some of the unique features of this book include the following:

- ▶ Detailed discussion of the predevelopment stages of voice-based applications to provide explicit guidelines that clarify subsequent techniques and processes

- ▶ Exhaustive examination of such issues as user interface and design considerations

- ▶ Extensive coverage of VoiceXML 2.0 and related technologies such as speech recognition grammar format and CCXML

- ▶ Systematic and detailed analysis of all major functionalities of VoiceXML 2.0

- ▶ Four ready-to-use case studies covering major development aspects along with detailed code analysis

Every program and code snippet in this book is tested in the DreamTech Software Research Lab, and you can directly use them in your applications.

This book also contains a host of useful tips and last minute solutions that will prove to be quite handy in developing voice-based applications in VoiceXML.

Prerequisites for Using This Book

Most of the programs in this book use VoiceXML and related technologies. The book provides extensive and specifically planned coverage of VoiceXML that primarily aims at application developers as its target audience. You should be well acquainted with web technologies such as HTML and ASP before reading this book.

The book is designed in such a fashion that even if you have little or no prior experience in developing voice applications, you should not have any difficulty in learning the subject. Yet, any experience with or knowledge of voice-based systems such as IVRs will serve to steer you faster through the book.

It is assumed that you are familiar with the Extensive Markup Language (XML) and its syntax. Some prior experience in working in an XML-based language will help you to grasp the subject faster and avoid common mistakes such as improper syntax.

What Is The Target Test Platform?

All of the sample programs and code snippets based on the VoiceXML in this book were fully tested on a desktop PC using Motorola Application Development Kit version 3.0. In addition, the VoiceXML grammars and the sample code in Chapter 5 were tested using the Tellme Network online testing facility called Tellme Studio. All the code in Chapter 10 was tested using the Windows 2000 Server with the Microsoft Web Telephony engine installed on it. And finally, the code in Chapter 12 was tested using the Motorola Application Development Kit version 2.0.

What Is Special About the Accompanying Programs?

Every chapter contains a set of instructions for executing the code it contains. These sets of instructions were developed based on test executions, taking care to make them complete and explicit.

You can download the sample code and programs from Osborne's web site at http://www.Osborne.com.

How Do I Contact the Authors?

If you have any queries or points for discussion, please do contact us. Our mailing address is admin@dreamtechsoftware.com. We will be pleased to inform and enlighten you to the best of our aptitude.

Introduction

TDreamTech Software India, Inc. is a software solution and service provider that succeeded in commanding a strong global presence in a competitive environment just a short while after its inception.

We provide a broad range of services and offer a dynamic blend of consulting and system integration solutions to help corporations design and implement innovative business strategies on the fast track of e-economy.

Our objective is to go beyond the obvious conventions. A futuristic vision motivates the globally acclaimed software products of DreamTech Software. Our talented pool of 40-strong professionals spares no pains in striving to create and provide competitive solutions for the latest software driven areas.

DreamTech Software has already distinguished itself with an excellent track record of publishing books on advanced technologies, including XML and XSLT, WAP, Bluetooth, and 3G and peer-to-peer networking.

The success of DreamTech's endeavors to provide world-class software products can be gauged by the fact that its clientele already includes some of the most distinguished names in IT-related publishing and IT-based solutions.

Web and Voice Technologies

IN THIS CHAPTER:

Ⅰn this chapter, we present an account of the evolution of modern voice technologies and the basic techniques involved in electronic communication through the medium of voice.

By the late 20th century, the computer distinguished itself as a key player in every human activity, be it business, research, engineering, or entertainment. What gave the computer even greater importance was the invention of the World Wide Web. By bringing the entire globe under its orb, the World Wide Web opened before us a new world characterized by the use of computer applications in every field.

Voice and web technologies assumed a definite shape in the last decade of the 20th century and soon sparked a series of unprecedented changes in the way people interact long distance. Today there are a host of competent technologies, such as VoiceXML, that facilitate fast and accurate transfer of information all over the world.

Here you'll learn about VoiceXML, a novel and interesting technology, beginning with a glimpse of the history of its evolution and a brief introduction.

Introduction to Telephone Systems

In 1886, the Bell Telephone Company introduced a 50-line magneto switchboard in Canada. This instrument, which was used to switch calls between two towns of Canada, marked the beginning of the present day worldwide telephony networks. In later years, particularly in the early 20th century, the telephone industry witnessed a remarkable growth. Thanks to this growth, telephones today have become an inseparable part of our lives, and the telephony networks, by connecting almost the entire world, have virtually turned the world into a global village. You will be able to appreciate these networks by going through the following discussion, which focuses on the key aspects of telephone systems.

Public Switched Telephone Network

Although the Public Switched Telephone Network (PSTN) is today's most popular architecture for worldwide telephony environments, the first-ever telephone architecture, invented by Alexander Graham Bell, was not based on the PSTN model. Bell's architecture was based on the *interconnected model*. With this architecture, to facilitate a telephone call between two persons, one located at, say, Dallas and the other at Seattle, their telephone instruments need to be connected through a dedicated wire. The visual layout of Bell's interconnected telephone model is shown in Figure 1-1.

Within the first few months of working with the interconnected model, it became obvious that this model was incapable of meeting the exacting and ever-increasing demands of the world of communication. A major shortcoming was that it called for an increase in the number of connecting wires with the rising number of subscribers, which would mean managing a complex network of wires. Consequently, a more efficient system became necessary. Soon, another breakthrough came with the introduction of switching technology in the telephone system architecture.

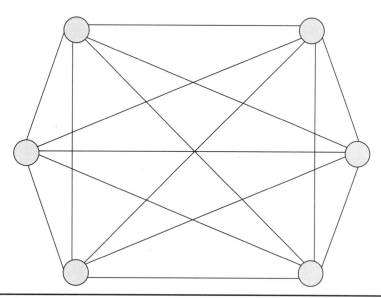

Figure 1-1   *Bell's interconnected telephone model*

This new system featured a *central office*, and every subscriber was connected to this office through a copper wire, rather than to one another as in the interconnected model. Figure 1-2 shows a schematic representation of this system.

In the *centralized switching system*, a caller is first connected to the switching office operator, and then the operator manually connects the caller to the desired receiver using a simple jumper cable system. Before long, such switching offices were set up in most areas and had people asking for long-distance calls between cities or states. With this increased

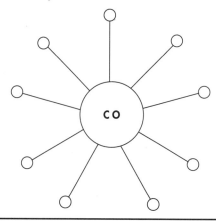

Figure 1-2   *Centralized switching system model*

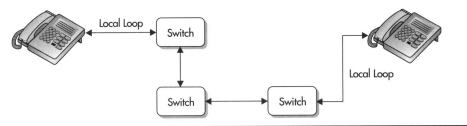

Figure 1-3   *A call passes through multiple switches before connecting to the receiver.*

demand, the problem faced in Bell's architecture resurfaced. Each central office was required to be connected to switching offices located in other cities or states, for which intercity or interstate cables had to be laid. To overcome this problem, a second level of switching was introduced. This was soon followed by more advanced levels of switching systems.

Today, the telephony architecture is based on a multiple-level hierarchy that works through multiple-level switching offices distributed around the world. Each telephone is usually connected with a pair of copper wires to the nearest local central office, at a distance of about 1 to 5 km. Let's see how this current model actually works.

Every phone is connected to a *connecting office* (CO) via a local loop system. The CO switch supplies a small amount of current to the line connected to the telephony device. All telephony devices are equipped with an on/off switch, often called a *hook switch*. When you put down the receiver on the cradle, the hook switch is turned off to disconnect the flow of current.

When the subscriber picks up the phone, the hook switch closes to complete the circuit. This results in current flow between the local loop and the instrument, thereby facilitating a call. To make a call, two types of dialing systems are used—the *touch-tone dialing system* and the *pulse-based dialing system.*

Let's examine how a simple call is placed on the network. Each telephone has a uniquely assigned number for its identification over the network. The number is generally seven digits. The first three digits serve to identify the switch and the remaining identify the line number attached to the switching equipment. For example, if the number is 1234567, then the digits 123 identify the corresponding switch and the digits 4567 identify the line number attached to the switch. A call can be passed on to multiple switches for connecting to the receiver device. This process is schematically shown in Figure 1-3.

Apart from the PSTN model, a few other models of telephone architecture do exist. However, these serve special purposes, and are not intended for supplying telephone services to the masses.

Introduction to Computer Telephony

The latest development in telecommunication is *computer telephony*, and its popularity is rising by the day. Whenever a computer or a computer-based device is used to handle any kind of telephony call, we consider the process an example of computer telephony.

Computer telephony is a very general term; but when we talk about computer telephony integration, it means that a computer, and not a manual legacy switching system, controls the switching process.

Internet Telephony

Internet telephony is one of the newest and most sought after telecom technologies. Ever since its launch, this technology has found increasing favor with corporate companies and programmers.

In this system, the traffic of a telephony call either partially or fully carries over the Internet in the form of *data packets*, which are similar for all kinds of data transmitted over the Internet. This system was first launched in February 1995 by a company named VocalTech Inc., which employed this system in its Internet phone software. The demands of this software are modest—you just need a sound card, speakers, microphone, and a voice-capable modem to run this software. The software first compresses the voice signals and translates them into IP packets for transmission over the Internet. This PC-to-PC Internet telephony works successfully only if both parties use the same Internet phone software and possess the minimum infrastructure.

In a very short period, Internet telephony advanced in leaps and bounds. Many software companies now offer a variety of PC telephony software endowed with exciting features. However, gateway servers are poised to don the role of leader by offering an interface between the Internet and the PSTN network. The gateway servers are well equipped with advanced voice cards that enable users to communicate via normal telephony devices. The model of the gateway architecture is depicted in Figure 1-4.

Internet telephony is beset with some basic problems such as inadequate quality of sound due to limitations imposed by Internet bandwidth and audio compression methods that are still wanting. However, Internet telephony within an intranet helps save on long-distance telephone bills by offering the facility of point-to-point calls via the gateway servers connected to the LAN. The components of an Internet telephony gateway are shown in Figure 1-5.

Suppose User A in New Delhi wants to make a point-to-point phone call to User B located somewhere in Singapore. User A picks up the phone and dials an extension to connect with the gateway, which houses the telephony board and compression-conversion software. This gateway converts the analog signals to digital and transmits the call over the IP-based WAN

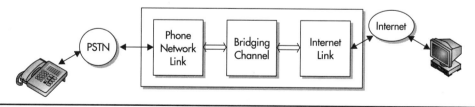

Figure 1-4   *Internet telephony gateway architecture*

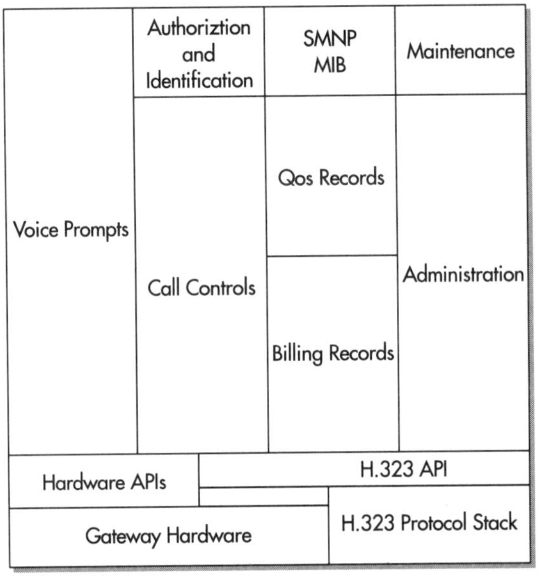

Voice Prompts
Authoriztion and Identification
SMNP MIB
Maintenance
Call Controls
Qos Records
Billing Records
Administration
Hardware APIs
H.323 API
Gateway Hardware
H.323 Protocol Stack

Figure 1-5 *Internet telephony gateway components*

to another gateway situated in Singapore. The gateway in Singapore converts the digital signals back into analog signals and delivers them to User B. The standard model of phone-to-phone connection using the IP networks is shown in Figure 1-6.

IT Network Server
IT Name Server
Internet
Ethernet Switch
IP Router
IT Gateway
Origination ISP
Calling Party
Telephone
PSTN
IP Router
Ethernet Switch
IT Gateway
Destination ISP
Calling Party
Telephone
PSTN

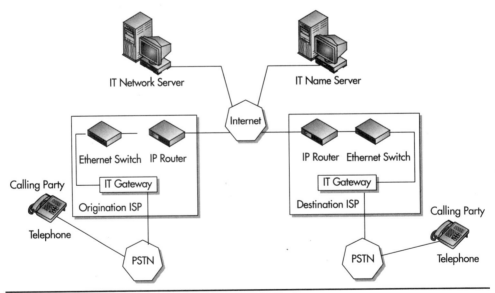

Figure 1-6 *IP network phone-to-phone connection*

Figure 1-7   *H.323 implementation*

The Internet, which is a network integrating within itself millions of networks, is gaining in popularity with every passing day, and consequently the traffic over the Web is increasing at a rapid pace. This has given rise to the problem of congestion over the Web, which causes delay in transmitting data packets over the networks. Such network delays often cause packets to be lost during transmission. The Internet is a packet-switched-based or connectionless network, wherein the individual packets of each voice signal travel over separate networks only to be reassembled again in the proper order at the final destination. Developers working on IP telephony (telephony over IP-based networks) use a variety of speech-compression methods. This lack of standardization renders many Internet telephony products nonoperable with one another.

To overcome this major problem, in May 1996, the International Telecommunications Union (ITU) came up with the *H.323 specification*—a standard that defines how voice, data, and video traffic is to be transmitted over IP-based networks. H.323 is the most widely adopted standard in the industry as of now. A visual representation of a standard H.323 implementation is presented in Figure 1-7.

Interactive Voice Response Systems

Interactive voice response (IVR) systems are automated systems that can interact with callers and provide them with the required information. The IVR systems have been in use for over a decade now. These are primarily used by call center operators and big companies to handle the large number of calls received in their customer care departments. These systems are also employed in telephone banking and various reservation services, and for providing stock quotes over the telephone.

A modern IVR system has the following basic features:

▶   Caller-independent voice recognition facility

▶   Multiple language support

▶   Capability to integrate with other IVR platforms

Most of the IVR systems use a simple touch-tone or Dual Tone Multiple Frequency (DTMF) user interface. In this type of interface, a user simply dials a telephone number and a computer picks up the call and starts the automated dialog process. An automated speech interface guides the user to enter choices using the keypad of the telephone device. Once the session is over, the IVR system disconnects the call. A simple example of this type of conversation is given here:

IVR system	"Welcome to the system, for weather information press 1, for traffic enquiry press 2, or press 3 to quit."
User	Presses 1 on keypad.
IVR system	"Welcome to the weather system. For current weather press 1, press 2 for weather forecast, or press 3 to go back."
User	Presses 1 on keypad.
IVR system	"A maximum of 40 degrees and a minimum of 33 degrees is expected. Thanks for using the system."

By the 1980s, the DTMF-based user interface became a de facto standard for IVR systems. However, this interface was soon to be replaced by a technique capable of recognizing the human voice with better accuracy. In the late 1980s, the Advance Research Project Agency (ARPA) funded some of the organizations working on the development of computer-based speech recognition systems. These organizations came out with early speech recognition systems that were not very advanced and could recognize input only from a specific number of callers or human voices. However, modern IVR systems handle a large numbers of users effectively because they are able to recognize voice inputs supplied by different callers, by interpreting them using highly advanced techniques like artificial intelligence (AI). Despite remarkable advances in speech recognition technology, DTMF-based IVR systems still survive, as they are less expensive and faster to develop and implement compared to natural language recognition-based or directed dialog-based IVR systems. An estimated comparison graph of development expenses is shown in Figure 1-8.

The speech recognition facility has added a new dimension to IVR development and implementation. Many factors contributed to the success of IVR systems and their popularity in the corporate sector. Some of these factors are listed here:

► The most significant benefit offered by IVR systems is the diminishing cost of operations with increased customer participation.

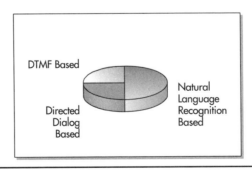

Figure 1-8 *IVR systems development expenses*

▶ With fast, increasing processing power, speech recognition systems are becoming more and more accurate.

▶ From the customer's point of view, IVR systems have proved their worth by providing 24/7 services.

Speech Synthesis Process and Engines

Today, *speech synthesis* has become an indispensable part of our day-to-day life. It's being increasingly used to provide customer care solutions via call centers, telephone banking facilities, and many other consumer-oriented utilities. Speech synthesis is the process of producing artificial computer-controlled human voice, also called *text-to-speech technology*. Let's take a look at the developments in the field of speech synthesis over the past two centuries. Efforts began in the 18th century in some parts of Europe to generate human voice using machines. Christian Gottlieb Kratzenstein, a Russian professor of physics in Copenhagen, built a machine in 1773 that could successfully pronounce vowels by using resonance tubes connected with organ tubes. About the same time, Wolfgang Von Kempelen tried to build a speaking machine, and he published details of his machine in 1791. Von Kempelen's machine was the first that could produce whole words and short sentences.

In the 19th century, other similar devices were built, but they did not contribute significantly to the development of speech synthesis technology. However, in 1835, Joseph Feber made a device that was a remarkable improvement over the previous ones. In 1922, James Stewart introduced one of the first electrically controlled synthesis machines. The machine that is considered the first fully developed speech synthesizer, known as VODER (Voice Operating Demonstrator), was introduced by Homer Dudley in 1939.

By around 1970, the research work on speech synthesis systems became closely associated with computer technology. Computers were increasingly used to implement speech synthesis for practical purposes in a real-world environment, and several systems for converting text to speech were developed.

The Process of Speech Synthesis

These days, plenty of speech synthesis systems are available in the market, and they offer good quality and almost 100 percent accuracy. In addition, they support various languages with good fidelity. Figure 1-9 presents a normal speech synthesis process.

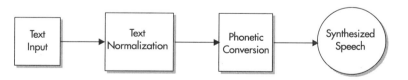

Figure 1-9   *Normal speech synthesis process*

Next, let's discuss the process of speech synthesis step by step.

Text Input and Text Normalization

A speech synthesis software or program takes input mostly from a text file. While receiving the input, most speech synthesis systems convert the text into Unicode or any other native format. Once the input has been received, text normalization takes place. In this process, all abbreviations are written in full form in the context of their usage in text. For example, Ms. Angie is converted to Miss Angie so it will be pronounced as such instead of being pronounced "Ms. Angie." Apart from the textual data, numerical data also needs to be normalized in the context of its usage. Thus, $255 is pronounced as "dollar two hundred fifty five," whereas ZIP 255 may be pronounced as "ZIP two five five." Similarly, the textual data 52% is converted into fifty two percent while synthesizing the output.

Phonetic Conversion and Synthesized Speech

Once all the text is normalized, the process of *phonetic conversion* begins, which involves converting every word to its phonetic equivalent. At this stage, the context of the sentences is also an important consideration. Let's clarify the concept of sentence context using the following two sentences:

▶ You are coming, Anna.

▶ You are coming, Anna?

The first sentence represents a command to Anna, whereas the second sentence is a question. These aspects need to be considered carefully for the accurate generation of synthesized speech.

The last step is generating the waveform or any audible form of the phonetic data using prestored audio elements and a rule-based concatenation of the elements by means of a concrete logic system and artificial intelligence.

Speech Recognition Process

Speech recognition process is often referred to as *automatic speech recognition* (ASR). This technology is used to understand human voice and to interact with humans using verbal commands. For example, a telephone banking system interacts with its users and asks for their account numbers and passwords. Such systems speak to the users by means of speech recognition software and can understand human voice. Through these systems, users can perform transactions using speech instead of pressing buttons on the keypad.

Today, the latest speech recognition systems claim to offer an accuracy of more than 60 to 70 percent even under adverse conditions such as poor sound quality and insufficient speaker voice clarity. Speech recognition systems are available even for languages like Chinese and Japanese, which are considered complex languages as they use a large number of character sets and have large vocabularies. Figure 1-10 shows a diagrammatic representation of the speech recognition process.

Now we'll discuss the major steps involved in speech recognition (as demonstrated in Figure 1-10) to understand the process of speech recognition.

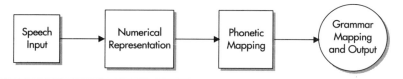

Figure 1-10   *Speech recognition process*

Speech Input and Numerical Representation

The first step in the process of speech recognition is capturing user input and converting it into digital format. This process is called *digitization of speech*. In telephony networks, the digitization process takes place immediately after the system prompts the user for entry because most telephony networks do not use digital technology to transmit voice packets across networks. Even if you are using an IP-based telephony product, it will digitize all the voice samples before transmitting them over the network.

The second step is the transformation of the digital data into sets of numbers. Such sets represent the pitch combination and contain detailed information regarding the pitch levels at different stages of the session.

Phonetic Mapping and Output

Phonetic mapping is the third major step in the speech recognition process. In this process, the spectral analysis information (set of numbers) is rendered into the closest and the best possible phoneme results. This is the most vital step as it directly influences the accuracy of the speech recognition capability of the system. Phonetic mapping results in the generation of a qualifier set of phoneme strings. Every string has its own score that indicates its proximity to the spoken word or text.

In the last step of the speech recognition process, these sets of phonemes are matched against the provided grammar library to select the closest option available based on the grammar. Consider the following example to understand phonetic mapping:

Write	Score	45%
Wright	Score	30%
Right	Score	75%

Now, look at the grammar that defines a set of expressions for an element named choice:

```
$choice = (right    |    wrong    |    none );
```

In this case, when the system performs matching, it picks the best option based on the grammar and produces the result shown here:

Right   Score   75%

The system recognizes the word *right* when processing the input.

Voice Markup Languages

The history of Voice Markup Languages is not very old. The development of Voice Markup Languages started in 1995 when AT&T Bell laboratories started a project called PhoneWeb. The aim was to develop a markup language like HTML for defining voice markup for voice-based devices such as telephones and voice browsers.

When AT&T Bell Labs split into two companies, both companies continued their work on the development of a Voice Markup Language and both came up with their own versions of Phone Markup Language (PML). Later, in 1998, Motorola came up with a new voice markup language called VoxML. This language is a subset of XML and enables the user to define voice markup for voice-based applications. Soon IBM also joined the race with the launch of SpeechML, the IBM version of Voice Markup Language. Other companies such as Vocalis developed their own versions of this language. In the following few sections, we discuss some of these languages briefly.

SpeechML

In early 1999, IBM launched *SpeechML*, an XML-based markup language for defining voice markup for existing web content. This suite from IBM has a voice browser that interprets and understands SpeechML. Just as HTML is used to build web-based visual content, SpeechML is used to build web-based voice applications.

JSML

Java Speech Markup Language (JSML) was introduced by Sun Microsystems. JSML is a subset of XML. Authoring JSML documents can be easily done by using any plain text editor such as Notepad or an XML editor like XML SPY present on the desktop of your system. Every JSML document contains various elements for defining voice markup and for interacting with the user of the application. JSML uses Unicode character sets to define the contents so that developers are able to create applications compatible with most of the popular languages.

JSML makes it possible for applications to annotate text with additional information that serves to improve the quality and genuineness of computer-generated speech. Documents written in JSML may include information about paragraphs, sentences, and special processing instructions for some content of a document. Pronunciation of words and phrases, emphasis on words, and control on the pitch are also possible with JSML, as shown in the following example:

```
<SENT>This is simple sentence <EMP>generated using JSML</EMP> language.</SENT>
```

JSML may be used for text in Japanese, Spanish, Hindi, Hebrew, English, Dutch, German, and all such languages that are supported by Unicode character sets. However, a single JSML document should contain the markup of only a single language. Applications are therefore required to manage and control the speech synthesizers if multiple language output is required. Figure 1-11 shows the workflow of JSML.

TalkML

TalkML was introduced by HP Labs. It is also a subset of XML and has been designed for voice browsers. TalkML is primarily intended for the following devices:

- ► Interactive voice response systems
- ► Smart phones
- ► Mobile devices
- ► Voice browsers

A remarkable feature of TalkML is that it supports more natural dialog-based interaction than DTMF-based voice applications. TalkML also allows developers to display visual contents on small devices such as cell phones, and the process is controlled through Cascading Style Sheets (CSS), making it easy for users to understand the spoken dialog.

VoxML

Motorola Inc. developed *VoxML* in September 1998 in its bid to capture the market of voice-based development systems. Motorola named it "the Markup Language for Voice Applications." The main objective of launching VoxML was to offer users a platform to develop voice-based applications as easily as they develop web-based applications using HTML and CSS.

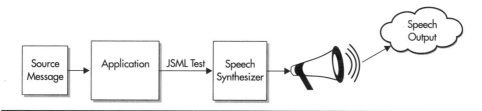

Figure 1-11   *JSML workflow*

VoxML follows the syntactic rules of XML. Each VoxML document consists of some dialogs and forms for interacting with the user and some elements for prompting the user for input.

Following is a sample VoxML document:

```
<?xml version="1.0"?>
<DIALOG>
    <STEP NAME="init">
        <PROMPT> Welcome to VoxML example.<BREAK SIZE="LARGE"/> </PROMPT>
        <INPUT TYPE="NONE" NEXT="#nextstep"/>
    </STEP>
    <STEP NAME="nextstep">
        <PROMPT>
            Please choose from the following options. The available options are:
movies, travel.
        </PROMPT>
        <INPUT TYPE="OPTIONLIST">
            <OPTION NEXT="movies.vml"> movies </OPTION>
            <OPTION NEXT="travel.vml"> travel </OPTION>
        </INPUT>
    </STEP>
</DIALOG>
```

As seen in this example, the first line contains an XML version declaration. Following this, the dialog for interacting with the user begins. VoxML blazed a trail in the development of voice-based application, and many developers were encouraged to create more and more voice-based applications using VoxML.

The major components of the VoxML development platform are listed here and also depicted in Figure 1-12.

▶ External web server

▶ Motorola VoxML development node

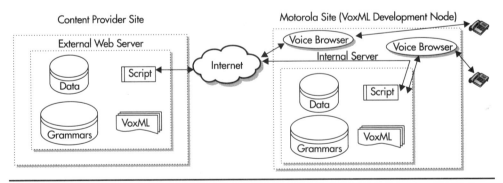

Figure 1-12 *VoxML platform components*

Introduction to VoiceXML

The VoiceXML Forum is an organization founded by Motorola, IBM, AT&T, and Lucent to promote voice-based development. This forum introduced a new language called *VoiceXML* based on the legacy of languages already promoted by these four companies. In August 1999, the VoiceXML Forum released the first specification of VoiceXML version 0.9. In March 2000, version 1.0 was released. Then in October 2001, the first working draft of the latest VoiceXML version 2.0 was published. A lot more on this front is expected in the near future.

Different Implementations of VoiceXML

These days, many companies provide VoiceXML solutions to implement complete VoiceXML-based application for an enterprise. Every company extends the VoiceXML by introducing custom tags of objects, which can be used for developing applications. Some of the popular implementations of VoiceXML are listed here:

- ▶ Tellme Studio (http://studio.tellme.com)
- ▶ VoiceGenie (http://www.voicegenie.com)
- ▶ Nuance (http://www.nuance.com)
- ▶ BeVocal (http://www.bevocal.com)
- ▶ IBM WebSphere Voice Server
  (http://www-3.ibm.com/software/speech/enterprise/ep_11.html)
- ▶ HeyAnita (http://www.heyanita.com)

Most of the companies responsible for these implementations also provide facilities for developers to test their applications. Motorola provides a desktop simulator for testing VoiceXML applications in a simulated environment. You can download this software from the following web site: http://developers.motorola.com/developers/wireless/.

Nuance also offers a large number of tools for VoiceXML-based development including voice browsers, a VoiceXML editor, grammar development tools, voice servers, and several other tools that are of great help in developing VoiceXML-based applications.

Every VoiceXML document contains a top-level root element, and all the other elements come under this top-level element. Every document starts with the VoiceXML version declaration at the top level as shown in the following line of code:

```
<vxml version="1.0">
```

Following is a sample VoiceXML document:

```
<?xml version="1.0"?>
<vxml version="1.0">
<form>
<block>Hello to the Voice World</block>
</form>
</vxml>
```

Commercial Aspects of VoiceXML

VoiceXML is one the most sought after technologies for voice-based applications, such as interactive voice response systems and call center systems. VoiceXML has the potential to boost the development of voice-based applications just as HTML gave a fillip to the development of web-based applications. Here are some of the possible areas in which VoiceXML can be used commercially:

► Interactive voice response systems that provide various kinds of information to the clients of an enterprise

► Call centers

► Telephone-based banking applications

► Ticket reservation services

► Services such as voice-activated dialing and voice mail services, which are in increasing demand

A major advantage of VoiceXML is that it provides web content over a simple telephone device, making it possible to access an application even without a computer and an Internet connection. VoiceXML finds ready acceptance in the business world due to the following reasons:

► Providing a voice-based interface with the web interface is an advantage to the visually challenged, who cannot use a visual interface.

► It is also possible to use the application for accessing a web-based interface even while on the move through a mobile phone, which is much easier to carry around than a personal computer.

► The number of telephone users is far greater than the number of people who use personal computers or the Internet. Thus, by using VoiceXML applications, you can reach out to more customers than is possible by using the Internet.

Implementation Possibilities of VoiceXML

As discussed previously, the major advantage of VoiceXML is that it can provide information to those who do not have access to computers or the Internet. Information is provided using a voice-based interface, which is easily accessible through simple telephony networks. Various service providers are now able to offer their services to a mass market of users, which was not possible in the past. Some of the possible scopes are listed here:

► Applications using the synthesized speech technology

► Machine-human interaction using DTMF-based interface

► Machine-human interaction using the natural language recognition-based interface

Information available in other forms of media such as audio files and HTML pages can also be served by extracting such information and then converting it into synthesized speech via text-to-speech technology.

Summary

In this chapter, we first presented a brief account of the telephony networks that are predecessors of voice communication networks. We then explained Internet telephony and discussed some major issues associated with it. Following this, we described interactive voice response systems and the relevance of such systems in the present scenario. From here, we moved to our discussion on speech synthesis process and speech recognition process. We proceeded to discuss some of the markup languages that were in vogue before the advent of VoiceXML. We then discussed in detail the VoiceXML markup language, its technical aspects and commercial possibilities. We also focused on some innovative features of VoiceXML features that distinguish it from other languages.

Designing Guidelines for Voice Applications

I n this chapter, we discuss some of the vital aspects involved in the initial stages of designing a voice application. Specifically, we examine the basics of voice sites. We also show you how to conduct an analysis of your target audience, outline content management and organization, design navigation flow, and plan dialog management—all important issues to consider before you actually start developing your voice application.

Understanding Voice Sites

The first step towards developing a successful voice application is a proper perception of the concept of voice sites. A *voice site* may be defined as an environment wherein the medium of voice is used for communication. Voice sites are accessible from any telephony device connected to Public Switched Telephony Network (PSTN) architecture. For accessing a voice site, the user dials a specified number from his or her telephony device and is connected to a server. This server, referred to as a *voice server*, consists of the following major components:

▶ A voice browser

▶ Text-to-speech engines

▶ Speech recognition engines

Let's take a closer look at how these components work in a voice server. The voice browser is a vital component of a voice server. It enables the user to interact with a voice site by providing audio prompts and recognizing user input, which is also in the voice format. When the user connects to a voice server, the voice browser receives the call and by utilizing text-to-speech engines and prerecorded audio files, it interacts with the user. To recognize user input, which is in the form of spoken words or phrases, the voice browser uses speech recognition engines. If the user provides input through the keypad of a telephony device, the voice browser uses Dual Tone Multiple Frequency (DTMF) tone detection technology for recognizing the user input. Following is a sample of a typical conversation between a user and the voice browser:

▶ **System**   "Welcome to voice portal. For weather information, say 'weather'; for movie information say 'movies'; and to exit say 'exit.'"

▶ **User**   "Weather."

▶ **System**   "Welcome to weather section. The maximum temperature expected today is around 32 degrees Celsius and the minimum is around 26 degrees Celsius."

▶ **System**   "Thanks for using the application, now terminating the application."

Each of the three main components of the server play a particular role in bringing about the preceding conversation. After the user connects with the server, the voice browser receives the call and starts a new session for the user. In the next step, the voice browser uses the text-to-speech engine to prompt the greeting message and all the available options. When the user selects any option using spoken input, the voice browser recognizes the spoken phrase using the speech recognition engine. It then executes the commands associated with the recognized phrase. Once this process is over, the voice browser again uses the text-to-speech engine to prompt the thanks message to the user and terminates the application.

Now that we have briefly described the working of the voice server, let's proceed to discussing the various factors involved in designing and developing a voice application. The first and the foremost parameter involved in designing and developing a voice application is the target audience. Correct identification of the target audience is a mandatory prerequisite for the commercial success of any voice application.

Identifying the Target Audience

Before you can begin creating a voice application, you need to lay the groundwork based on inferences drawn from a meticulous analysis of the application's target audience or primary users. To identify the target audience, focus your research streams to collect data on the following parameters:

▶   Types of callers

▶   Age groups of callers

The following discussion will enable you to understand how these two parameters affect the design of an application.

Types of Callers

Among a host of users in a typical environment, all users or only some of them may use your voice application. You may be required to serve callers of many types. Each type of caller has some distinct qualities that affect their assessment of an application. We focus on two broad categories—beginners and experienced callers.

Beginners

Beginners constitute the first and the largest category of callers. Though some of them may have some prior experience with voice applications, most of them will be using a voice application for the first time. They aren't very familiar with speech synthesis prompts and might encounter difficulty in recognizing them.

Another common problem associated with beginners is their inability to interact properly with the system by providing the correct spoken input. They often tend to use words like *ummm…* and *ahh…* while providing the spoken input. It's difficult for the speech recognition system to understand such words. The following sample dialog illustrates the lack of proper interaction between a user and a system because of the anomaly in the user input, the user being a beginner.

▶   **System**   "What kind of pizza would you like?"

▶   **User**   "*Ummm…* plain cheese pizza."

▶   **System**   "I am not able to understand what you have said."

Here are some important points that you need to consider while designing an application for beginners:

▶ Make your dialogs clear and effective. Maintain good phonetic clarity and use short dialogs.

▶ Keep the grammar design clear and simple. Include all the phonetic possibilities of any spoken word expected from the user.

▶ Design clear and effective error messages for the system to ensure that the user is provided proper guidance whenever an error message is served.

▶ Design an exhaustive and effective help system that provides clear-cut instructions so as to bail out the user from any possible difficulty in interacting with the application.

▶ Inform the user regarding the functions of universal access commands such as "exit" or "help" so that he or she can avail themselves of the full benefit of these features.

Experienced

It's relatively easy to design and develop a voice application that is intended for experienced users. While designing a voice application that targets experienced users, you'll find the following tips helpful:

▶ Experienced users always expect a good dialog design with clear and to-the-point information in prompts.

▶ Such users are used to the DTMF tone system. Therefore, it's good to incorporate both the dialog-based and the DTMF-tone-based input facilities in your application.

▶ Include more keywords in the grammar for quick navigation and selection of choices to save the user's time and effort.

▶ Use specific error messages and a point-to-point help system. Avoid elaborate and confusing help messages.

After identifying the category of callers—whether beginners or experienced users—for your voice application, the next step is to identify the age group(s) of callers and analyze their personality traits. Callers belonging to different age groups such as kids, teenagers, adults, and so on have some distinct personality traits that affect their interaction with the voice site.

Serving Different Age Groups of Callers

To develop a voice application to serve a particular category of audience, first collect data regarding the characteristics of the age group of expected callers. Design the dialogs and prompts based on this data. The following discussion of the distinct characteristics of some of the main age groups and what they expect from a voice application will help you in this regard.

Kids

Kids always relish some kind of entertainment, so while designing a voice application for kids, include some humorous dialogs and anecdotes that will amuse them.

Here are some of the points you should consider while developing a voice application for kids:

▶ Design attractive and fanciful dialogs to impress kids and to help them use the application effortlessly.

▶ In error messages, address kids in an informal and friendly manner as in the following dialog:

   ▶ **System** "Please choose between one or two."

   ▶ **User** "Three."

   ▶ **System** "Oh, my dear, your choice is not available, please select again."

   ▶ **User** "Two."

   ▶ **System** "That's cool. You chose the right one."

Teenagers

If you're planning to develop a voice application for teenagers, such as one for a music store, consider the following points:

▶ Avoid lengthy dialogs because teenagers always want things to happen fast and easily.

▶ Use the mixed approach of DTMF and synthesized dialogs frequently, because most teenagers are adept at using the keypad system.

▶ Use hot words for terminating the session and for easy navigation between the application in any situation while accessing the application.

Adults

The category of adults, consisting of diverse subgroups, needs careful handling while developing a voice application. The subgroups range from experienced callers to first-time callers. Some subgroups may be defined by the profession of its members. Among the callers, there could be business executives, field persons, doctors, and so on. If the subgroup differentiation is based on age, there could be categories such as those of youngsters, middle-aged persons, and persons over 50 years of age. While developing a voice application for adults, consider all these groups. You should adhere to the following guidelines while designing a voice application for adults:

▶ Keep the dialogs short and easy to understand so that users need not listen carefully every time they access the application. Avoid taxing the memory of users as much as possible.

▶ Always provide an alternative method like a DTMF-based system for accessing the application.

▶ If possible, detect the user when he or she accesses the application with the help of calling line identification methods and personalize the application for specific settings.

Besides the considerations based on the age of callers, there are some common rules you must follow while designing a voice application. These rules, which apply to all age groups and categories, are described here:

▶ After designing the prompts, implement them and start the audible test by listening to them repeatedly. Some of the dialogs may appear flawless on paper, but when you listen to them, they may not be quite clear, and the user may have difficulty understanding them.

▶ Avoid using words that aren't easily understood while pronounced using the synthesized speech system, such as the use of "hair" and "here" in the same sentence.

▶ While interacting with the application, the user must have the facility to terminate the application and end the call at any stage of the session.

▶ Provide an option to replay system prompts at every stage of the application since users are always liable to miss information while listening to the prompts.

▶ Provide an exhaustive help system that will address all the problems a user may encounter in a session. The help system should also be easily accessed from any stage of the session.

Content Management

Once you're through with the analysis of the target audience and have given due attention to their age-specific needs in your design, the next step to consider is content management. Content management is a high-attention area and demands scrupulous planning.

Starting from Scratch

Before you begin work related to your application's contents, check on the following: Are you going to build the voice application starting from scratch? Does your client or company already have a web site or an interactive voice response (IVR) system, the content of which you may use partly?

Today, most companies have a web site, and some of them even have an IVR system in their customer care departments. If your client company already has a presence on the Internet, you stand to gain advantages such as the following:

▶ Since most of the research work has already been done for the existing system, you need not conduct an exhaustive research. This way, you gain on time and effort.

▶ A good amount of content as well as clear guidelines are available for developing the rest of the content.

On the other hand, if you are required to develop the contents of the application from scratch, you have to plan and design everything, such as the content type you propose to launch on the site, the scheme for presenting that content type, and so on. In the discussions that follow, we focus on two cardinal aspects of content development:

►   Deciding on the contents

►   Organizing the contents

Deciding on the Contents

Deciding the nature of the contents is a crucial step in the content development cycle. The research conducted on the target audience and the types of services you plan to offer to your clients are two definite pointers that ease this task. In the following sections, we discuss some of the common criteria, as listed here, to be observed while deciding on the contents for a voice application:

►   Choose the right information.

►   Always check for content accuracy.

►   Avoid repetition in the text.

►   Check for the content relevance and update it regularly.

Choose the Right Information

Choosing the right information without losing track of the target audience is the first step towards making the contents appealing to your audience. Localization and personalization of content are imperative for creating a good voice application. For example, if you're developing a weather information service for a company situated in Richmond, the primary target audience is the local community. Take care to provide the weather information forecast for Richmond in the first few prompts. Refrain from asking the user for too many inputs for selecting a city or state.

You must ensure that the information your application provides is unique and of special value compared to that of already deployed applications provided by your competitors. This will give your application an edge over the others.

Content Accuracy

Make sure that your content is 100 percent accurate. Inaccurate information will discourage users from using the application. Such information is liable to cause serious losses to both your company and your clients.

Avoid Repetitive Content

Make sure that no information is repeated within the application. Repetitions are liable to confuse and disconcert the user who navigates through the application. Users get a negative impression and they would not make use of your application regularly.

Content Relevancy

Keeping content current is an important task in content management. Always provide up-to-date information by refreshing content frequently. For instance, if you're providing a movie ticket reservation facility, update your database on a minute-to-minute basis to ensure that the data your application provides represents the latest ticket reservation status.

Organizing the Contents

Once you're through with the content designing part, move on to organizing the content that you have decided to provide to the users through your voice application. Content organization makes an impression, good or bad, on users right in their maiden interaction with your application. It is based on this impression that they will appraise your application.

The success of even the most popular portals and search engines may be attributed to systematic organization of contents. Most web sites follow their own customized content organization patterns. Yet any good content organization scheme is characterized by some definite features such as those listed here:

▶   Content must be accessible through the minimum number of mouse clicks.

▶   The home page must be accessible from anywhere in the site through a single mouse click.

▶   There should be no broken or orphan links anywhere in the site.

When you're developing voice applications, all the criteria for effective content organization with regard to web sites apply, only the mouse clicks are replaced by the hot words. A few of the more popular patterns for content organization are described in the following section.

Sequential Structure of Content Organization

In the past, this was the most widely used method for developing voice applications. It's still the simplest method as far as developers are concerned. In sequentially structured content, the caller will interact with the application in a sequential manner using prompts one after the other and following a restrained track. This structure doesn't offer much latitude to the caller for navigating within the application.

This type of content organization is suitable for applications that provide only one service to the users, such as a movie ticket reservation system, as shown in the following sample dialog:

▶   **System**   "Welcome to the movie reservation system. Say 'booking' for reservation, or say 'exit' for terminating the application."

▶   **User**   "Booking."

▶   **System**   "There are 15 tickets available right now. Say the number of tickets you want to book or say 'exit.'"

▶   **User**   "Exit."

▶   **System**   "Thanks for using the application. Have a good day."

As evident in this sample dialog, with this structure there is a very little space for the user to move around within the application. Most of the time, the user has only two choices. The sequential structure is, indeed, quite simple, and the user becomes familiar with the application in a few calls. However, this structure doesn't involve much user participation. Since there isn't much spoken user input, the interaction lacks the intimacy of natural conversation.

Hierarchical Structure of Content Organization

In the hierarchical structure of content organization, a simple tree method is used to organize the contents. This organization is often employed when an application offers more than one service to choose from. In this structure, a list of services is sorted out based on their priority with regard to a particular context or their use or on any other logical criteria. For example, if you're offering net banking service through your voice application, you may want to adopt the hierarchical structure. Consider a sample dialog of a voice banking service:

▶ **System**   "Welcome to the Voice Bank."

▶ **System**   "Please choose one of the following options: Press 1 or say 'account balance' for checking account balance. Press 2 or say 'statement' for getting details of your current account statement. Press 3 or say 'schemes' for information about different offers and plans. Press 4 or say 'exit' to close this application."

▶ **User**   "Schemes."

▶ **System**   "Press 1 or say 'deposit' for information about different deposit schemes. Press 2 or say 'loans' for various loan schemes. Press 3 or say 'exit' to go back to the main menu."

▶ **User**   "Exit."

The hierarchical dialog structure is schematically represented in the diagram shown in Figure 2-1.

Mixed Approach

Nowadays, a single voice application is often expected to dispense a variety of services. In such cases, the mixed approach proves to be both effective and user friendly. In this method, the major categories of services are identified and these form the topmost hierarchy level. Once the user selects one of these, the rest of the processing will be carried out using the sequential structure.

The main benefit of the mixed approach is that by providing a sorted list of all the services offered by the application, you refrain from confusing the user with too many choices and options, although the application offers a variety of services.

Design Time Considerations

Whatever approach you adopt for organizing the content, you must also take into account some basic considerations and design norms that cannot be compromised. They are to be observed as much as possible, for any deviation from them will affect the content organization adversely.

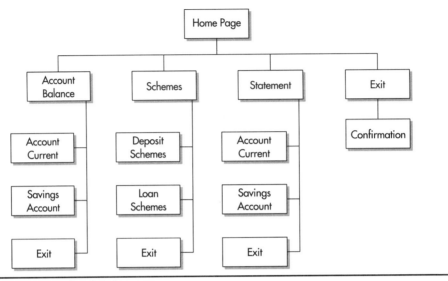

Figure 2-1 *Hierarchical dialog structure*

Consistency Make sure that your content organization adheres to a consistent pattern. If you use two or more patterns to organize your application's contents, then you have to ensure that the mixed pattern doesn't confuse the user. Avoid mixing more than one approach haphazardly at various stages of the session. This will leave the user confused and hamper smooth and fast interaction. For any number of options offered, the last option must be for terminating the application. As already mentioned, content organization is the first thing about an application that concerns users. If the content organization impresses them, your voice application receives a fillip.

Skilled Organization of Contents Whatever approach you choose for content organization, ensure that it is implemented with meticulous attention paid to the last detail. Take care to avoid broken or orphan links. Access to the main menu and termination of the application must be possible at any stage during an ongoing session.

Once the contents have been properly managed in accordance to a scheme that will suit the application, the next design consideration is working out the dialog flow and creating the navigation architecture for the application. We discuss these aspects of voice sites in the sections that follow.

Designing the Dialog Flow

To construct some good dialogs for your voice application, it's recommended that first you sketch on paper the initial prompts and dialogs contemplated as separate units and then integrate them according to your needs.

A *flowchart* represents a visual image of all the dialogs and prompts in the application and the sequence in which they are executed. You can also use any flowcharting software such as SmartDraw for designing and creating your flowcharts easily. Before making the flowchart, break down your dialogs and prompts into smaller segments so that they can be easily integrated into a compact and coherent system.

Two kinds of dialog designs are popular these days:

- ▶ Directed dialogs
- ▶ Mixed initiative dialogs

Directed Dialogs

In this design, a series of direct dialogs and prompts constitute the application. Such a design provides a limited number of choices and options, and the session proceeds as directed by the application depending on the option selected by the user. The following provides a sample of directed dialog-based conversation:

- ▶ **System**   "Welcome to the Voice restaurant system. Please choose one of the following pizza types: Press 1 or say 'cheese.' Press 2 or say 'plain pizza.' Press 3 or say 'classic pizza.' Press 4 or say 'exit' to quit the application."

- ▶ **User**   "Cheese."

- ▶ **System**   "Press 1 or say 'large' for a large-size pizza. Press 2 or say 'medium' for a medium-size pizza. Press 3 or say 'small' for a small-size pizza. Press 4 to go back to main menu."

- ▶ **User**   "Medium."

- ▶ **System**   "You have chosen a small-sized cheese pizza, is this right? Press 1 or say 'confirm' to confirm your order. Press 2 or say 'no' to discard the order and go back to main menu."

- ▶ **User**   "No."

- ▶ **System**   "Going back to main menu."

As is obvious from the preceding sample dialog, with the directed dialog design, at every step the dialog is directed by the application, and at every step the user has a fixed number of choices to select from. Now, let's examine an application that uses the mixed initiative dialog pattern.

Mixed Initiative Dialogs

This dialog design represents the latest method of using dialogs in a voice application. In this method, natural, language-based dialogs are spoken by the user, and the system understands the user input. All dialogs are directed by the caller, and the system gathers the necessary information from the spoken input and asks the user for any additional information required. A major challenge to this technology is the effectiveness it demands of the system in correctly interpreting the user input from among a wide range of possible user inputs and prompts.

Consider the following sample dialog that uses the mixed initiative dialog pattern for a restaurant service application that delivers pizzas to the user's home.

▶ **System** "Welcome to the Voice restaurant system. Please place your order."

▶ **User** "Please deliver three small cheese pizzas."

▶ **System** "You have ordered three small cheese pizzas, correct?"

▶ **User** "Yes."

▶ **System** "Thanks for using the system."

As the preceding example shows, the expected user is experienced and handles the situations easily.

Although a voice application based on the directed dialog system is relatively easy to develop and to manage, such an application may not find favor with experienced and frequent callers.

On the other hand, a voice application using the mixed initiative dialog system provides a natural interface to callers, and they can get their tasks done within a few steps. However, this system encounters a major problem when the speech recognition technology fails to filter out the desired option from the spoken input. The probability for this is high when the grammars aren't clearly written, causing the error margin to increase. The mixed initiative dialog system works well with experienced callers who are able to interact with the application effectively. Now, let's proceed to discussing the navigation architecture of voice sites.

Designing the Navigation Architecture

The navigation structure of a voice site plays a major role in the success of a voice application. To enable users to navigate through your application with ease, observe the following guidelines:

▶ Users must always be able to move around within the application by using hot words.

▶ Provide globally accessible voice-activated links for accessing the help feature and for terminating the application at any stage.

▶ Organize information in such a way that the users are able to locate and use it easily.

▶ Design a multilayered navigation structure and make cross-section navigation possible.

Design small dialog segments for your voice application. This approach facilitates reusing these segments at many instances across the site. Make sure that every dialog segment is complete in every respect and can be used as a stand-alone unit if required at more than one place.

Dialogs Description

Always provide clear and descriptive titles to all your dialog segments so that the user can access most of the information easily and without having to resort to the help system. Titles of the dialog segments must clearly reflect the task that the dialog segment will discharge. Otherwise, the user won't be able to get the desired information through dialog segments.

Don't mix up voice links and dialog titles. This will create confusion as illustrated in the following example:

Dialog	Bad Example	Preferred Way	Voice Link
Welcome dialog	"Welcome to voice shopping main menu."	"Welcome to voice shopping."	"Main menu."

In this example, we have used the phrase "main menu" as a voice link to access the welcome dialog in the application. However, the voice link is mixed up with the dialog title.

Bridging the Delay Factor

If a transaction involves some processing on the server before executing a dialog, there will be a delay or idle time during which the processing takes place. This moment of silence may be unsavory to most users. So, while designing dialogs, use some audio clips to fill dialog interchange time and processing periods. If the user requests the termination of the application, use a sound clip before announcing the session termination. The audio clips could be the brand audio of your company, a simple beep, or anything else. Besides making the session lively, a sound clip during the interval of processing will convey to the user that the input supplied is being processed. In addition, if you're transferring a call to some other application, play some sounds while the transferring process is going on in the server.

The use of audio clips helps you enhance the quality of your voice application by providing the following advantages to the user:

▶ By playing audio clips, you can easily fill the time lag between the execution of two processes.

▶ Designing different sounds for different events such as error notification, successful process completion, and so on will provide the user a hint regarding the forthcoming dialog, thereby helping him or her get ready to reply quickly.

You should observe the following precautions while using audio clips in your application:

▶ Avoid using too many audio clips in the site; this will overload the application as well as confuse the user.

▶ Take care to make the audio clips consistent within an application. For instance, you should not use two different audio clips for error messages at two different locations within the same voice application.

Using Voice-Activated Links

Voice-activated links provide an effective means of connecting different modules of voice application. Voice links work exactly like hyperlinks in a web site. Look at the following example:

```
Welcome to our portal <a href="index.htm"> click here </a>home page.
```

In the preceding example, the text "click here" works as a hyperlink. When the user clicks the link, he or she is taken to the file associated with this hyperlink. Users can identify the hyperlinks easily on a web page, as they appear in a pattern different from that of the general text. However, in the case of voice links, there is no arrangement to render them visually distinct. Hence, you need to insert some aural indication before and after a voice link for its identification as illustrated in the following example:

```
Welcome to voice portal, check your <sound>mail<sound> and
do <sound>shopping<sound> without any hassle
```

In the preceding example, the words "mail" and "shopping," which are part of a sentence, also work as voice links. The user can say either "mail" or "shopping," respectively, for checking their mail or buying some goods from the store.

To design effective voice links for an application, keep in mind the following guidelines:

▶ Make sure that the word or the sentence used as a voice link is clearly audible and can be easily recognized by the user.

▶ A link should contain enough information about the dialog or section that the user will be connected to by the execution of that link.

▶ Avoid use of voice links in situations where three or more choices are presented because many users won't be able to recognize or extract all the links from the spoken text in such cases.

▶ If there are three or more choices, use the menu-based model to enable the user to get the desired information.

Globally Accessible Commands

Today, generally you'll find a link to the home page on every page of a particular web site. Voice applications also have some special sets of commands that are accessible anytime during a session. These globally accessible commands are provided as a functionality of the voice browser. There are two main categories of global commands:

▶ Application-specific global commands

▶ Voice browser-provided global commands

Application-Specific Global Commands

You can provide application-specific global commands by defining their hot words and grammar in the application root file. When you define hot words in the root file, their corresponding commands are available for use throughout the application session. These commands are used to access the main menu of the application, invoke the help system, or terminate the application in any situation and location. However, the scope of these commands is limited to their respective applications. You cannot use commands defined in one application in another.

Voice Browser-Provided Global Commands

Most voice browsers also provide a set of global commands that are accessible across an application. These commands are mainly used for accessing the voice browser main menu by speaking some predetermined hot words. These commands can be accessed anytime while using the application, which is served by a voice browser, irrespective of whether the application also provides similar commands for such functionality.

Migration from the Existing System

Most companies these days have their own web sites. Some of them also have interactive voice response systems running successfully in their networks. Customers of such companies are used to their own systems and are liable to feel uncomfortable when they switch over to a new system. You need to make some special considerations while developing a voice application for users who are already acclimatized to some other scheme for interaction.

When you plan to build a voice application by integrating an existing system, take the following points into account while building the voice interface of the application.

If the existing application is a touch-tone-based system, you can consider developing a touch-tone-based voice interface for your application, as users will be comfortable with it. Use of the directed dialog system will also prove a good choice in such cases.

However, if an existing IVR system is being incorporated, the mixed initiative dialog system is the better alternative, because it will enable the user to interact with the application easily and complete tasks quickly and efficiently.

If your voice application is to integrate an existing web site, the voice interface must be similar to the visual interface of the web site. You should replace most of the visual elements such as menus, links, and forms by their counterparts using VoiceXML. In the discussion that follows, we explain how various visual elements of the web site are replaced by their counterparts in a voice application using the VoiceXML elements and different dialog methods. In web sites, the most common elements for collecting data, showing contents, and getting user input are as follows:

► Menus for navigation
► Hyperlinks for navigation
► Forms for collecting data

We discuss the voice equivalents of these elements in the upcoming sections.

Menus for Navigation

In web sites, menus are used for navigating within the site. Menus provide impressive visual assistance to the user by incorporating images and colors to display the contents. The web site menus might have a multilayered architecture.

In the case of voice applications, multilayered menus are liable to confuse the user and render the application interface cumbersome. While building a menu-based system for a voice application, choose a properly organized dialog design system, based on your needs.

It will be worthwhile to consider the following points while designing menus for navigating within a voice application:

▶ Avoid lengthy menus such as those in web sites. A good menu-based system contains a maximum of four choices for one function.

▶ Concentrate on the prompts and design them effectively to impart clear-cut information.

Hyperlinks for Navigation

In web sites, we use hyperlinks for navigating between different sections. Similarly, to facilitate navigation in your voice application, you have to include a good number of voice links while designing dialogs. You should define the grammar of these voice links in the root-level document so that they can be accessed anytime during the session.

Forms for Collecting Data

Forms are used for collecting data from the user and for posting the collected data to a server for processing. In VoiceXML, we have several elements under the forms section to collect various kinds of data from the user. In most web sites, forms are lengthy and take time to fill out, but since they are in a visual medium, users can go about this without difficulty. However, in the case of voice applications, lengthy forms are to be avoided. While designing the forms, take care to keep them as short as possible and ask the user only for the necessary information.

Now, we take to the final stage in designing your voice application—developing dialogs and prompts. We have discussed two types of dialog patterns—directed dialog systems and mixed dialog systems. In the following section, we explore how to design dialog languages so that they seem natural to users.

Designing Dialogs and Prompts

The design of dialogs constitutes an important aspect of the voice personality of an application. The dialog design should consider such parameters as the voice gender, age factor, intonation, and so on. Since users have to interact directly with the prompt dialogs, designing the prompts is also a significant factor in shaping the overall impression an application creates. Let's take a closer look at designing the voice personality of the application and designing the prompts separately in the following sections.

Designing the Voice Personality

The voice personality of an application has an immediate impact on the user. Whether synthesized speech or a set of prerecorded messages is used, the personality of the voice system plays an important role in the success of the application. Users always consider the voice system as the voice of a person from the company. Some other important things users notice are

▶ Gender of the person

▶ Age and the accent of the person

While selecting a personality for the voice system, you must pay attention to the following aspects:

▶ Select the personality that suits your company's brand image and the services you're planning to offer by the voice application. For example, if you're planning to sell cosmetics through the voice application, use a female voice for the system. Similarly, an application offering a pizza delivery service must have a voice personality different from the one used for online banking services.

▶ Analyze your target audience. Collect information about the geographical locations of the expected audience, their speech culture, and their accent. For example, if you're planning to design an application for an audience in Florida and your system uses an African accent, callers will find it difficult to interact with the system.

▶ Also, keep in mind the age factor of the voice you intend to use in your system. For example, an application targeting kids doesn't have any room for an experienced adult male voice for providing information.

▶ Always take into account the branding strategies of your company and clients when you choose the voice personality.

The following qualities are expected in a well-selected and designed personality:

▶ The selected personality should match the needs of the target audience in every respect.

▶ The accent must be clear to enable even nonexperienced callers to easily understand the prompts and dialogs.

▶ While prompting and speaking dialogs, the voice personality should take care to keep the environment lively.

▶ Make sure that the personality meets the brand image requirement of the company.

Next, we examine the various types of prompts and how they can be designed to create a lasting and fair impression on the user.

Designing the Prompts

In a voice application, you need to include a number of prompts, each of which carry some information for the user. Here, we discuss the four main types of prompts used in voice applications, visually represented in Figure 2-2:

▶ Preliminary prompts

▶ Middle-level prompts

▶ Error messages

▶ Help messages

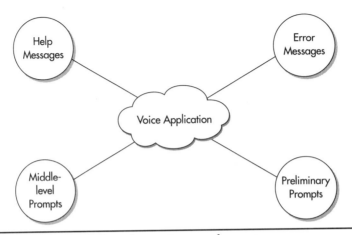

Figure 2-2 *Voice applications rely on four main types of prompts.*

Preliminary Prompts

Preliminary prompts come into action when an application starts or at the beginning of a new dialog, which starts a new section within the application. These prompts are also referred to as *welcome messages*. Their main purpose is to provide basic, but sufficient, information about the system to users and instruct them on using the application. A single application might contain more than one preliminary prompt. Preliminary prompts, though mostly short, are perfect sentences with respect to grammar and language.

Middle-level Prompts

Middle-level prompts are among the most important prompts in the entire voice application scenario as they direct the user, from time to time, to complete transactions by providing information about various ongoing activities. Middle-level prompts are used for collecting the information and executing related activities. These prompts are also used to provide information regarding the processing being carried out in the server. For example, if the system is transferring a call to another system, middle-level prompts are used to inform the user about the call transfer, as shown in the following example:

▶ **Middle-level prompt** "Please hold the line while your call is being transferred to an attendant."

Error Messages

Error messages constitute a vital segment of any voice application. They come into action when the user makes any mistake while interacting with the application. For example, if the user provides unacceptable input while filling out a form, the system notifies the user by prompting an error message. Give due importance to the following guidelines while developing error messages:

- ▶ Error messages are used to notify the user about the error. Hence, they have to be clear and concise.

- ▶ Error messages should not contain any confusing details about the error, rather they should just guide the user in performing the correct transaction.

- ▶ Avoid mixing up different error messages by using similar sentences. Make sure that distinct sentences are used for all possible errors.

Help Messages

Help messages form the periphery of the prompts design process. When the user encounters a problem while interacting with the application, he or she may browse the help section to find the solution to the problem. Through help messages users can learn how to use the system effectively. Help messages are mostly designed in a computer-directed dialog pattern.

Summary

This chapter detailed some of the preliminary design considerations involved in developing a voice application. We began by discussing the various components of a voice application. You then learned how a voice application functions. Building on this information, we examined the various parameters one by one. You learned the significance of conducting a thorough and comprehensive study of prospective clients and the relevance of the inferences drawn, as well as the techniques involved in content management. After this, we delved into the processes of planning dialogs, inventing an effective scheme of dialog flow, and some of the popular patterns of dialog distribution.

Lastly, we showed you the voice personality factor and the attributes that constitute the voice personality of an application such as voice gender, intonation, accent, the strain of dialog scripts, the design and organization of prompts, and so on. This chapter, in essence, presented an exhaustive account of the tasks involved in the preproduction phase of a voice application.

CHAPTER

3

Working with VoiceXML

IN THIS CHAPTER:

Architecture of VoiceXML

Application Overview

The Concept of Voice Dialogs

Execution Process of VoiceXML Documents

Executing a Multidocument-based Application

Navigation in VoiceXML

Getting Input from the User

Types of Form Items

Form Interpretation Algorithm

Summary

I n this chapter, we focus on four major issues that form the basis of developing a voice application: the architecture of VoiceXML, VoiceXML applications and document structure, input techniques and form items, and the form interpretation algorithm. Each section of this chapter covers one core functionality of VoiceXML. Along with the explanation of each function, we furnish sample code to aid better understanding of the concepts we explore. We also examine various common VoiceXML techniques in the context of each of these four topics.

Architecture of VoiceXML

The architecture of VoiceXML is very similar to that of standard web applications. As you know, in the case of web applications, all the HTML documents reside on a server. When a user requires some documents from the server, he or she sends a request to the server by using software called a *browser* or *user agent*. Upon receiving the user request through the browser, the server starts processing the required documents and sends the result to the browser as its response. The browser forwards this response to the user.

In VoiceXML applications, just as in web applications, documents are hosted on the web server. In addition to a web server, a VoiceXML architecture houses another server, the voice server, which handles all interactions between the user and the web server. The voice server plays the role of the browser in a voice application, interpreting all spoken inputs received from the user and providing audio prompts as responses to the user. In the case of voice applications, the end user need not have any high-end computer and sophisticated browsing software. He or she can access the voice application through a simple telephony device connected to the PSTN architecture. Figure 3-1 shows the architecture of a voice application.

As evident from Figure 3-1, the standard implementation architecture of a voice application includes the following components:

▶ Web server

▶ VoiceXML interpreter

▶ PSTN network

▶ Client device

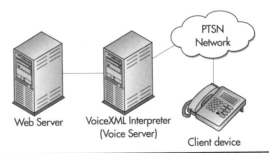

Figure 3-1 *Architecture of a voice application*

We've already discussed PSTN networks and client devices in Chapter 1. Here, we explore the first two components in the following sections.

Web Server

The web server stores all the VoiceXML and related documents. It receives requests from the voice server and processes them using business logic. The result is sent as a response to the voice server. The web server sometimes also works as a database server for the application, facilitating database-related processing in the application by using business logic. In some cases, the database server is maintained separately and the web server communicates with the database server for database-related processing.

VoiceXML Interpreter

The VoiceXML interpreter is one of the most important components of the voice server. It communicates with the user and processes all user inputs and then passes on user requests to the web server for further processing. It also provides a voice-based interface for application users by generating synthesized speech using text-to-speech technologies.

Application Overview

In VoiceXML, an *application* refers to a set of interlinked documents, all of them referencing a root-level document called the *application root document*. All applications begin functioning from the root-level document. Once the root-level document is loaded on the server, the variables and hot words defined in it are always accessible throughout the user's session with the application, even if they aren't defined in specific documents. Figure 3-2 shows the application structure. Before delving into the application structure detailed in this figure, let's briefly touch on document structure.

VoiceXML documents consist of a series of interlinked documents. Every VoiceXML document contains a top-level element and certain other elements under the top-level

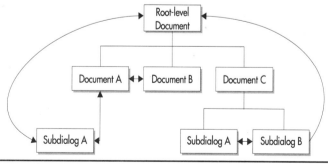

Figure 3-2   *VoiceXML document structure*

element. All the dialogs in a document are processed in sequential order after the initiation of the top-level element. In the next section, we introduce you to the concept of dialogs.

The Concept of Voice Dialogs

A VoiceXML document is subdivided into a series of dialogs and subdialogs. *Dialogs* contain information for processing a particular transaction as well as information regarding the next dialog to be called upon completion of an ongoing transaction.

Subdialogs are mostly treated as functions that are used for specific tasks such as calculating the age of a person based on his or her date of birth. Subdialogs are called from their parent dialogs, and they return output to their respective parent dialogs after completing the assigned task.

In VoiceXML, two types of dialogs are used for interacting with the users. *Forms*, the first type, are used to define the interaction with users for collecting input from them using predefined grammars and field items. *Menu-based dialogs* are used to provide a series of options and perform the transaction corresponding to a selected option.

Now that we've described the architecture of a VoiceXML application, how its different components work to serve the required information, and the concept of dialogs in VoiceXML, we next examine the process of executing VoiceXML documents. We also show you how a complete VoiceXML application is executed on the server.

Execution Process of VoiceXML Documents

When the voice server processes a VoiceXML document, the processing is done in sequential order—from the top of the document to the end of the document. Listings 3-1a and 3-1b show a simple and easy-to-understand interface for the process of document execution in VoiceXML.

Listing 3-1a: *Simple Document Execution in VoiceXML 1.0 (example3-1a.vxml)*

```
<?xml version = "1.0"?>
<vxml version = "1.0">
      <var expr = "'This is first form in the document'" name = "variable" />
      <form>
            <block>
                  <prompt>
                        <value expr = "variable" />
                  </prompt>
                  <goto next = "#secondform" />
            </block>
      </form>
      <form id = "secondform">
```

```
            <block>
                    This is the second form in the document
            </block>
        </form>
</vxml>
```

Listing 3-1b: *Simple Document Execution in VoiceXML 2.0 (example3-1b.vxml)*

```
<?xml version = "1.0"?>
<vxml version = "2.0">
        <var expr = "'This is the first form in the document'" name = "variable" />
        <form>
            <block>
                    <prompt>
                            <value expr = "variable" />
                    </prompt>
                    <goto next = "#secondform" />
            </block>
        </form>
        <form id = "secondform">
            <block>
                    This is the second form in the document
            </block>
        </form>
</vxml>
```

As you can see in Listings 3-1a and 3-1b, we declare the XML version in the very first line and then the VoiceXML version for the VoiceXML interpreter. Next, we declare variables that hold a value and then we add two forms in the document. The first form is used for prompting the value of a variable. In the next step, controls are transferred to the second form using the <goto> element. In the second form, we just prompt the user with some information regarding the current location. Here's a step-by-step description of the execution process in this example:

1. The voice browser loads the document into memory.

2. The voice browser checks for the valid XML and VoiceXML declarations.

3. All the variables are initialized and assigned the given values, if any.

4. The first form is loaded and the content of <block> element executed. Then the voice browser loads the second form by transferring controls to it, after executing the <goto> element.

5. The voice browser unloads the first form, loads the second form, and executes the second form's contents.

6. The second form and the document are unloaded from memory and the execution process is terminated.

Attribute	Description	Optional
version	Defines the version number of this particular document. Its possible value is either 1.0 or 2.0.	No
base	Defines the base URI.	Yes
lang	Defines the language and locale type for this document.	Yes
application	Defines the URI of the root document for this document, if any exist.	Yes

Table 3-1   *Attributes of <vxml>*

All VoiceXML documents start with the XML declaration followed by the <vxml> declaration, which also works as the top-level element for all kinds of VoiceXML documents. Table 3-1 provides a description of the attributes of <vxml> elements.

You have just seen the execution of a single VXML document. Now we'll turn to the execution of a multidocument VXML application. As the following section clarifies, the execution process of a multidocument application is quite different from that of a single document, because in the former case it's possible to simultaneously load more than one document in the memory.

Executing a Multidocument-based Application

In simple applications, every VoiceXML document works as a stand-alone document and doesn't contain links to any other document at its root-level document. When developing a large application, you need to work with various documents. In such cases, you can choose the multidocument-based application structure. In this structure, a document is defined as a root-level document and all other documents refer to it using the application attribute in the <vxml> top-level element.

In multilevel document applications, every time a document is loaded on the server, the server also loads its application-level root document, if any, defined in the application attribute of the <vxml> element. The application-level root document always remains loaded in memory until another document that doesn't contain links to any root-level document becomes the root-level application document.

In a multidocument application, a maximum of two documents can be loaded in memory at any given time. Of these two, only one will be available at a time for the execution process on the server. Some of the important transactions that may occur between two documents during a session of a multidocument application are explained in the following sections.

Root to Root-level Transaction

In this transaction, both the documents are treated as root-level documents. For example, Document A calls Document B, which doesn't contain the application attribute in the <vxml> element. In this case, Document B is also loaded as the root-level document and Document A is unloaded from the server for that particular session.

Root-level Documents to Sublevel Documents

In this type of transaction, one document is a root-level document and the other a sublevel document, which contains the application attribute in the <vxml> element. Both the documents are loaded on the server, and the user processes the sublevel document.

Sublevel Document to Sublevel Document

Both the documents involved in this transaction are sublevel documents, and both use the same document as the root-level document. In this case, only the context of the root-level document is preserved.

So much for the execution process of simple and multidocument VXML applications. Next, we focus on the navigation process in VoiceXML.

Navigation in VoiceXML

Transferring a user from one document to another document or to a subdialog on user request is part of the navigation mechanism. In a VoiceXML application, a user can navigate using the <menu> or the <link> element. With VoiceXML applications, the menu-driven system is the most widely used system for navigation. It enables the user to navigate through the application as easily as on a web page created using HTML. Listings 3-2a and 3-2b illustrate the menu-driven navigation, which uses the <menu> element.

Listing 3-2a: *The <menu> Element in VoiceXML 1.0 (example3-2a.vxml)*

```
<?xml version = "1.0"?>
<vxml version = "1.0">
    <menu scope = "dialog">
        <prompt>
            Please select one of the following options: weather report or
news.
        </prompt>
        <choice next = "#form1">
            weather report
        </choice>
        <choice next = "#form2">
            news
        </choice>
        <nomatch>
            <reprompt />
        </nomatch>
    </menu>
    <form id = "form1">
        <block>
            You selected weather report.
```

```
                            <disconnect />
                    </block>
            </form>
            <form id = "form2">
                    <block>
                            You selected news.
                            <disconnect />
                    </block>
            </form>
</vxml>
```

Listing 3-2b: *The <menu> Element in VoiceXML 2.0 (example3-2b.vxml)*

```
<?xml version = "1.0"?>
<vxml version = "2.0">
        <menu scope = "dialog">
                <prompt>
                        Please select one of the following options: weather report or
news.
                </prompt>
                <choice next = "#form1">
                        weather report
                </choice>
                <choice next = "#form2">
                        news
                </choice>
                <nomatch>
                        <reprompt />
                </nomatch>
        </menu>
        <form id = "form1">
                <block>
                        You selected weather report.
                        <disconnect />
                </block>
        </form>
        <form id = "form2">
                <block>
                        You selected news.
                        <disconnect />
                </block>
        </form>
</vxml>
```

As seen in Listings 3-2a and 3-2b, the user is offered a simple menu containing two choices. When the user selects any of the available choices, a form is called to prompt the user with the select option. The output of these examples is depicted in Figure 3-3.

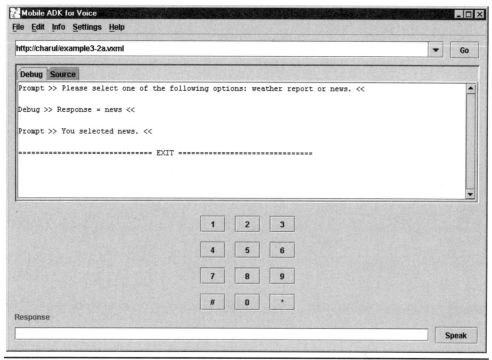

Figure 3-3   *Output of Listings 3-2a and 3-2b*

The <link> Element in VoiceXML 1.0

You can also use the <link> element for navigation in a VoiceXML application. The <link> element also contains grammar for recognizing user input. Table 3-2 describes the attributes of the <link> element in VoiceXML 1.0.

In Listing 3-3a, we use the <link> element according to the standards of VoiceXML version 1.0 and the grammar type employed is JSGF.

Listing 3-3a: *The <link> Element in VoiceXML 1.0 (example3-3a.vxml)*

```
<?xml version = "1.0"?>
<vxml version = "1.0">
     <link next = "http://charul/example3-1a.vxml">
          <grammar type = "application/x-jsgf">
               home | main menu
          </grammar>
          <dtmf>
               2
          </dtmf>
     </link>
```

```
        <menu scope = "dialog">
            <prompt>
                Please select one of the following options: weather report or
news </prompt>.
            <choice next = "#form1">
                weather report
            </choice>
            <choice next = "#form2">
                news
            </choice>
            <nomatch>
                <reprompt />
            </nomatch>
        </menu>
        <form id = "form1">
            <block>
                You selected weather report.
                <disconnect />
            </block>
        </form>
        <form id = "form2">
            <block>
                You selected news.
                <disconnect />
            </block>
        </form>
</vxml>
```

In Listing 3-3a, once the document is loaded on the server, the user can choose home or the main menu for accessing the home page of the application. In this application, we use the first example (shown in Listing 3-1a) as a URI for the next attribute. When the user speaks "home" or "main menu," the application loads the filename example3-1a.vxml.

The output of this example is shown in Figure 3-4.

Attribute	Description	Optional
next	Used to define the target URI.	No
expr	Used when the URI is generated dynamically.	Yes
event	Used to throw the event if user input matches the grammar.	Yes
caching	Used for the caching.	Yes
fetchaudio	Used for defining the URI of the audio clip when the fetching process is done.	Yes
fetchtimeout	Used for defining the time before throwing the error.badfetch event when the content isn't available.	Yes
fetchint	Used to determine when the content can be fetched.	Yes

Table 3-2 *Attributes of the <link> Element in VoiceXML 1.0*

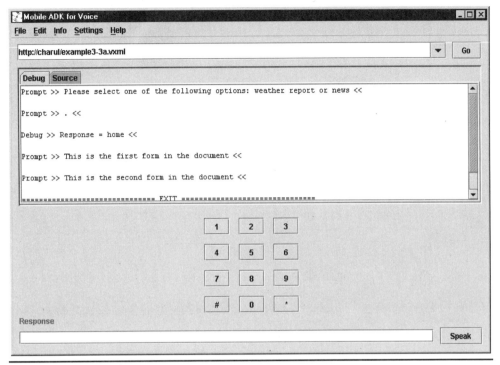

Figure 3-4   *Output of Listing 3-3a*

The <link> Element in VoiceXML 2.0

The <link> element of VoiceXML 2.0 is quite different from that of VoiceXML 1.0. Two more attributes are added to this element in version 2.0. In addition, a new format for writing the grammar is introduced in version 2.0. Table 3-3 describes the newly added attributes in the <link> element.

Attribute	Description	Optional
dtmf	Used to define the DTMF key for this particular link. It is equivalent to a defined DTMF grammar for the link.	Yes
maxage	Indicates the willingness to use content whose maximum age is not greater than the time specified.	Yes
maxstale	Indicates the willingness to use content that has exceeded the expiration time.	Yes

Table 3-3   *Attributes of the <link> Element in VoiceXML 2.0*

In Listing 3-3b, we demonstrate how the <link> element of VoiceXML 2.0 is used to accomplish the same task as achieved by the <link> element of VoiceXML 1.0.

Listing 3-3b: *The <link> Element in VoiceXML 2.0 (example3-3b.vxml)*

```
<?xml version = "1.0"?>
<vxml version = "2.0">
      <link next = "http://charul/example1a.vxml" dtmf = "1">
            <grammar mode = "voice">
                  <rule id = "root" scope = "public">
                        <one-of>
                              <item>
                                    home
                              </item>
                              <item>
                                    main menu
      </item>
                        </one-of>
                  </rule>
            </grammar>
      </link>
      <menu scope = "dialog">
            <prompt>
                  Please select one of the following options: weather report or
news.
             </prompt>
            <choice next = "#form1">
                  weather report
            </choice>
            <choice next = "#form2">
                  news
            </choice>
            <nomatch>
                  <reprompt />
            </nomatch>
      </menu>
      <form id = "form1">
            <block>
                  You selected weather report.
                  <disconnect />
            </block>
      </form>
      <form id = "form2">
            <block>
                  You selected news.
                  <disconnect />
```

```
            </block>
        </form>
</vxml>
```

The preceding code is almost similar to that of Listing 3-3a. The only difference is that the <link> element has been changed according to the VoiceXML 2.0 standards and it now follows the rules of a valid XML application for writing the grammar. Listing 3-3b gives the same result as Listing 3-3a when run on the system (refer back to Figure 3-4).

Links can also throw an event when matched instead of sent to a new document on the server. For example, when the user says "exit," the <link> element is used to throw the event and then it's used with the <catch> element to terminate the application. The following sample code demonstrates this process:

```
<link event = "exit">
        <grammar mode = "voice">
                <rule id = "root" scope = "public">
                        <one-of>
                                <item>
                                        terminate
                                </item>
                                <item>
                                        exit
                                </item>
                        </one-of>
                </rule>
        </grammar>
</link>
```

With the preceding sample, we conclude our discussion of the VXML application structure and navigation techniques. In the next section, we take up another major aspect of VoiceXML applications—methods of collecting data from the user.

Getting Input from the User

In HTML, you employ forms to collect the user's data using various field and input types. After collecting the data using an HTML-based form, you post that data to the server using the <submit> element. The server does the rest of the processing and stores the data in the database. VoiceXML also follows the form-based structure for collecting various types of data from the user and submitting it to the server. In VoiceXML, forms are treated as key components for developing applications.

In VoiceXML, data is collected using the <form> element and its subelements such as fields and the like. Table 3-4 provides descriptions of the <form> element attributes.

Attribute	Description	Optional
id	Used for defining the name of the form. The form name is used for referencing the form at other places within the document.	Yes
scope	The value of the scope attribute decides the scope of the form grammar. For example, if the scope is "document," then the document containing this form is a root-level document. So the form grammar is alive during the complete session while accessing the application and can be accessed from any document or subdialog within the application.	Yes

Table 3-4   *Attributes of the <form> Element*

Types of Form Items

Two types of form items are available in VoiceXML for working with the <form> element: field items and control items. *Field items* are used to collect data from the user and *control items* carry a block of code for completing a specific task. Let's take a closer look at both these form items.

Types of Field Items

In VoiceXML, field items are used to specify a field item variable for collecting information from the user. All the field items are equipped with well-designed prompts and grammar to help the user make a choice from the available options. Listed here are all the available field items:

► <field> element

► <record> element

► <transfer> element

► <object> element

► <subdialog> element

We discuss these elements in the following sections in detail, illustrating the use of each element with relevant sample code. Some of the examples are provided in both versions of VoiceXML for your reference.

The <field> Element

The <field> element comes under the form items section in VoiceXML, and it works as a subelement of the <form> element. You use the field element to define an input field for collecting user data. The defined input field is stored in a variable so that it can be submitted to the server or can be used anywhere in the document. Table 3-5 describes all the attributes of the <field> element.

Attribute	Description	Optional
name	Used to define the name of the variable for storing the information. The name must be a unique variable name in the scope of the same form.	No
expr	Used to define the initial value of the declared variable.	Yes
cond	Provides a boolean condition to check whether the form item is visited or not.	Yes
type	Used to define the type of the data that you are going to collect from the user for this specific item.	No
slot	Used for defining the name of the grammar slot to be used.	Yes
modal	This is a boolean type attribute. If the value of the modal attribute is false, all the currently active grammars are kept alive while collecting the data from the user of this particular field item. If the value is set as true, then only the field grammar is activated and all the other activated grammars are temporarily disabled until the data is collected.	Yes

Table 3-5   *Attributes of the <field> Element*

While collecting data from the user, you also have to specify the type of data so that the voice browser is able to recognize and process the data after collecting it. The different types of data are described in Table 3-6.

As described in Table 3-6, seven data types are available in VoiceXML for collecting user information. The only missing major data type is a character data type for storing large or small character data while working with the <field> element. In the absence of a character

Data Type	Description
boolean	Used to simulate a yes-and-no type of environment for the specific field.
date	Used to collect the user input in date format. Four digits are used for the year, two digits each for the month and the day.
digits	Used for collecting numerical data from the user in the form of DTMF input or voice input. For example, the user may say "two seven nine" to enter 279.
currency	Used for collecting currency type data from the user.
number	Used for collecting number type data from the user. For example, if the user says "two hundred seventy nine," the system will parse the input to 279. This data type also supports decimal points between numbers. For example, if the user says "two hundred seventy point fifty," the system will parse the input to 270.50 while processing it.
phone	Used for collecting phone numbers from the user. The accepted input depends on local information and may vary with different platforms.
time	Used to collect time information from the user in the form of phrases and DTMF-based input. The syntax for representing the time may vary with different platforms and depends on the locale.

Table 3-6   *Data Types*

data type, the only way to store or gather large amounts of character data is to use the <record> element and then submit the collected data to the server.

Next, we show you code samples for each data type to illustrate the process of collecting various types of data from the user.

Collecting the Boolean Type Data   In Listing 3-4, we are seeking user permission for transferring a call to another destination by using the boolean type field.

Listing 3-4:   *Collecting Boolean Type Data (example3-4.vxml)*

```
<?xml version = "1.0"?>
<vxml version = "2.0">
        <form id = "select">
                <field name = "transfer" type = "boolean">
                        <prompt>
                                <voice gender = "male" category = "adult">
                                        Do you want to transfer this call to
                                                <emphasis level = "strong">
                                                        Timothy
                                                </emphasis>
                                        for further assistance ?
                                </voice>
                        </prompt>
                        <filled>
                                <prompt>
                                        You have selected
                                                <value expr = "transfer" />
                                </prompt>
                        </filled>
                </field>
        </form>
</vxml>
```

In Listing 3-4, we've defined a <field> item and specified the type as boolean for simulating a yes/no condition because the user can select only one choice. After collecting the input from the user, we prompt him or her for information about the selected choice. If the user says "yes," then the value of the selected variable becomes true. If the user says "no," the value corresponding to false is assigned to the selected variable defined in the <field> element. The output of this code is shown in Figure 3-5.

Collecting the Phone Type Data   For collecting phone numbers from the users, you use the phone data type. In Listings 3-5a and 3-5b, we demonstrate how to collect user data using the phone type and then play back the collected data.

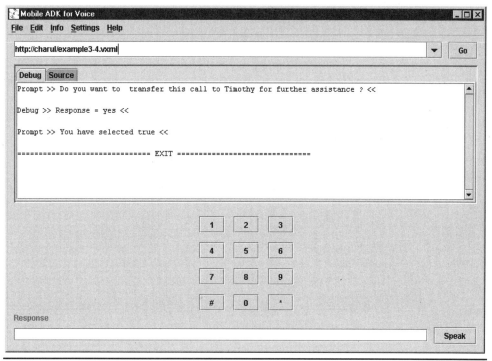

Figure 3-5   *Output of Listing 3-4*

Listing: 3-5a: *Collecting Phone Type Data in VoiceXML 1.0 (example3-5a.vxml)*

```
<?xml version = "1.0"?>
<vxml version = "1.0">
      <var name = "telno" />
      <form id = "input">
            <field name = "number" type = "phone">
                  <prompt>
                        Please press the number you want to dial
                  </prompt>
                  <nomatch>
                        <reprompt />
                  </nomatch>
                  <noinput>
                        <reprompt />
                  </noinput>
            </field>
            <filled>
                  <if cond = "number.length == 7">
```

```
                              <assign expr = "number" name = "document.telno" />
                              <goto next = "#confirm" />
                              <else />
                              <audio>
                                    This is an invalid entry
                              </audio>
                              <clear namelist = "number" />
                              <goto next = "input" />
                        </if>
                  </filled>
            </form>
            <form id = "confirm">
                  <field name = "verify" type = "boolean">
                        <prompt>
                              Please confirm the number
<value expr = "document.telno" />
                              . say yes or no
                        </prompt>
                        <filled>
                              <if cond = "verify == true">
                                    <prompt>
                                          Now dialing the number
      </prompt>
                                    <else />
                                    <prompt>
                                          Terminating the application
                                    </prompt>
                                    <throw event = "telephone.disconnect.hangup" />
                              </if>
                        </filled>
                  </field>
            </form>
</vxml>
```

Listing: 3-5b: *Collecting Phone Type Data in VoiceXML 2.0 (example3-5b.vxml)*

```
<?xml version = "1.0"?>
<vxml version = "2.0">
      <var name = "telno" />
      <form id = "input">
            <field name = "number" type = "phone">
                  <prompt>
                        Please press the number you want to dial
                  </prompt>
                  <nomatch>
                        <reprompt />
                  </nomatch>
```

```
                <noinput>
                        <reprompt />
                </noinput>
        </field>
        <filled>
                <if cond = "number.length == 7">
                        <assign expr = "number" name = "document.telno" />
                        <goto next = "#confirm" />
                        <else />
                        <audio>
                                This is an invalid entry
        </audio>
                        <clear namelist = "number" />
                        <goto next = "input" />
                </if>
        </filled>
    </form>
    <form id = "confirm">
        <field name = "verify" type = "boolean">
                <prompt>
                        Please confirm the number
                        <say-as type = "telephone">
<value expr = "document.telno" />
                        </say-as>
                        . say yes or no
                </prompt>
                <filled>
                        <if cond = "verify == true">
                                <prompt>
                                        Now dialing the number
                                </prompt>
                                <else />
                                <prompt>
                                        Terminating the application
        </prompt>
                                <throw event = "telephone.disconnect.hangup" />
                        </if>
                </filled>
        </field>
    </form>
</vxml>
```

The only difference between Listings 3-5a and 3-5b is the stage at which we prompt the user-collected data. In Listing 3-5b, we use the <say-as> element to define the pattern in which data is pronounced while generating the synthesized speech. Figure 3-6 shows the output of both examples after the user confirms a given number. Figure 3-7 displays the output when the user selects "no" and declines the given number.

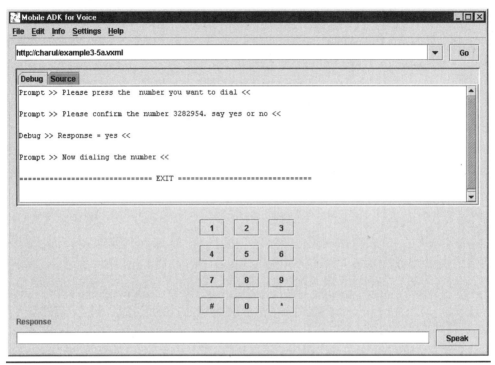

Figure 3-6 *Output of Listings 3-5a and 3-5b when user confirms phone number*

Collecting the Digits Type Data   Now, let's see how digit type data is received from the user using the <field> element. It must be noted that once you define the data type as digit, when the user says, "two five zero," the system will parse this input as a string of numbers and interpret it as 250. The valid patterns for giving input may vary for different platforms. In Listings 3-6a and 3-6b, we prompt the user to enter the number of desired cold drinks, and then to confirm the order.

Listing 3-6a: *Collecting the Digits Type Data in VoiceXML 1.0 (example3-6a.vxml)*

```
<?xml version = "1.0"?>
<vxml version = "1.0">
     <form id = "digitcheck">
          <block>
               Welcome to cold drink provider.
          </block>
          <field name = "digittype" type = "digits">
```

```
        <prompt>
                How many cold drinks you want to order?
        </prompt>
        <filled>
                <prompt>
                    You have ordered
                <value expr = "digittype" />
                    cold drinks.  These will be delivered shortly to
your house.
                </prompt>
        </filled>
    </field>
  </form>
</vxml>
```

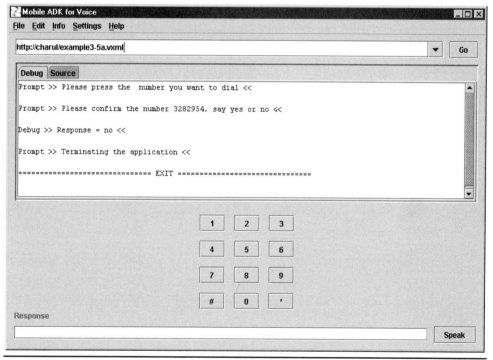

Figure 3-7   *Output of Listings 3-5a and 3-5b when user doesn't confirm phone number*

Listing 3-6b: *Collecting the Digits Type Data in VoiceXML 2.0 (example3-6b.vxml)*

```
<?xml version = "1.0"?>
<vxml version = "2.0">
      <form id = "digitcheck">
            <block>
                  Welcome to cold drink provider.
            </block>
            <field name = "digittype" type = "digits">
                  <prompt>
                        How many cold drinks you want to order?
            </prompt>
                  <filled>
                        <prompt>
                              You have ordered
                              <say-as type = "number">
                                    <value expr = "digittype" />
                              </say-as>
                              cold drinks.  These will be delivered shortly to
your house.
                        </prompt>
                  </filled>
            </field>
      </form>
</vxml>
```

The output of Listings 3-6a and 3-6b is shown in Figure 3-8. You can see in this figure that we give the input as "two five zero," and the system automatically converts it to 250 while handling the data. Remember, number choices can be entered only by saying single digits. Thus, the entry "three hundred and ten" isn't allowed. To enter this number, you have to say "three one zero."

Collecting the Time Type Data   When you need to collect time information from the user, define the type as time while defining the <field> element in your form. When users interact with the form, they can enter their choice by pressing the DTMF keys or by saying the desired choice in the format demonstrated in the example that follows. In addition, the time must be expressed in the 24-hour format.

For entering 5:21 A.M., you have to press the keys in the following order:

1. DTMF 0
2. DTMF 5
3. DTMF 2
4. DTMF 1

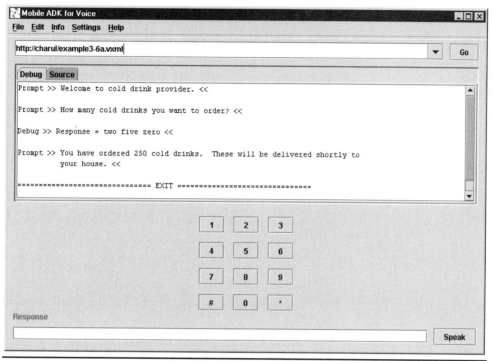

Figure 3-8   *Output of the Listings 3-6a and 3-6b*

The system on receiving this input will automatically convert it to 05:21 A.M. while parsing the data. If the user is to provide spoken input, he or she will have to say "five twenty one" to specify the time as 05:21 A.M. Listing 3-7 shows the function of time data type.

Listing 3-7:   *Collecting the Time Type Data (example3-7.vxml)*

```xml
<?xml version = "1.0"?>
<vxml version = "2.0">
     <form id = "digitcheck">
          <block>
               Welcome to Morning Alarm service
          </block>
          <field name = "digittype" type = "time" modal = "true">
     <prompt>
                    Please enter the time for wake up call
               </prompt>
               <filled>
                    <prompt>
```

```
        You have Selected
                        <say-as type = "time:hm">
                                <value expr = "digittype" />
                        </say-as>
                </prompt>
        </filled>
    </field>
</form>
</vxml>
```

In Listing 3-7, when you make your time selection, the system plays it back, adding a character after the time to represent the A.M. or P.M. status, as shown in Figure 3-9. For the P.M. status, the system adds the character "p" after the time, and for the A.M. status, the character "a" is added after the time.

Collecting the Number Type Data   While working with numbers, sometimes you require number inputs from the user that contain decimal points. To receive this type of input from the user, use the number type. While working with the number type, the user may say

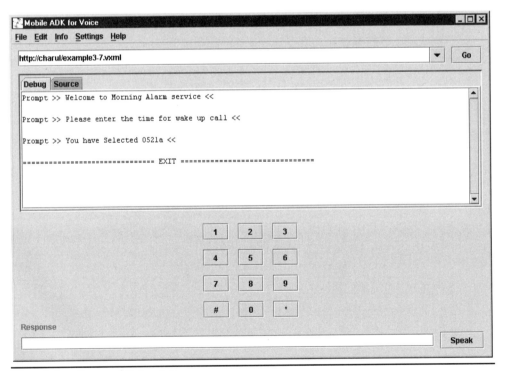

Figure 3-9   *Output of Listing 3-7*

"thirty five point one'' to represent 35.1. To supply this input, the user can also press the DTMF keys in the following order:

1. DTMF 3
2. DTMF 5
3. DTMF *
4. DTMF 1

Note that while entering the input from the keypad, the * button is used for specifying a decimal point between two numbers. In Listings 3-8a and 3-8b, we prompt the user to say a number of choices. The user's choices are then played back.

Listing 3-8a: *Collecting the Number Type Data in VoiceXML 1.0 (example3-8a.vxml)*

```
<?xml version = "1.0"?>
<vxml version = "1.0">
    <form id = "numbercheck">
        <field name = "numbertype" type = "number">
            <prompt>
                Please select a number.
            </prompt>
            <filled>
                <prompt>
                    You have selected
            <value expr = "numbertype" />
                </prompt>
            </filled>
        </field>
    </form>
</vxml>
```

Listing 3-8b: *Collecting the Number Type Data in VoiceXML 2.0 (example3-8b.vxml)*

```
<?xml version = "1.0"?>
<vxml version = "2.0">
    <form id = "numbercheck">
        <field name = "numbertype" type = "number">
            <prompt>
                Please select a number.
            </prompt>
            <filled>
                <prompt>
```

```
                        <say-as type = "number">
            <value expr = "numbertype" />
                        </say-as>
                    </prompt>
                </filled>
            </field>
        </form>
</vxml>
```

The output of both these examples is displayed in Figure 3-10.

Collecting the Date Type Data   While working with date type data, just define the data type as date to get the input in date format. To enter the date using the keypad, the user has to observe the following pattern:

1. First four digits for the year
2. Next two digits for the month
3. Last two digits for the date

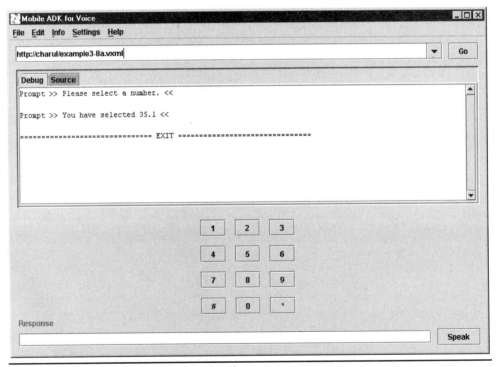

Figure 3-10   *Output of Listings 3-8a and 3-8b*

Once the user enters his or her choice, the system will return a string containing all eight digits—four for the year, and two each for the month and the date. Listing 3-9 demonstrates the process of receiving date type input from the user.

Listing 3-9:   *Collecting the Date Type Data (example3-9b.vxml)*

```
<?xml version = "1.0"?>
<vxml version = "2.0">
      <form id = "datecheck">
            <field name = "datetype" type = "date">
                  <prompt>
                        Please enter your birth date.
                  </prompt>
                  <filled>
                        <prompt>
                              Your birth date is
                              <value expr = "datetype" />
                        </prompt>
                  </filled>
            </field>
      </form>
</vxml>
```

Figure 3-11 shows the output of this example.

With Listing 3-9, we come to the end of our discussion on all major data types available in the <field> element. Now, we consider another constituent of the <field> element, shadow variables. Read on to learn about these variables.

Shadow Variables in the <field> Element   The <field> element shadow variables (prefaced by name$) use the following properties when the user fills the field element by DTMF or spoken input. All these variables are available only in read mode.

▶ **name$.confidence**   Defines the recognition confidence level of the given input. Contains a floating-point value between 0.0 and 1.0. The value 0.0 represents the minimum level of confidence, whereas the value 1.0 represents the highest level of confidence.

▶ **name$.utterance**   Provides the raw string of words that were recognized from the user input.

▶ **name$.bargeinscore**   Provides the confidence level of the barge in. Contains a floating-point value between 0.0 and 1.0, where the value 0.0 stands for the minimum confidence level and the value 1.0 denotes the maximum level of confidence.

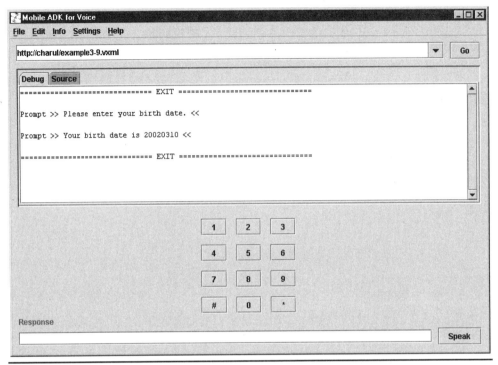

Figure 3-11   *Output of Listing 3-9*

▶ **name$.rawresults**   Provides the complete result from ASR in the form of [?][slot1:]value1[:score1]+ [?][slot2:]value2[:score2]+. where ? implies an ambiguous match, and all other optional parts are represent within [and].

▶ **name$.interpretation**   Contains the interpretation for this particular result. If the field slot matches one of the grammar slots, this value will always be the matched value. In case the field slot doesn't match any one of the grammar slots, the variable becomes an ECMAScript object.

Using Option List in <field> Element   Sometimes when working with the <field> element, you need to specify a set of predefined alternatives for this element. In such cases, the use of an option list is preferred to writing long grammars. An *option list* provides the user with a set of options from which he or she can select one. Listing 3-10a shows the use of a simple option list.

Listing 3-10a: *Option List in the <field> Element (example3-10a.vxml)*

```
<?xml version = "1.0"?>
<vxml version = "2.0">
```

```
            <form id = "option">
                  <field name = "optionlist">
                        <prompt>
                              Please select any one of the following options:
                              <enumerate />
                        </prompt>
                        <option>
                              red
                        </option>
                        <option>
                              blue
                      · </option>
                        <option>
                              green
                        </option>
                        <filled>
                              <prompt>
                                    You selected
                                    <value expr = "optionlist" />
                              </prompt>
                        </filled>
                  </field>
            </form>
</vxml>
```

In Listing 3-10a, we first provide the user with a list of available options by using the <enumerate> element and then play back the user's choice. The output of Listing 3-10a is shown in Figure 3-12.

You can also assign a DTMF value to each option in the options list by using the DTMF attribute of the <option> element. In such a case, to select an option, the user can either press the appropriate button on the keypad or give the spoken input. Listing 3-10b illustrates the use of the DTMF attribute with the <option> element.

Listing 3-10b: *Using Option List with DTMF Accessibility (example3-10b.vxml)*

```
<?xml version = "1.0"?>
<vxml version = "2.0">
      <form id = "option">
            <field name = "optionlist">
                  <prompt>
                        Select one of following options:
<enumerate />
                  </prompt>
```

```
                    <option dtmf = "1">
                          red
                    </option>
                    <option dtmf = "2">
                          blue
                    </option>
                    <option dtmf = "3">
                          green
                    </option>
                    <filled>
                          <prompt>
                                You selected
                                <value expr = "optionlist" />
                          </prompt>
                    </filled>
             </field>
      </form>
</vxml>
```

Figure 3-12   *Output of Listing 3-10a*

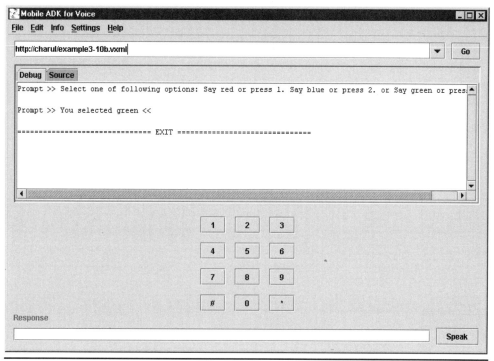

Figure 3-13   *Output of Listing 3-10b*

The output of Listing 3-10b is shown in Figure 3-13.

The <record> Element

In VoiceXML, the <record> element is used to collect data from the user in the form of an audio file, and all the recorded data is stored in a variable. You can post this data on the server and save the entire recording as a media file for later use. Attributes of the <record> element are described in Table 3-7.

Attribute	Description	Optional
name	Used to define the field item variable to store all the recorded data.	No
expr	Used to define the initial value of the variable.	Yes
modal	This is a boolean type attribute. If the value of the modal attribute is false, all the currently active grammars are kept alive while collecting the data from the user for this particular field item. If the value is set as true, then only the field grammar is activated, and all the other activated grammars are temporarily disabled until the data is collected.	Yes

Table 3-7   *Attributes of the <record> Element*

Attribute	Description	Optional
cond	Provides a boolean condition to check whether the form item is visited or not.	Yes
beep	If the value of the beep attribute is true, a tone is inserted before the start of recording. The default value is false.	Yes
maxtime	Defines the maximum time length for the recording.	Yes
finalsilence	Defines the interval of silence indicating the end of the spoken input from the user.	Yes
dtmfterm	If the value of dtmfterm is true, then the user is able to terminate the recording by pressing a button on the keypad of the telephone. The DTMF tone isn't considered part of the recorded speech.	Yes
type	Defines the media type of the recording result. This may vary with different platforms.	Yes
dest	Defines the URI destination of the recording for the streaming servers kind of services.	Yes

Table 3-7   *Attributes of the <record> Element* (continued)

If you plan to build a voice-based messaging service, you will find the <record> element quite handy for recording the user message and saving it on the server for later use. In Listing 3-11, we explain the function of the <record>element.

Listing 3-11:   *Using the <record> Element (example3-11.vxml)*

```
<?xml version = "1.0"?>
<vxml version = "2.0">
    <form>
        <record beep = "true" name = "greeting" maxtime = "50s" dtmfterm =
"true">
            <prompt>
                At the tone, please say your greeting.
</prompt>
            <noinput>
                I didn't hear anything, please try again.
        </noinput>
        </record>
        <field name = "confirm" type = "boolean">
            <prompt>
                Your greeting is
                <value expr = "greeting" />
                        .
        </prompt>
            <prompt>
```

```
                    To keep it, say yes. To discard it, say no.
        </prompt>
                <filled>
                    <if cond = "confirm">
                        <submit next = "upload1.asp" method = "post" enctype
= "multipart/form-data" namelist = "greeting" />
                    </if>
                    <clear />
                </filled>
            </field>
        </form>
</vxml>
```

In Listing 3-11, we prompt the user to record a greeting message. Once the user records the message, we play back the message to the user and ask for confirmation to save this message on the server. If the user agrees to save the message on the server, we post all the data on the server by using the <submit> element. Figure 3-14 shows the entire process of recording and saving the greeting message of Listing 3-11.

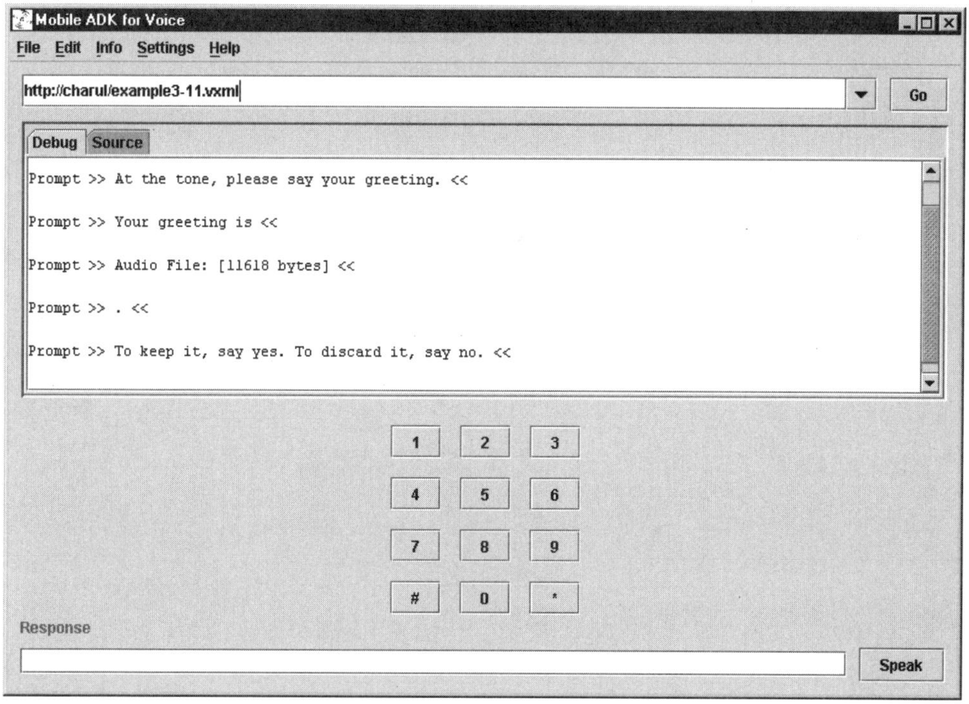

Figure 3-14   *Output of Listing 3-11*

The <record> element also contains the following shadow variables, which are available after the recording is over.

- ▶ **name$.duration**   Returns the total duration of the recording.

- ▶ **name$.size**   Returns the size of recording in bytes.

- ▶ **name$.termchar**   If the termination process is done using the DTMF key, this variable returns the value of the key pressed for terminating the recording.

- ▶ **name$.dest**   If the destination of the recorded speech has been redirected using the dest attribute, this shadow variable will return the redirected URI reference.

The <transfer> Element

Sometimes an application needs to transfer the current call to a third party for interaction with the application's user. An example of this would be transferring a call to a customer care executive for personally handling a particular matter by interacting with the application's user. In VoiceXML, the <transfer> element provides the facility to transfer calls to a third party using the telephony network. There are two types of call transfers:

- ▶ **Bridge transfer**   In a bridge transfer, the user's original session is kept on hold during the user's session with the third party. The user will return to the original session after his or her session with the third party.

- ▶ **Blind transfer**   In a blind transfer, the user's original session will end once his or her call is transferred to the third party, and the platform will throw a telephone.disconnect.transfer event. If anything remains to be executed in the original session, the execution process will be completed. However, in no case will the call with the original party be resumed.

The <transfer> element isn't a mandatory element. Most platforms support this element because it is a desirable feature. The attributes of the <transfer> element are described in Table 3-8.

Attribute	Description	Optional
name	Used to define the field item variable to store the result data.	No
expr	Used to define the initial value of the variable.	Yes
cond	Provides a boolean condition to check whether the form item is visited or not.	Yes

Table 3-8   *Attributes of the <transfer> Element*

Attribute	Description	Optional
dest	Used to define the destination URI in the form of a telephone number or IP-based telephone number.	Yes
destexpr	Used to define an ECMAScript script expression with the URI of the destination as the value.	Yes
bridge	Used to determine the next step after the call is connected to a third party. If the value of the bridge attribute is true, then the original session is suspended for the time the call is connected to the third party.	Yes
connecttimeout	Used to define the time to wait when the system is trying to transfer the call to the third party.	Yes
maxtime	Used to define the maximum allowed time for the transferred call. This attribute comes into action only when the value of the bridge is true.	Yes
transferaudio	Used to define the URI of the audio file to play from the third-party server until the third party responds to the call.	Yes

Table 3-8   *Attributes of the <transfer> Element* (continued)

In the <transfer> element, like other form elements, one field is used to store the result of the call transfer if it's a bridge transfer. In case of a blind transfer, the field item variable remains undefined. For a bridge transfer, the possible values of the field item variable are listed in Table 3-9.

Value	Description
busy	The third party has refused the call, resulting in the status being busy.
noanswer	There is no answer from the third party within the time specified by the connecttimeout attribute.
network_busy	The network that is used for transferring the call is busy.
near_end_disconnected	The call is completed but is terminated by the caller.
far_end_disconnect	The call is completed but is disconnected by the callee.
network_disconnect	The call is completed and is disconnected by the intermediate network.
maxtime_disconnect	The maximum allowed time for a call specified by using the maxtime attribute is over, and the call is disconnected by the network.
unknown	If the result is unknown to the system, then this value will be returned.

Table 3-9   *Possible Values of Field Item Variables in Bridge Transfer*

Listings 3-12a and 3-12b show the use of the <transfer> element with most of its major attributes.

Listing 3-12a: *Using the <transfer> Element in VoiceXML 1.0 (example3-12a.vxml)*

```
<?xml version = "1.0"?>
<vxml version = "1.0">
    <form id = "transfer">
            <var expr = "0" name = "duration" />
            <block>
                <prompt>
                    Please wait while your call is being transferred to our
customer care department.
                </prompt>
            </block>
            <transfer dest = "tel:+091-011-3243077" name = "transcall" bridge =
"true" connecttimeout = "5s">
                <filled>
                    <assign expr = "transcall.duration" name = "duration" />
                    <if cond = "transcall == 'busy'">
                        <prompt>
                            Sorry, all of our customer care team members
are currently busy, please try again later.
                        </prompt>
                        <elseif cond = "transcall == 'noanswer'" />
                        <prompt>
                            Sorry, our working hours are from 9:00AM to
6:00PM, please try between that time.
                        </prompt>
                        <elseif cond = "transcall == 'network_busy'" />
                        <prompt>
                            Our network is currently busy , please try
after some time.
                        </prompt>
                        <elseif cond = "transcall == 'maxtime_disconnect'"
/>
                        <prompt>
                            Sorry, the maximum allowed time duration for
the call is over now.
                        </prompt>
                    </if>
                </filled>
            </transfer>
            <block>
                Thanks for using the application.
            </block>
    </form>
</vxml>
```

Listing 3-12b: *Using the <transfer> Element in VoiceXML 2.0 (example3-12b.vxml)*

```
<?xml version = "1.0"?>
<vxml version = "2.0">
     <form id = "transfer">
          <var expr = "0" name = "duration" />
          <block>
               <prompt>
                    Please wait while your call is being transferred to our
customer care department.
               </prompt>
          </block>
          <transfer dest = "tel:+091-011-3243077" name = "transcall" bridge =
"true" transferaudio = "welcome.wav" connecttimeout = "5s">
               <filled>
                    <assign expr = "transcall.duration" name = "duration" />
                    <if cond = "transcall == 'busy'">
                         <prompt>
                              Sorry, all of our customer care team members
are currently busy, please try again later.
                         </prompt>
                    <elseif cond = "transcall == 'noanswer'" />
                    <prompt>
                              Sorry, our working hours are from 9:00AM to
6:00PM, please try between that time.
                    </prompt>
                    <elseif cond = "transcall == 'network_busy'" />
                    <prompt>
                              Our network is currently busy, please try
after some time.
                    </prompt>
                    <elseif cond = "transcall == 'maxtime_disconnect'"
/>
                    <prompt>
                              Sorry, the maximum allowed time duration for
the call is over now.
                    </prompt>
                    <elseif cond = "transcall == 'unknown'" />
<prompt>
                              Sorry, we are not able to process your request
because of some unknown reason.
                    </prompt>
                    </if>
               </filled>
          </transfer>
          <block>
               Thanks for using the application.
          </block>
     </form>
</vxml>
```

The output of Listings 3-12a and 3-12b is shown in Figure 3-15.

The <transfer> element also has one shadow variable, which is described here:

▶ **name$.duration**   This shadow variable returns the duration of a successful call in seconds.

Inside the <transfer> element, some events can also fire specific tasks such as disconnecting the call. All the events that can be thrown inside the <transfer> elements are listed here:

▶ **telephone.disconnect.hangup**   This event is thrown when the caller has hung up the phone.

▶ **telephone.disconnect.transfer**   This event is thrown when the caller has been redirected to another location and will not return.

▶ **error.telephone.noauthorization**   If the caller isn't permitted to call the destination, then this event will be thrown.

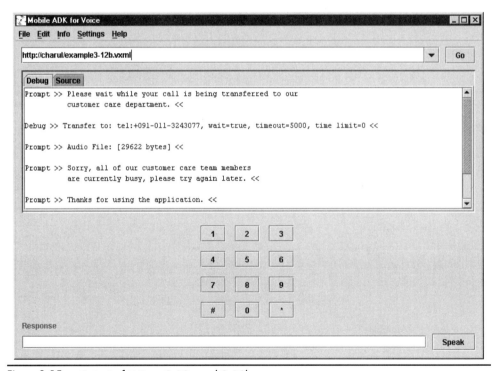

Figure 3-15   *Output of Listings 3-12a and 3-12b*

- ▶ **error.telephone.noroute**   This event will occur when the platform isn't able to call the destination.

- ▶ **error.telephone.beddestination**   If the destination URI isn't available (malformed), this event is thrown.

- ▶ **error.telephone.nosource:**   If the platform isn't able to allocate resources to transfer the call to the destination, this event will be thrown.

- ▶ **error.telephone.protocol.nnn**   If the telephony protocol stack raises an unknown exception that doesn't match any other error.telephone events, then this event will be thrown.

The <object> Element

In HTML, you use the <object> tag to include external objects such as ActiveX objects to increase the performance and the processing speed of complex transactions. External objects are also employed as reusable components and for writing the complex business logic required to perform the desired operations. VoiceXML has a corresponding element, the <object> element, which increases the functionality and performance of applications by using platform-specific objects. Table 3-10 provides a description of the attributes of the <object> element.

Attribute	Description	Optional
name	Used to define the variable. The type of the variable is defined by the object.	No
expr	Used to define the initial value of the variable.	Yes
cond	Provides a boolean condition to check whether the form item is visited or not.	Yes
classid	Used to define the URI where the object is implemented.	No
codebase	Used to define the base path, which resolves the relative URIs defined in the classid.	Yes
codetype	Defines the content type of expected data while downloading the object specified via the classid attribute.	Yes
data	Defines the URI of the location where the object data exists. In the case of a relative URI, this will be resolved using the codebase attribute.	Yes
type	Used to define the content type of data defined in the data attribute.	Yes
archive	Used to define a list of URIs of archives containing the object-relevant resources.	Yes
fetchint	Used to determine when content can be fetched.	Yes
fetchtimeout	Used for defining the time before throwing the error.badfetch event, when the content isn't available.	Yes
maxage	Indicates the willingness to use content whose maximum age isn't greater than the time specified.	Yes
maxstale	Indicates the willingness to use content that exceeds the expiration time.	Yes

Table 3-10   *Attributes of the <object> Element*

If you refer to an unknown object by using the <object> element, the error.unsupported.object event is thrown. Listing 3-13 shows an example of the <object> element.

Listing 3-13:   *Using the <object> Element (example3-13b.vxml)*

```
<?xml version = "1.0"?>
<vxml version = "2.0">
      <form id = "object">
            <object data =
"http://www.dreamtechsoftware.com/voicexml/objects/stringparse.jar" name =
"string" classid = "method://parse_string/parse_return">
                  <param expr = "document.name" name = "fname" />
                  <param expr = "document.lname" name = "lname" />
            </object>
      </form>
</vxml>
```

The <subdialog> Element

In VoiceXML, the <subdialog> element is used to invoke a dialog that has been called from some other location. When the <subdialog> element is called, a new execution process starts. This process contains all the declarations and state information for the dialog. The subdialog execution process will continue until it reaches the <return> element. The <return> element is used to end the process and return the controls to the main dialog.

When the subdialog execution process ends, it returns to the calling dialog. The context for that particular subdialog will be destroyed, and the execution process of the main dialog will resume with the <filled> element. When you invoke a subdialog, the context of the subdialog and the main dialog will stay alive independently. The instances of variables of both the contexts are different and cannot be shared with each other. In the scope of a subdialog context, the standard rules for the grammars, events, and so on apply.

There are some basic differences between subroutines and subdialogs. Subroutines are able to access variable instances in their calling routine, whereas subdialogs don't have access to the variable instances in their calling dialogs. Subdialogs are the most convenient way to build a library of reusable components. Table 3-11 describes the attributes of the <subdialog> element.

Attribute	Description	Optional
name	Used to define the variable that holds the result when returning to the main dialog.	No
expr	Used to define the initial value of the variable.	Yes
cond	Provides a boolean condition to check whether the form item is visited or not.	Yes
namelist	Has the same functionality as the namelist attribute in the <submit> element. Provides a list of variables to submit.	No

Table 3-11   *Attributes of the <subdialog> Element*

Attribute	Description	Optional
src	Used to define the URI of the subdialog.	No
method	Used to define the method of request from the available methods of get and post.	No
enctype	Used to define the type of media encoding.	Yes
fetchaudio	Used for defining the URI of the audio clip when the fetching process is over.	Yes
fetchint	Used to determine when content can be fetched.	Yes
fetchtimeout	Used for specifying the time before throwing the error.badfetch event when the content isn't available.	Yes
maxage	Indicates the willingness to use content whose maximum age isn't greater than the time specified.	Yes
maxstale	The maxstale attribute indicates the willingness to use content that exceed the expiration time.	Yes

Table 3-11 *Attributes of the <subdialog> Element* (continued)

In subdialogs, the <param> element is used to pass parameters to the subdialog at the time of invoking it. All parameters, which are passed using the <param> element, must be declared in the subdialog using the <var> element. If the variable isn't declared in the subdialog, a semantic error occurs. If you declare a variable in the subdialog and no <param> element is associated with it, the value of the expr attribute is assigned to the variable. However, if the <param> element is found, then the value of expr is ignored.

Listings 3-14a and 3-14b illustrate the use of the <subdialog> element. In the first document, shown in Listing 13-14a, we invoke a subdialog, and in the second document, shown in Listing 13-14b, we collect information. We then return to the main dialog where we play back the collected information.

Listing 3-14a: *Using the <subdialog> Element (example3-14.vxml)*

```
<?xml version = "1.0"?>
<vxml version = "2.0">
     <form id = "sub">
          <block>
               <prompt>
                    Now transferring to the subdialog to collect the
information.
               </prompt>
          </block>
          <subdialog src = "http://charul/subdialog.vxml" name = "result">
               <filled>
                    <prompt>
                         Welcome back to the main dialog. Your age is <value
expr = "result.age" />.
```

```
                            </prompt>
                    </filled>
                </subdialog>
        </form>
</vxml>
```

Listing 3-14b: *Subdialog Document (subdialog.vxml)*

```
<?xml version = "1.0"?>
<vxml version = "2.0">
        <form id = "subdialog">
                <field name = "age" type = "digits">
                        <prompt>
                                Please say your age
                        </prompt>
                        <filled>
                                <return namelist = "age " />
                        </filled>
                </field>
        </form>
</vxml>
```

The output of both Listing 3-14a and 3-14b is shown in Figure 3-16.

Types of Control Items

In VoiceXML, two types of control items are available under the <form> element:

►   <block> element
►   <initial> element

Let's take a closer look at each of these elements.

The <block> Element

The <block> element is a child of the <form> element and is used to build a block of executable contents. It contains the code employed for prompting the user and for computation. The <block> element isn't used for collecting information from the user through the field element. The following sample code shows the most basic use of the <block> element:

```
<block>
        Hello world
</block>
```

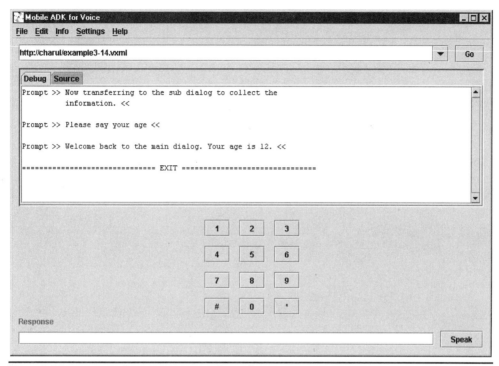

Figure 3-16   *Output of Listings 3-14a and 3-14b*

On execution of the preceding code, the system will display a "Hello world" message. If you are using the <block> element, then the form item variable value is automatically set to true before the execution of the <block> element. The attributes of the <block> element are described in Table 3-12.

The <initial> Element

When you are using the mixed initiative form approach in VoiceXML, the <initial> element comes into action. It's executed when the user is initially prompted for some general information but has not reached the directed mode phase of the application. If the user has reached the directed mode, the server side controls the process, and the initial element has no role. The <initial> element doesn't have grammars or any <filled> element like other form items.

Attribute	Description	Optional
name	Used to find out whether this block is eligible for execution or not.	No
expr	Used to define the initial value of the variable.	Yes
cond	Provides a boolean condition to check whether the form item is visited or not.	Yes

Table 3-12   *Attributes of the <block> Element*

Attribute	Description	Optional
name	Used to track whether the <initial> element is eligible for execution or not.	No
expr	Used to define the initial value of the variable.	Yes
cond	Provides a boolean condition to check whether the form item is visited or not.	Yes

Table 3-13 *Attributes of the <initial> Element*

Table 3-13 describes the attributes of the <initial> element.

When the <initial> element is executed in the application, no field grammar is active, and if any event occurs between executions, then the relevant event handler is executed. Listing 3-15 shows the use of the <initial> element.

Listing 3-15: *Using the <initial> Element (example3-15b.vxml)*

```
<?xml version = "1.0"?>
<vxml version = "2.0">
     <form id = "collectinformation">
          <grammar src =
"http://www.dreamtechsoftware.com/voicexml/grammar/example15b.grxml" type =
"application/grammar+xml" />
          <block>
               Welcome to the highway restaurants locater.
     </block>
          <initial name = "entered">
               <prompt>
                    Please  indicate the starting and ending points of your
journey by saying from starting point to ending point.
               </prompt>
               <nomatch count = "1">
                    For example "from New Delhi to Agra".
          </nomatch>
          </initial>
          <field name = "startingpoint">
               <grammar src =
"http://www.www.dreamtechsoftware.com/voicexml/grammar/example15b1.grxml" type =
"application/grammar+xml" />
               <prompt>
                    Please say your starting point.
               </prompt>
          </field>
          <field name = "endingpoint">
               <grammar src =
"http://www.www.dreamtechsoftware.com/voicexml/grammar/example15b2.grxml" type =
"application/grammar+xml" />
               <prompt>
```

```
                    Please say your ending point.
                </prompt>
            </field>
        </form>
    </vxml>
```

Form Interpretation Algorithm

The *form interpretation algorithm* (FIA) is used to control the interaction between a user and a form in VoiceXML. The FIA also controls the execution process of menu items. While controlling a menu item, the FIA handles it as a form element containing a single field item. The choice elements build the <filled> element during the execution process of a menu item.

While executing the forms in a VoiceXML document, the FIA is responsible for handling the following tasks:

- ▶ Initialization of the <form> element and its subelements
- ▶ Prompting the user and handling the execution of the <prompt> element
- ▶ Activating grammars and mapping the inputs from grammars
- ▶ Controlling all other form activities

The FIA includes the following four phases in a complete life cycle:

- ▶ Initialization phase
- ▶ Select phase
- ▶ Collect phase
- ▶ Process phase

We explain these phases in the following sections.

Initialization Phase

This is the first phase in the life cycle of FIA. The *initialization phase* represents the time the document is being loaded on the server and the form is being initialized. The initialization process of a form is controlled within the initialization phase itself. Here are the steps involved in the initialization phase:

1. The form initialization process starts by loading the content in sequential order.
2. All the declared variables are initialized in the following manner:
    - ▶ Check for the expr attribute. If the attribute contains a value, that value is assigned to the variable.
    - ▶ If no expression is defined, the variable is initialized as undefined.

3. The available form items are initialized in document order with the counter set to 1.

4. If the current form is initialized as a result of any previous input provided by the user in the last form, the session moves to the process phase directly after the initialization process.

Figure 3-17 visually depicts the initialization phase.

Select and Collect Phases

Once the initialization phase is over, the next phase in the FIA is the *name selection phase*, or *select phase*. The main objective of the select phase is to control the process of selecting form items based on their order in the document. The select phase includes the following steps:

1. If any <goto> element existed in the previously selected form, it selects the specified form in the last <goto> element.

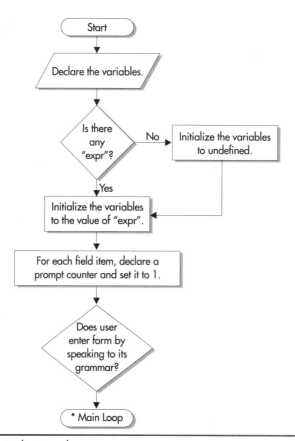

Figure 3-17   *The initialization phase*

2. In cases where the <goto> element doesn't exist in the last form, the first form item with the unsatisfied guard condition is selected in the document order.

3. If none of the form items have an unsatisfied guard condition, the FIA performs an <exit/> operation.

After the completion of the select phase, the control is transferred to the *collect phase*. In the collect phase, the FIA is responsible for collecting all input from the user. In this phase, all the events are also collected for the process phase.

Figure 3-18 shows the select and collect phases.

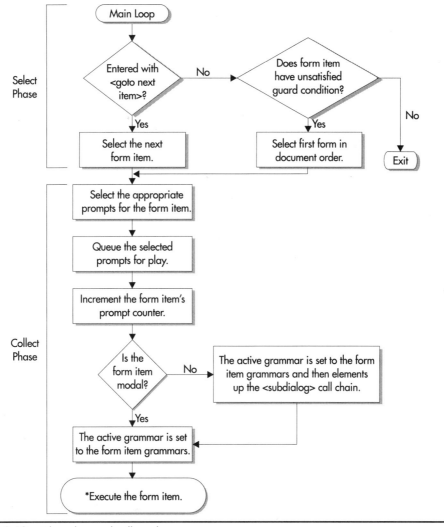

Figure 3-18   *The select and collect phases*

Process Phase

The main objective of the *process phase* is to process all the collected data in the collect phase as well as conduct the processing on the events collected during the collect phase.

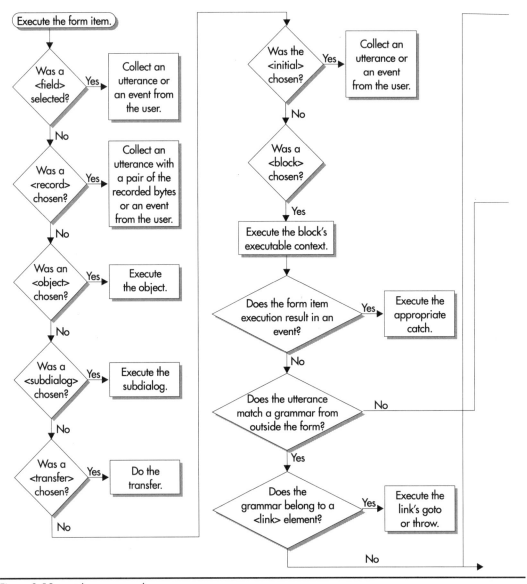

Figure 3-19a   *The process phase*

After the completion of the process phase, controls are again transferred to the select phase for a new cycle. Figures 3-19a and 3-19b depict the process phase.

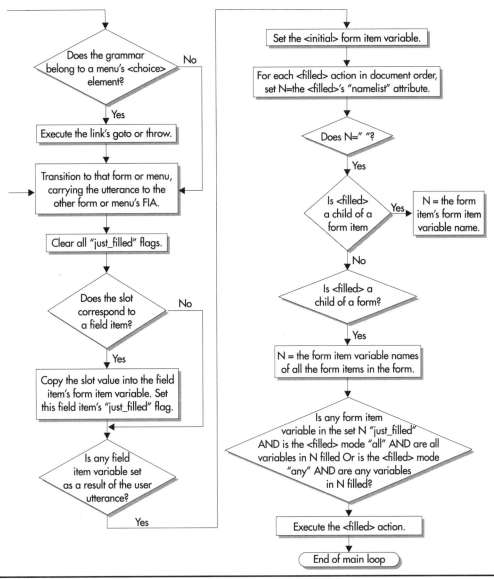

Figure 3-19b   *The process phase* (continued)

Summary

In this chapter, we discussed the form items and the techniques of getting user input in VoiceXML at length. We examined all the available form items and included illustrative examples. We also showed you the document structure and the document execution process in VoiceXML. This chapter provides a complete reference for understanding forms in VoiceXML and how they actually work and collect input from the user. Towards the end of the chapter, we explained the form interpretation algorithm.

Advanced Elements of VoiceXML

I n this chapter, we proceed to discuss some of the advanced features offered by the VoiceXML language for handling complex situations. Although we have shown you how to build simple VoiceXML documents, we have yet to take up topics such as event handling and variables. When you start building large-scale voice applications, you need to have a closer and more accurate control over the application for ensuring sound performance. Large-scale applications often require judiciously planned usage of features such as error handling and resource fetching, as well as more versatile prompts created by using various speech markup language elements.

We begin our discussion with the various types of forms and processes for event handling, for managing the various events that are likely to arise in the course of an advanced VoiceXML application. Following this, we take a look at the various types of variables supported by the VoiceXML language. Later on the techniques for caching and fetching resources and the various elements that constitute the speech markup are described.

Types of Forms

Two different types of forms are used in voice applications, each based on a different approach: directed forms and mixed initiative forms. In all the examples considered so far, we have employed forms based on the directed approach. Such forms are used to build a computer-directed interaction voice interface for an application. With directed forms, all the form items are executed in sequential order starting from the top. The computer controls and directs the selection of form items. Listings 4-1a, 4-1b, and 4-1c together show an example of a directed form used to build a restaurant finder service.

Listing 4-1a: *Using a Directed Form (directed_form.vxml)*

```
<?xml version = "1.0"?>
<vxml version = "2.0">
    <form id = "restaurant_finder">
        <block>
            Welcome to the Restaurant Finder service.
        </block>
        <field name = "state_locater">
            <prompt>
                Please say the name of a country.
            </prompt>
            <grammar src =
http://www.dreamtechsoftware.com/voicexml/countrynames.grxml" type =
"application/grammar+xml" />
        </field>
        <field name = "city_locater">
            <prompt>
                Please say the name of a city.
        </prompt>
```

```
                    <grammar src =
http://www.dreamtechsoftware.com/voicexml/citynames.grxml" type =
"application/grammar+xml" />
            </field>
            <block>
                    <submit next =
http://www.dreamtechsoftware.com/voicexml/restaurant.asp" namelist = "city_locater
state_locater" />
            </block>
        </form>
</vxml>
```

Listing 4-1b: *State Names Grammar for the Directed Form (countrynames.grxml)*

```
<?xml version = "1.0"?>
<grammar root = "statenames" version = "1.0" xml:lang = "en-US">
      <rule id = "statenames" scope = "public">
            <one-of>
                    <item tag = "france">
                            france
                    </item>
                    <item tag = "england">
                            england
                    </item>
                    <item tag = "norway">
                            norway
                    </item>
            </one-of>
      </rule>
</grammar>
```

Listing 4-1c: *City Names Grammar for the Directed Form (citynames.grxml)*

```
<?xml version = "1.0"?>
<grammar root = "maingrammar" version = "1.0" xml:lang = "en-US">
      <rule id = "maingrammar" scope = "public">
            <one-of>
                    <item tag = "paris">
                            paris
                    </item>
                    <item tag = "london">
                            london
                    </item>
                    <item tag = "oslo">
```

```
                    oslo
                </item>
            </one-of>
        </rule>
</grammar>
```

In this example, all interaction between the user and the system is guided by the computer, and the processing is done in sequential order from top to bottom. Here is the output of Listings 4-1a, 4-1b, and 4-1c:

▶ **System**   "Welcome to the restaurant finder service."

▶ **System**   "Please say the name of a country."

▶ **User**   "India."

▶ **System**   (A nomatch event is thrown.) "Service for this country isn't currently available. Please say the name of country."

▶ **User**   "France."

▶ **System**   "Please say the name of a city."

▶ **User**   "Paris."

▶ **System**   "There are 40 Food Plaza restaurants in Paris. You can choose any of the restaurants from the Food Plaza chain to get 30 percent discount on all items."

Mixed Initiative Forms

In applications that use forms based on the mixed initiative approach, the conversation between the user and the computer can be directed by either the user or the system. All forms that are based on the mixed initiative approach contain at least one or more <initial> elements to start the conversation and collect input from the user. In addition, one or more form-level grammars can exist within the same document to collect data pertaining to more than one field item from a single user utterance.

Activating more than one form-level grammar in a single document helps the user get things done much faster as compared to the directed forms approach. Listing 4-2 shows a refurbished version of the earlier code example using the mixed initiative approach.

Listing 4-2:   *Using a Mixed Initiative Form (mixed_form.vxml)*

```
<?xml version = "1.0"?>
<vxml version = "2.0">
    <form id = "restaurant_locater">
        <grammar src = "http://www.dreamtechsoftware.com/voicexml/main.grxml"
type = "application/grammar+xml" />
        <initial name = "begin">
```

```
        <prompt>
                Please say the name of the country and the city in which
you would like to find a restaurant.
        </prompt>
    </initial>
    <field name = "country">
        <prompt>
                Please say the name of a country
        </prompt>
    </field>
    <field name = "cityname">
        <prompt>
                Please say the name of a city
                <value expr = "state" />
        </prompt>
        <filled>
                <submit next =
"http://www.dreamtechsoftware.com/voicexml/restaurant.asp" namelist = "cityname
statename" />
        </filled>
    </field>
    </form>
</vxml>
```

In this listing, we have enhanced the restaurant finder service by using the mixed initiative form approach. Here, the interaction between the user and the system is guided by both the computer and the user, enabling the user to get things done faster as compared to the directed form approach. Here is the output of Listing 4-2:

▶ **System**   "Please say the name of the country and the city in which you would like to find a restaurant."

▶ **User**   "Paris, France."

▶ **System**   "There are 12 restaurants in Paris that we have found in our database. For Indian food, do visit Shalimar restaurant."

Event Handling in VoiceXML

In VoiceXML, every session of interaction between a user and an application is marked by several types of events. For instance, if the user provides unacceptable input or if there is a semantic error in the document, the system will throw a related event to execute the predetermined course of action for that event. You can also use the <throw> element for throwing an event. All the thrown events are caught using the <catch> element. In the section that follows, we present a detailed analysis of the complete process.

The <throw> Element

The <throw> element in a VoiceXML document is used for throwing an event whenever necessary during the user's interaction with the application or for performing other tasks. The <throw> element can be used to throw the following two types of events:

▶ Predefined events

▶ Application-defined events

Table 4-1 describes all attributes of the <throw>element for VoiceXML 2.0.

When a user interacts with an application, several events can be thrown by the platform. All these events are predefined for specific occurrences that could take place in a session. Table 4-2 presents brief descriptions of some predefined events in VoiceXML 2.0.

VoiceXML also contains a set of predefined errors. Table 4-3 carries brief descriptions of the predefined errors in VoiceXML 2.0.

The <catch> Element

The <catch> element in VoiceXML contains a set of executable codes that are executed when particular events occur. Suppose user input doesn't match the grammars prescribed for the field containing the input, and this happens three times repeatedly. In each instance, the time platform will generate a nomatch event. When the count of the nomatch event exceeds the allowed limit of three inputs, the <catch> element may be used to trace the nomatch event

Attribute	Description
event	Used to define the name of the event that is being thrown. For example, <throw event="nomatch"> is used for throwing the nomatch event.
eventexpr	Used to define an ECMAScript expression evaluating the name of the event being thrown.
message	Used to provide additional information regarding the thrown event. This attribute varies from platform to platform.
messageexpr	Used to define an ECMAScript expression evaluating the message.

Table 4-1   *Attributes of the <throw> Element*

Event	Description
cancel	This event occurs when the user requests to stop the current record.
telephone.disconnect.hangup	This event occurs when the user hangs up the phone and the application is terminated.
noinput	This event occurs when the user fails to provide the input within the time limit set by the timeout attribute.
telephone.disconnect.transfer	This event is associated with the <transfer> element. When you transfer a call to a third party as a blind transfer using the <transfer> element, the call isn't returned to the original called party. The platform throws this event.
help	The platform throws this event when the user prompts for the help feature.
nomatch	If the user input doesn't match the grammar associated with the field containing the input, the system throws the nomatch event.
exit	If the user requests to exit from the application, the platform throws the exit event.
maxspeechtimeout	If the user input length exceeds the limit defined in the maxspeechtimeout attribute, the platform throws this event.

Table 4-2   *Predefined Events in VoiceXML 2.0*

Error	Description
error.badfetch	The platform throws this error when the system fails to fetch the document from the specified address. Some possible causes of such a failure are: the document is missing at the specified address, the document or URI is malformed, a communication problem occurred in the network, and so on.
error.badfetch.http error.badfetch.protocol	If the system is unable to fetch some content, the interpreter provides detailed information about the specific protocols for which the problem was encountered.
error.semantic	During the parsing of a VoiceXML document, if a runtime error such as an error due to improper nesting of elements occurs, the system throws error.semantic.

Table 4-3   *Predefined Errors in VoiceXML 2.0*

Error	Description
error.noauthorization	If the user tries to perform some action on the server for which he or she isn't authorized, then error.noauthorization is thrown. For example, if the user, by using the <transfer> element, tries to transfer a call to some number to which he or she has no access rights, this error will occur.
error.unsupported.format	If you try to process an object that isn't supported on the server, then this error is thrown. For example, if you are recording audio from the user using the record element and you specify an unsupported format for saving the recorded message, then the platform will throw this error.

Table 4-3   *Predefined Errors in VoiceXML 2.0* (continued)

and its occurrence and perform the necessary action accordingly. Listing 4-3 explains the use of the <catch > element in a VoiceXML document.

Listing 4-3:   *Using the <catch> Element (example4-3b.vxml)*

```
<?xml version = "1.0"?>
<vxml version = "2.0">
    <form id = "checkday">
        <field name = "dayofweek">
            <prompt>
                Please say the name of the current day.
        </prompt>
            <grammar>
                <rule id = "root" scope = "public">
                    <one-of>
                        <item tag = "monday">
                            Monday
                        </item>
                    </one-of>
                </rule>
            </grammar>
            <nomatch>
                Sorry you have selected the wrong day
    <reprompt />
            </nomatch>
            <noinput>
                I did not hear anything
```

```
                    <reprompt />
            </noinput>
            <help>
                    Please say the name of current day such as Sunday,
Wednesday, and so on
            </help>
            <catch count = "3" event = "nomatch noinput">
        <prompt>
                        Sorry you have exceeded the maximum limit allowed
for inputs
            </prompt>
            </catch>
        </field>
        <block>
            You have chosen
            <value expr = "dayofweek" />
        </block>
    </form>
</vxml>
```

In this example, we prompt the user to enter the name of the current day. When the user supplies the input, we check whether the input conforms to the grammar prescribed for the field. It's possible that the user may provide an unacceptable input more than three times or that he or she doesn't provide the input at all even after being prompted three times. In such cases, we use the <catch> element to capture the generated events on the server and to count the number of times an invalid input is provided. If the number of unacceptable inputs exceeds the set limit, a message is served to the user. Figure 4-1 shows the function of the <catch> element in Listing 4-3. This example has been tested using the VoiceXML terminal facility offered by Tellme Networks on its web site.

As you have seen in Listing 4-3, the <catch> element can detect more than one event in one instance. You can also catch all events by keeping the event attribute empty. Table 4-4 describes all the attributes of the <catch> element.

Every element uses the <catch> element defined in its parent element. Thus, if you define the <catch> element before a field item and then subsequently within the field item, you can throw the same event at any stage. The <catch> element defined previously is used to catch every occurrence of the event. While processing the <catch> element, the selection algorithm selects the <catch> elements in sequential order. If by mistake an event is thrown within the <catch> element that is intended to catch that event, an infinite loop results and the platform produces a semantic error notification. This situation is illustrated in the following code:

```
<catch event="abc">
    <throw event="abc"/>
</catch>
```

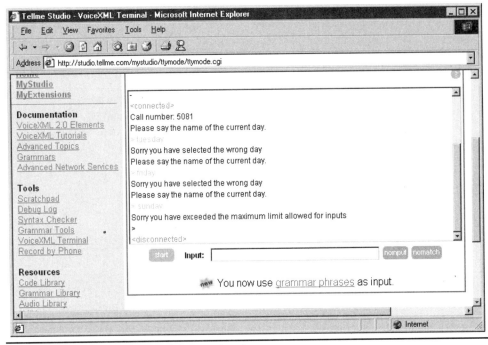

Figure 4-1   *Displaying the use of the <catch> element*

Most VoiceXML platforms provide certain default <catch> elements and some of the actions associated with them. Table 4-5 describes default <catch> elements and the predefined actions they address.

Attribute	Description
event	Used to define the name of the <catch> event. If this attribute is left empty, all the events that occur during the document processing are caught. You may also provide a space-separated list of the events to be caught.
count	Used to define the occurrence of an event. This attribute allows you to perform a specific action every time the event occurs.

Table 4-4   *Attributes of the <catch> Element*

Element	Action
nomatch	Reprompts the user for valid input.
noinput	Reprompts the user to provide input.
error	Used to terminate the execution and exit from the interpreter. A notification is provided in audible form.
exit	Used to terminate the execution and exit from the interpreter.
telephone.disconnect	Used to terminate the execution and exit from the interpreter.
help	Used to invoke the default help section.

Table 4-5   *Predefined <catch> Elements*

Variables in VoiceXML

Unlike HTML, VoiceXML has the provision to declare variables and use them for storing data during a user's interaction with the application. VoiceXML variables are similar to ECMAScript variables, which are declared using a scripting language like JavaScript. You can access VoiceXML variables in the script and use the variables declared in the script in a VoiceXML document. The naming convention of VoiceXML variables conforms to the ECMAScript standard. The names of VoiceXML variables must be unique in their scope and should conform to the standard naming convention. The following code shows how a variable is declared in a VoiceXML document:

```
<var name="username"/>
<var name="username" expr="john smith"/>
```

If you declare a variable with its initial expression, it will hold the assigned value until another value is assigned to it by the <assign> element. All the variables declared in a VoiceXML document are processed in sequential order. The interpretation algorithm cannot be manipulated to initialize a variable before all previously declared variables have been initialized and loaded into memory. In VoiceXML, different types of variables may be declared depending on their scopes. Some variables are predefined for any VoiceXML document and are available whenever a process is being executed on the server. The session variables, for instance, fall under the category of predefined variables. Table 4-6 describes the scope of all variable types.

Scope	Description
application	The variables for an entire application are declared in the application-level root document using the <var> element, and these are available to all leaf documents of that particular application. You can access the application variable from any document or subdialog within the scope of the application.
session	In VoiceXML, every time an application is executed on the server, some session variables are available for use in the application. Session variables have read-only properties, and you cannot declare new session variables in a VoiceXML document. Session variables of a particular session are available within the entire session. However, cross-access (that is, accessing variables of one session through another session) isn't allowed.
document	Document-level variables are specifically declared in a particular VoiceXML document. When a document is executed on the server, its document-level variables are loaded into memory along with it. These can also be unloaded from memory.
dialog	In VoiceXML, you can also declare variables for each dialog. The variables declared under a particular dialog can be used only within the scope of that dialog.
anonymous	You can also declare variables within some special elements such as <block> and <catch>.

Table 4-6   *Possible Scopes for Variables*

Some standard application variables are available in VoiceXML for working with an application. Table 4-7 provides brief descriptions of these standard application-level variables.

Variable	Description
application.lastresult$	This is a read-only variable, and it stores the value of the last recognition occurring within the scope of an application.
application.lastresult$[i].confidence	This variable holds the value of the confidence level for a particular interpretation. Usually, its values range from 0.0 to 1.0. Value 0.0 represents the minimum level of confidence, and value 1.0 represents the maximum level of confidence. The values may vary on different platforms.

Table 4-7   *Predefined Application-level Variables*

Variable	Description
application.lastresult$[i].utterance	This variable holds the raw string of words recognized for a particular interpretation. The spelling and the tokenization process of the string may vary on different platforms.
application.lastresult$[i].inputmode	This variable holds information regarding the input mode of a particular recognition. The possible values can indicate DTMF or voice mode.
application.lastresult$[i].interpretation	This variable holds the interpretation information.

Table 4-7   *Predefined Application-level Variables* (continued)

The availability of session variables in VoiceXML depends on the type of platform and on the information available to the server from the network. Table 4-8 lists the available session variables.

Variable	Description
session.telephone.ani	This variable provides the number of the calling phone. It works only when the calling line identification service is available.
session.telephone.dnis	This variable provides the number dialed by the user. This information is available only when the dialed number identification service is provided.
session.telephone.iidigits	This variable provides information regarding the nature of the operating line of the call—whether the call has been made from a pay phone or a cellular phone. This information is available when the service is supported.
session.telephone.uui	This variable holds the additional information on the ISDN call setup provided by the calling party, which is available only if the service is supported.
session.telephone.rdnis	This variable provides the number from where the call was redirected to its current location or from where the transfer of the call was made. For example, if User A calls User B, and User B's telephone system forwards the call to another voice server, then the voice server accesses the information available in the session.telephone.rdnis variable, which would be the number of User B's system; session.telephone.dnis is the number of the voice server, and the number of User A is stored in the session.telephone.ani variable.

Table 4-8   *Predefined Session-level Variables*

Variable	Description
session.telephone.redirect_reason	This variable contains a string that indicates the reason for redirecting the call from the original location to the server. This variable is available whenever session.telephone.rdnis is invoked. Some of the possible predefined reasons assigned for redirecting a call are unknown, user busy, unavailable, time of day, do not disturb, away, unconditional, deflection, no answer, and out of service.

Table 4-8   *Predefined Session-level Variables* (continued)

If you are developing applications using the emulated environment, you may not be able to access most of the session variables that we just discussed. When it comes to document-level variables, you need to declare them in the specific document in which you intend to use them. If the document is a root-level application document, all the declared variables become application-level variables.

The dialog-level variables are declared under a particular dialog and are only available up to the scope of the dialog. Listing 4-4 involves both document-level and dialog-level variables.

Listing 4-4:   *Using Document and Dialog-level Variables (example4-4b.vxml)*

```
<?xml version = "1.0"?>
<vxml version = "2.0">
      <var name = "var1" />
      <form id = "form">
            <field name = "number" type = "number">
                  <prompt>
                        Tell me a number.
                  </prompt>
                  <filled>
                        <var name = "var2" />
                        <assign expr = "number" name = "var2" />
                        <assign expr = "'This is a document-level variable named
var1.'" name = "var1" />
                        <prompt>
                              <value expr = "var1" />
                              Next variable contains the value you entered
                              <value expr = "var2" />
                              is a dialog-level variable, named var2
                        </prompt>
                  </filled>
            </field>
      </form>
</vxml>
```

Figure 4-2 shows the output of this example.

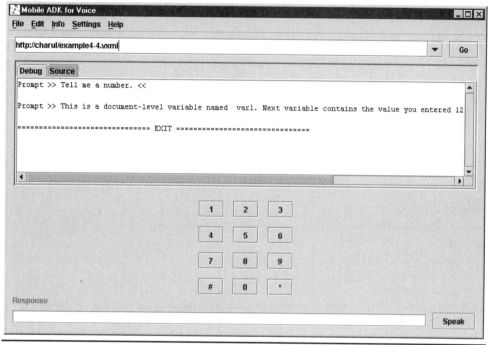

Figure 4-2 *Output of Listing 4-4*

Resource Fetching and Caching

In VoiceXML, you can fetch external documents and use their data in your application. These external documents may be audio files, grammars, or objects. Every fetch process has the following attributes, which set some conditions necessary for the successful completion of the fetch process.

- ► fetchtimeout
- ► fetchint
- ► maxage
- ► maxstale

fetchtimeout

By using the fetchtimeout attribute, you can set a specific time limit for the content-fetching process. If the platform isn't able to fetch the content within the specified time limit, the fetch process stops.

fetchint

The fetchint attribute is used to define the process of content fetching to the VoiceXML interpreter. For example, using the fetchint attribute you can inform the interpreter when the content should be fetched or whether the content was fetched at the time of page loading.

maxage

The maxage attribute is used to indicate that the document can use the content as long as the content expiration time doesn't exceed the specified limit.

maxsatale

Using the maxsatale attribute, you can use the content of a document whose expiration time has exceeded the specified time limit.

   You can play audio content during the fetch process by using the fetchaudio attribute. If this attribute isn't specified, no audio can be played during the fetch process. The fetchaudio attribute facilitates playing of audio clips while some documents are being fetched. This helps in keeping the session lively. Similarly, during a call transfer to a third party, an audio clip can be played using the fetchaudio attribute to inform the user processing is still happening on the server.

Caching in VoiceXML

Most browsers now use caching techniques to improve overall performance and save time while browsing web sites. Similarly, most voice browsers (VoiceXML interpreters) also employ caching techniques to enhance the performance of VoiceXML applications. In VoiceXML, it's also possible to control the caching process for every resource. For example, you can set the maxage attribute to a value greater than zero to fetch a new copy of the content if the content age expires in the cache, or through the maxstale attribute use content that isn't too stale. The latter alternative significantly improves the application's performance because a fresh copy of the content isn't required, which helps save time considerably.

Defining Prompts in VoiceXML

Prompts constitute a major consideration in the development of a voice application. Prompts are used to inform the user about activities occurring on the server. Through prompts, the user is also directed to provide required information while filling out forms. All prompts are deployed using the <prompt> element. Table 4-9 describes the attributes of the <prompt> element.

Attribute	Description
bargein	Used to control the possibility of interruption by the user during the prompt. If false, the user isn't able to interrupt the prompt in the middle. Default is true.
bargeintype	Used to define the type of the bargein attribute.
cond	Used to define any expression that indicates whether the prompt should be spoken.
count	Used to determine the number of occurrences of a prompt. Default value is 1.
timeout	If the timeout attribute is assigned some value and the user fails to provide the input within the time limit specified by this value, the <noinput> event is thrown.
xml:lang	Used to define the locale and the language settings for a particular prompt.

Table 4-9   *Attributes of the <prompt> Element*

The <prompt> element is very easy to use. In the following example, a basic prompt asks for the user name:

```
<prompt>
     Please say your name.
</prompt>
```

It isn't necessary to define the <prompt> element if you don't use any attribute of this element or if you want to play an audio file as the prompt message. In such cases, you may define the <audio> element in the following way:

```
<audio src="http://www.dreamtechsoftware.com/VoiceXML/voice.wav" />
```

While using speech markup elements, you need to define the <prompt> element. Otherwise, semantic errors are likely to be generated due to improper nesting of elements.

Using Speech Markup Elements

In the new framework of VoiceXML, speech markup elements are defined in the Synthesized Speech Markup Language (SSML). These elements may be used to control the behavior of prompts while generating synthesized speech. In the following discussion, we explain how some of the speech markup elements are used to control the audio rendering behavior of prompts.

The <paragraph> Element

The <paragraph> element is used to define the paragraph structure in the prompted text. The <p> element may also be used to describe a paragraph in a prompt. Table 4-10 describes the <paragraph> element attribute.

Attribute	Description
xml:lang	Used to define the locale and language settings for a specific paragraph. If this attribute isn't specified, default specifications will be used.

Table 4-10 *Attribute of the <paragraph> Element*

The following code snippet demonstrates the use of the <paragraph> element:

```
<prompt>
            <paragraph>
                    This is our first paragraph in the text.
            </paragraph>
        </prompt>
```

The <sentence> Element

The <sentence> element is used to define text being presented as a sentence. The <s> element can also be used to describe the sentence. The <sentence> element attribute is described in Table 4-11.

This code snippet demonstrates how the <sentence> element is used:

```
<prompt>
        <paragraph>
                This is our first paragraph in the text.
                <sentence xml:lang = "en:us">
                        Welcome to the first sentence in the document.
                </sentence>
        </paragraph>
    </prompt>
```

The <say-as> Element

The <say-as> element is used to define the type of the text enclosed within this element. This information, in turn, is used to define the pronunciation of the text. The <say-as> element is equipped with a wide variety of data format identifiers. With this element, you can interpret text using different variations, and the VoiceXML browser will generate the spoken output

Attribute	Description
xml:lang	Used to define the locale and language settings for a specific paragraph. If this attribute isn't specified, default settings will be used.

Table 4-11 *Attribute of the <sentence> Element*

Attribute	Description
sub	This attribute is used to define the text to be spoken as substitution for the text enclosed in the <say-as> element.
type	This mandatory attribute defines the format identifier for the pronunciation of the enclosed text.

Table 4-12   *Attributes of the <say-as> Element*

accordingly. While using the <say-as> element, it's necessary to include the type attribute that contains the format identifier for audio rendering of the enclosed text. Brief descriptions of the attributes of the <say-as> element are provided in Table 4-12, followed by a description of the format identifiers used in the type attribute in Table 4-13.

Type	Description
acronym	Defines the contained text as an acronym and tells the interpreter to pronounce the letters individually.
number	Used to define the numbers contained in the text. It has two possible format values: ordinal and digits. In the ordinal format, the text is pronounced as an ordinal, whereas in the digits format, the text is pronounced as a sequence of digits.
date	Defines the enclosed text as the date type of data. The possible format values are dmy, ym, md, y, and ymd. If none of these is specified, the system default value, which is based on the locale information, is used.
time	Defines the enclosed text as a time of day.
duration	The contained text represents a duration in terms of hours, minutes, and seconds, using the format values hms, hm, h, m, s, and ms.
currency	Defines the enclosed text as a currency amount. Availability of the spoken output for different currencies depends on the platform used.
measure	Describes the text as a measurement.
telephone	Describes the text as a telephone number.
name	Describes the text as the name of a person, organization, company, and so on.
net	Defines the text as an Internet URL, the possible format values being e-mail and URL.
address	Describes the text as a postal address.

Table 4-13   *Format Identifiers Used in the <say-as> Element*

Listing 4-5 shows the <say-as> element in action.

Listing 4-5:   *Using the <say-as> Element (example4-5b.vxml)*

```
<?xml version = "1.0"?>
<vxml version = "2.0">
      <form id = "firstform">
            <block name = "firstblock">
                  <prompt>
                        The current time is
                        <say-as type = "time:hms">
                              13:22:25
                        </say-as>
                        and your currently billed amount is
                        <say-as type = "currency">
                              $42.12
                        </say-as>
                              .
                  </prompt>
            </block>
      </form>
</vxml>
```

The output of Listing 4-5 is shown in Figure 4-3.

The <voice> Element

The <voice> element plays an important role in effecting improved personalization of your voice application prompts so as to create a good impression on the user. This element is used to specify the characteristics of the voice actor for producing output. It may be used to specify the gender, age, and other parameters of your voice actor. The availability of the <voice> element varies with different platforms. Some platforms may not support the <voice> element. In such cases, the voice actor characteristics cannot be configured using this element. Table 4-14 describes the attributes of the <voice> element.

Attribute	Description
age	Used to specify the age level of the voice actor. The specified values are always integer values.
gender	Used to specify the gender of the voice actor. The two possible values are male and female. The availability of the gender attribute, however, depends on the VoiceXML platform implementation.

Table 4-14   *Attributes of the <voice> Element*

Attribute	Description
category	Used to define the age category of the voice actor. This attribute is liable to be confused with the age attribute, but be aware that a marked difference exists between the two. The age attribute is used to define the age as an integer value, whereas the category attribute is used to define the age category as adult, child, and so on. For the category attribute, the possible values are child, teenager, adult, and elder.
name	Used to define the name of the voice actor to be used for the prompts. The implementation of this attribute depends on whether different voice actors have been installed and are available on the platform.
variant	Used to provide the other variants of voice characteristics of the same voice character installed on the system if available. This attribute always assumes an integer value.

Table 4-14   *Attributes of the <voice> Element* (continued)

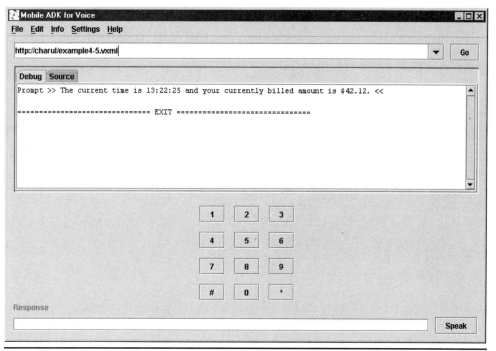

Figure 4-3   *Output of Listing 4-5*

Listing 4-6 demonstrates how you would use the <voice> element.

Listing 4-6: *Using the <voice> Element (example4-6b.vxml)*

```
<?xml version = "1.0"?>
<vxml version = "2.0">
      <form id = "firstform">
            <block name = "firstblock">
                  <prompt>
                        <voice gender = "male" category = "adult">
                              Welcome to the Voice book shop. Please choose one
from the following choices.
                        </voice>
                        <voice gender = "male" variant = "2" category = "adult">
                              Technical books, Social books
                        </voice>
                  </prompt>
            </block>
      </form>
</vxml>
```

The output of this example is shown in Figure 4-4.

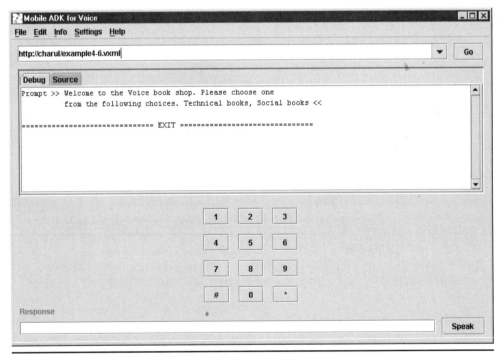

Figure 4-4 *Output of Listing 4-6*

The <emphasis> Element

The <emphasis> element facilitates imparting emphasis to the text content while generating audio using the text-to-speech synthesizer. The text-to-speech synthesizer imparts stress to the text at the time of speech generation depending on the value assigned to the emphasis level. The <emphasis> element has only one attribute, which is described in Table 4-15.

Listing 4-7 illustrates the use of the <emphasis> element in speech generation.

Listing 4-7:   *Using the <emphasis> Element (example4-7b.vxml)*

```
<?xml version = "1.0"?>
<vxml version = "2.0">
      <form id = "firstform">
            <block>
                  <prompt>
                        Welcome to
                        <emphasis level = "strong">
                              Monday night
                        </emphasis>
                        shopping festival.
                  </prompt>
            </block>
      </form>
</vxml>
```

The output of this example is shown in Figure 4-5.

The <break> Element

The <break> element is used to provide a pause between a pair of words or between two sentences. If you don't define the <break> element, the speech synthesizer automatically introduces pauses and breaks between words and sentences depending on the context of the language. This element contains two attributes, which are described in Table 4-16.

Attribute	Description
level	Used to provide the level of emphasis required for the contained text. Its possible values are none, strong, moderate, and reduced.

Table 4-15   *Attribute of the <emphasis> Element*

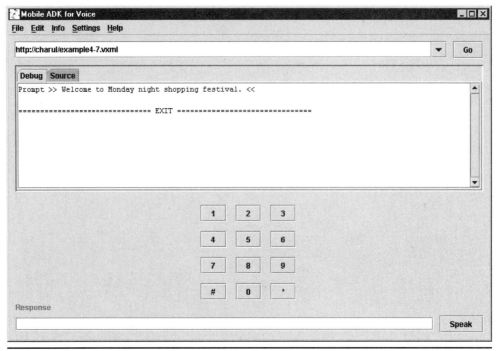

Figure 4-5 *Output of Listing 4-7*

Attribute	Description
size	Used to define the size of the break. Possible values for this attribute are none, small, medium, and large.
time	Used to define the time span of the break by providing a value in milliseconds, such as 20ms.

Table 4-16 *Attributes of the <break> Element*

Listing 4-8 illustrates the use of the <break> element.

```
<?xml version = "1.0"?>
<vxml version = "2.0">
      <form id = "firstform">
            <block>
                  <prompt>
                        Welcome to Monday night shopping festival.
      <break size = "large"/>
                        This shopping festival is brought to you by Indian sales
chain.
                  </prompt>
            </block>
      </form>
</vxml>
```

The <prosody> Element

The <prosody> element occupies a paramount position among the SSML elements used for speech markup. This element is used to control some vital parameters that constitute the generated speech—for example, parameters such as speech rate, pitch rate, pitch range, volume of speech output, and so on. Table 4-17 describes the attributes of the <prosody> element.

Attribute	Description
pitch	Used to control the pitch while prompting the contained text. Possible values are high, medium, low, and default.
range	Used to define the range of pitch for the contained text. Possible values are low, high, medium, and default.
rate	Used to define the speech rate at the time of prompting the text. Possible values are fast, slow, medium, and default.
duration	Used to define the duration of time during which the synthesizer speaks out of the contained text. This attribute conforms to the format of milliseconds, such as 250ms.
volume	Used to define the level of volume for the contained text. Possible values are silent, soft, medium, loud, and default.
contour	Used to define a set of possible targets for specified intervals in the spoken output. The contour attribute has a pair of values (10%, +25%), where the first value represents the percentage of the interval and the second value the pitch, in the form of permitted formats such as absolute values, descriptive values, relative values, and so on.

Table 4-17   *Attributes of the <prosody> Element*

In the <prosody> element, if you define both the duration and the rate attributes, then the duration attribute overrides the rate attribute because of its higher precedence. This happens in the case of pitch and range attributes when the contour attribute specifies values for the pitch and the range. The availability of various attributes of the <prosody> element varies on different platforms. Listing 4-9 illustrates how the <prosody> element is used to control both the pitch and the volume of the contained text.

Listing 4-9:   *Using the <prosody> Element (example4-9b.vxml)*

```
<?xml version = "1.0"?>
<vxml version = "2.0">
    <form id = "firstform">
        <block>
            <prompt>
                <prosody pitch = "50" volume = "high">
                    Welcome to Monday night shopping festival.
</prosody>
                This shopping festival is brought to you by Indian sales
chain.
            </prompt>
        </block>
    </form>
</vxml>
```

The <audio> Element

The <audio> element is one of the most commonly employed among the speech markup elements. This element is used to play back an audio clip whenever necessary. The <audio> element can also be used to fill the latency period while processing a transaction on the server. This element is an empty element and doesn't require the use of the closing tag. Table 4-18 describes the attributes of the <audio> element.

Attribute	Description
expr	Used to defined the initial value of the variable.
fetchint	Used to determine when content can be fetched.
fetchtimeout	Used for specifying the time before throwing the error.badfetch event, when the content isn't available.
maxage	Indicates the willingness to use content whose maximum age isn't greater than the time specified.
maxstale	Indicates the willingness to use content that has exceeded the expiration time.
src	Used to define the URI of the desired audio clip for playback.

Table 4-18   *Attributes of the <audio> Element*

The following code illustrates the use of the <audio> element:

```
<audio src="http://localhost/welcome.wav" />
```

Alternative text, which is text used by the voice server when the audio clip isn't available on the specified location defined in the src attribute, may be defined using the <audio> element. For defining alternative text, the <audio> element is used as an empty element. The following sample code demonstrates the procedure for providing alternative text using the <audio> element:

```
<audio src="http://localhost/welcome.wav">
      Welcome to the voice shopping center
</audio>
```

This concludes our discussion on speech markup elements. From here, we move on to examining at length other elements of VoiceXML, such as the executable elements.

Other Elements in VoiceXML

Among the executable contents provided by VoiceXML, the executable elements are quite important from the application development point of view. The term *executable content* refers to a block of executable code. An example would be code that appears in the <block> element, which we discussed in Chapter 3. The following elements are covered in this section:

- ► <assign>
- ► <clear>
- ► <if>
- ► <script>
- ► <exit>

The <assign> Element

The <assign> element is used to assign a value to a variable. If you have declared a variable, you can assign a value to the variable using the <assign> element within the scope of the variable. Table 4-19 provides a description of the attributes of the <assign> element.

Attribute	Description
expr	Used to assign a value to the variable
name	Use to define the name of the variable to which the value is being assigned

Table 4-19   *Attributes of the <assign> Element*

The following sample code illustrates the usage of the <assign> element:

```
<assign name="var1" expr="'hello'"/>
```

The <clear> Element

The <clear> element is use to reset values of form item variables to the undefined status and reinitialize values of the prompts counter for form items that are reset. See Table 4-20 for a description of the attribute for the <clear> element.

Here's how you use the <clear> element:

```
<clear namelist ="var1 var2 var3"/>
```

The <if> element

The <if> element is used to set a logical condition. You can also use the <else> and <elseif> elements to enhance the functionality of the <if> element while building the logical condition. Following is sample code that illustrates the usage of the <if> element as well as that of the <else> and the <elseif> elements:

```
<if cond="var1 > 60">
<prompt>The value of var1 is now exceeding the limit of 60.</prompt>
<throw event="help"/>
</if>
<if cond="var1 < 55">
<prompt>The value of var1 is less than 55.</prompt>
<else/>
<prompt>The value of var1 is now greater than 55.</prompt>
</if>
<if cond="color == 'red'">
<prompt>The value of color is red.</prompt>
<elseif cond="color == 'green'"/>
<prompt>The value of color is green.</prompt>
<elseif cond="color == 'blue'"/>
<prompt>The value of color is blue.</prompt>
<else/>
<prompt>Please select any of the following colors. Red, Green, and Blue. </prompt>
</if>
```

Attribute	Description
namelist	Used for defining the names of all the form item variables that need to be reset.

Table 4-20 *Attribute of the <clear> Element*

The <script> Element

As mentioned earlier in this chapter in the section "Variables in VoiceXML," VoiceXML supports ECMA-based scripting. You can write scripts for handling small logical operations such as string parsing. This element enables the use of client-side scripts in VoiceXML documents. The <script> element can be a part of a form or can be used within executable content such as the <block> element. The major difference between the HTML <script> element and the VoiceXML <script> element is that the <script> element in VoiceXML doesn't have a type attribute that needs to be defined. All scripts written using this element follow the same scope measurements as the <var> element. Descriptions of the attributes for this element are provided in Table 4-21.

Listing 4-10 illustrates how to use the <script> element.

Listing 4-10:   *Using the <script> Element (script.vxml)*

```
<?xml version = "1.0"?>
<vxml version = "2.0">
    <script>
        <![CDATA[
function multiply(n)
{
return 2 * n;
}
]]>
    </script>
    <form id = "form">
        <field name = "no" type = "number">
            <prompt>
                Tell me a number and I'll multiply that number by 2.
            </prompt>
            <filled>
                <prompt>
                    You have entered
                    <value expr = "no" />
                    and the resulting number after multiplication is
                    <value expr = "multiply(no)" />
                </prompt>
            </filled>
        </field>
    </form>
</vxml>
```

Attribute	Description
src	Used for defining the URI of the script, if an external script file is used.
charset	Used to define the encoding of the script.
fetchint	Used to determine when content can be fetched.
fetchtimeout	Used for defining the time before throwing the error.badfetch event when the content isn't available.
maxage	Indicates the willingness to use content whose maximum age isn't greater than the time specified.
maxstale	Indicates the willingness to use content whose age exceeds the limit of expiration time.

Table 4-21   *Attributes of the <script> Element*

Figure 4-6 shows the output of Listing 4-10.

The <exit> Element

The <exit> element is used to terminate all currently loaded documents and return the controls to the interpreter context. If the controls are returned to the interpreter context, the interpreter may terminate the call or may perform any other option. Table 4-22 describes the attributes of the <exit> element.

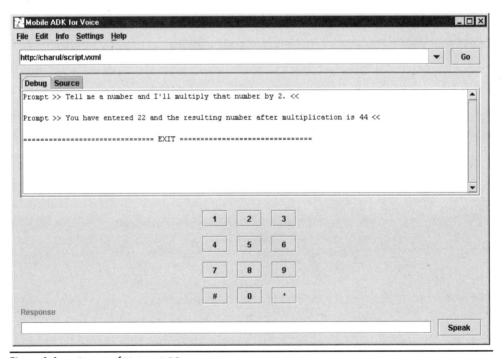

Figure 4-6   *Output of Listing 4-10*

Attribute	Description
namelist	Used for defining the names of all form item variables to be returned to the interpreter context.
expr	Used to define the returned expression.

Table 4-22   *Attributes of the <exit> Element*

Summary

This chapter presented a discussion on some of the advanced features involved in the development of a highly scalable and extensive voice application. We first discussed the two types of forms based on the approach adopted in creating them. We clarified how the functionality of an application may be enhanced by using mixed initiative forms in place of directed forms, which we had used prior to this chapter. We then explained the various event handling techniques and how these techniques may be used to achieve good control over the voice application. Subsequently, we showed you the variables and the techniques for resource fetching and caching that are imperative for developing complex documents and involving the logic for advanced applications. We concluded by describing the various speech markup elements that prove handy in defining prompts in VoiceXML and some of the more significant executable elements available in VoiceXML.

CHAPTER 5

Grammars in VoiceXML

This chapter focuses on the importance of grammars in VoiceXML. We explain the usage of grammars while discussing their role in voice application development. Grammars are always one of the most important parts of the dialog design of a voice application. Although our discussion is primarily based on the grammar standard meant for VoiceXML 2.0, we also touch on the previous style of grammar writing and syntaxes. The chapter also covers the scope of grammars and preparing grammars.

The Role of Grammars in VoiceXML Applications

Grammars facilitate the real-world use of VoiceXML applications. They pave the way for users' interactions with such applications. While writing grammars for your application, you must ensure that the user isn't forced to interact with a system full of computer-directed dialogs. Applications using computer-directed dialogs most likely won't be popular among users, for people instinctively favor the natural way of speaking even if they are interacting with a computer using a voice application.

While receiving input from users, allow them to speak naturally. Use grammars to extract the desired phrases from the given input. Understand that this is the key role that grammars play in enabling the user to interact with a voice application through natural speech.

The <grammar> Element in VoiceXML 1.0

In VoiceXML, you use the <grammar> element to define grammars for form items and other elements. Grammars define the keywords and a set of acceptable inputs that a user can use to interact with the application. The two main grammar formats used in the VoiceXML 1.0 are as follows:

▶ Java Speech Grammar Format

▶ Nuance Grammar Specification Language

You can use <grammar> elements to define both internal and external grammars in a document. You can also define grammars for DTMF-based input. The following sample code shows you how to define inline grammar:

```
<grammar  type = "application/x-jsgf" scope = "dialog">
          inline grammar
</grammar>
```

To define any external grammar, follow this syntax:

```
<grammar  type = "application/x-jsgf" scope = "dialog" src=URI of the grammar
file">
```

Table 5-1 describes the attributes of the <grammar> element.

Attribute	Description	Optional
src	Used to define the URI of the grammar file in case of external grammars.	Yes
scope	Used to define the scope of the grammar. If the document-level scope is defined, the grammar will be active in all the dialogs of the same document. In a root-level application document, the grammar will be active in all the leaf documents. Otherwise, the scope will be limited to its parent document.	Yes
type	Used to define the MIME type of grammar. If not specified, then the system will try to determine the MIME type automatically.	Yes
caching	Used for caching.	Yes
fetchint	Used to determine when content can be fetched.	Yes
fetchtimeout	Used for defining the time before throwing the error.badfetch event when the content isn't available.	Yes

Table 5-1   *Attributes of the <grammar> Element in VoiceXML 1.0*

The code in Example 5-1a illustrates the use of the <grammar> element to define the inline grammar for the <field> item.

Example 5-1a: *Using Inline Grammar (example5-1a.vxml)*

```
<?xml version = "1.0"?>
<vxml version = "1.0">
    <form id = "weather">
        <field name = "city">
            <prompt>
                Please say Mumbai or New Delhi.
            </prompt>
            <grammar type = "application/x-gsl">
                [mumbai (new delhi)]
            </grammar>
            <nomatch>
                Information is not available for this city
                <reprompt />
            </nomatch>
        </field>
        <filled namelist = " city  ">
            Weather details for
            <value expr = "city" />
            <if cond = "city == 'new delhi'">
                <prompt>
                    It is currently 42 degrees in
                    <value expr = "city" />
```

```
, and a bright sunny day.
                        </prompt>
                        <elseif cond = "city == 'mumbai' " />
                        <prompt>
                                It is currently 37 degrees in
                                <value expr = "city" />
                                and showers are expected in the evening
                        </prompt>
                </if>
        </filled>
    </form>
</vxml>
```

Grammars in VoiceXML 2.0

VoiceXML 2.0 incorporates some major changes in the grammar writing process as compared to VoiceXML 1.0. In VoiceXML 2.0, a separate language is introduced for writing the grammar and defining its syntax. This language is called the *speech recognition grammar format*. A basic change brought about by this format is that it's now possible to write grammars in an XML-based format, as the speech recognition grammar format is an XML-based language.

VoiceXML 2.0 supports two formats of grammar writing—Augmented Backus-Naur Form (ABNF) syntax and XML-based syntax. The main goal of the speech grammar recognition format is facilitating the transformation into each of the two grammar writing formats of VoiceXML 2.0. The description of both these formats follows.

Augmented Backus-Naur Form Syntax

ABNF is a plain-text-based format for writing grammars in VoiceXML 2.0. This format is quite similar to the traditional format of Backus-Naur Form (BNF) grammars. The ABNF syntax is derived from the Java Speech Grammar Format, which is used throughout VoiceXML 1.0.

XML-based Syntax

The XML-based grammar writing format is a new feature in the VoiceXML 2.0 framework. This format is also based on the Java Speech Grammar Format as well as the TalkML and Pipebeach grammar formats.

The <grammar> Element in VoiceXML 2.0

In consonance with the changes in the grammar writing format of VoiceXML 2.0, the <grammar> element has also been changed to meet the new requirements. The new

<grammar> element is capable of handling the two grammar formats mentioned in the preceding sections, XML-based format and ABNF syntax.

Before going into a detailed discussion on grammars, let's take a look at the attributes of the <grammar> element, which are described in Table 5-2.

You may use both the internal and external grammars in a document according to your requirements. The following code snippet illustrates the procedure for defining inline grammars, followed by two code snippets illustrating the procedure for defining external grammars.

Attribute	Description	Optional
src	Used to define the URI, this dictates the location of the grammar file if you wish to use external grammars in your documents.	Yes
xml:lang	Used to define the locale and language information for both inline and external grammars. The default value is US ENGLISH, represented as en-us.	Yes
type	Used to define the MIME type of the grammar. If not specified, then the system will try to determine the MIME type automatically.	Yes
scope	Used to define the scope of the grammar. This attribute is used only in case of inline grammars. The two possible values for this attribute are dialog and document.	Yes
mode	Used to determine the mode of grammars, such as DTMF grammar or voice grammar. The possible values for this attribute are DTMF and voice.	No
version	Used to define the version information for the grammar. The default value of this attribute is 1.0.	Yes
root	Used to define the root rule of the grammar in the case of inline grammars.	Yes
fetchint	Used to determine when content can be fetched.	Yes
fetchtimeout	Used for defining the time before throwing the error.badfetch event when the content isn't available.	Yes
maxage	Used to indicate that the document can use the content as long as the content expiration time does not exceed the specified limit.	Yes
maxstale	Used to indicate that the document can use content whose expiration time has exceeded the specified time limit.	Yes
weight	Used to define the weight of a grammar. It only affects the processing of grammar, not the result. The default value of this attribute is 1.0. Remember, the weight attribute works only with the voice mode of grammars. Implicit grammars, such as in the <option> element, do not support the weight attribute.	Yes

Table 5-2   *Attributes of the <grammar> Element in VoiceXML 2.0*

Defining Inline Grammars (Voice Grammars)

```
<grammar mode = "voice" type = "application/grammar">
      sunday {sunday} |       monday {monday} |       tuesday {tuesday}
</grammar>
```

Defining External Grammars (XML-based Grammar Format)

```
<grammar src = "http://www.dreamtechsoftware.com/voicexml/main.grxml" type =
"application/grammar+xml" />
```

Defining External Grammars (ABNF Grammar Format)

```
<grammar type="application/grammar"
src="http://www.dreamtechsoftware.com/voicexml/main.grm"/>
```

DTMF Grammars

DTMF grammars play an important role in enhancing the performance of your application by making the interface quickly accessible and easy to use. The mode attribute is used to define grammar as DTMF grammar. While working with DTMF grammars, the xml:lang attribute of the <grammar> element isn't required, and if defined, this attribute is ignored at the time of execution. You can define DTMF grammars in the same way as we define voice grammars in Examples 5-2a and 5-2b.

Example 5-2a: *Using DTMF Grammar (example5-2a.vxml)*

```
<?xml version = "1.0"?>
<vxml version = "1.0">
      <form id = "main">
            <field name = "colorchooser">
                  <prompt>
                        Press 1 to choose the red color
      </prompt>
                  <grammar src =
"http://www.dreamtechsoftware.com/voicexml/example5-2b.grxml" type =
"application/grammar+xml">
                  </grammar>
                  <nomatch>
                        <reprompt />
                  </nomatch>
            </field>
      </form>
</vxml>
```

Example 5-2b   *Using DTMF Grammar (example5-2b.grxml)*

```
<?xml version = "1.0"?>
<grammar  version = "1.0"  mode = "dtmf">
       <rule id = "main" scope = "public">
              <one-of>
                     <item tag = "red">
                            1
                     </item>
              </one-of>
       </rule>
</grammar>
```

The Scope of Grammars

The scope of a grammar defines the working criterion for its activation at the time of execution. To meet the requirements of your application, you can choose from many categories of grammars with different scopes. Grammars can be broadly categorized under the following four categories, depending on their scope:

► Field grammars

► Link grammars

► Form grammars

► Menu grammars

Field Grammars

Field grammars enable you to define a set of grammars for a particular field. The scope of field grammars is limited to within the <field> element in which they are defined. While working with the grammars of one <field> element, you cannot validate user input received by another <field> element. Example 5-3b should help you understand the procedure of using field grammars in your documents.

Example 5-3b: *Using Field Grammars (example5-3b.vxml)*

```
<?xml version = "1.0"?>
<vxml version = "2.0">
       <form id = "checkmonth">
              <field name = "monthofyear">
                     <prompt>
```

```
                    Please say the name of any month from march to july.
                </prompt>
                <grammar>
                    <rule id = "root" scope = "public">
                        <one-of>
                            <item tag = "march">
                                march
                            </item>
                            <item tag = "april">
                                april
                            </item>
                            <item tag = "may">
                                may
                            </item>
                            <item tag = "june">
                                june
                            </item>
                            <item tag = "july">
                                july
                            </item>
                        </one-of>
                    </rule>
                </grammar>
                <nomatch>
                    Sorry you have selected a wrong month.
                    <reprompt />
                </nomatch>
                <noinput>
                    I did not hear anything
                    <reprompt />
                </noinput>
            </field>
        <block>
            You have chosen
            <value expr = "monthofyear" />
        </block>
    </form>
</vxml>
```

Link Grammars

Link grammars are used to define acceptable input for the <link> element. The scope of
the link grammar is document level by default. If you are defining link grammars in any
application-level root document, then the grammars stay alive in all the loaded current

sublevel documents within the scope of the application. The following example clarifies the procedure for defining link grammars:

```
<link next = "http://www.dreamtechsoftware.com/voicexml/main.vxml">
    <grammar>
        main menu {} | home page {} | home {}
    </grammar>
</link>
```

Form Grammars

For form-level grammars, you may use either the document-level scope or the dialog-level scope. The following sections describe both these scopes.

Dialog-level Scope

This is the default scope assigned to any form-level grammar. If you classify the scope as being dialog level, the grammar in question will be active for the amount of time inherent in the scope of that particular form. Example 5-4b illustrates form-level grammars having a dialog-level scope.

Example 5-4b: *Using Form Grammar—Dialog Scope (example5-4b.vxml)*

```
<?xml version = "1.0"?>
<vxml version = "2.0">
    <form id = "checkmonth">
        <field name = "monthofyear">
            <prompt>
                Please say the name of any month from march to july.
            </prompt>
            <grammar scope = "dialog">
                march {march} | april {april} | may {may} | june {june} |
july {july}
            </grammar>
            <nomatch>
                Sorry you have selected a wrong month
            <reprompt />
            </nomatch>
        </field>
        <block>
            You have chosen
<value expr = "monthofyear" />
        </block>
    </form>
</vxml>
```

Document-level Scope

Form grammars with a document-level scope remain active throughout their associated document. You can access document-level grammars anywhere in the document after their initialization. If you defined the scope of the document but don't define any scope for a grammar, the platform will automatically assign the document scope to the grammars. Both these cases are illustrated in the following code snippets.

Grammar with a Document-level Scope

```
<form id = "checkmonth" >
    <field name = "monthofyear">
        <prompt>
            Please say the name of any month from march to july.
        </prompt>
        <grammar scope = "document">
            march {march} | april {april} | may {may} | june {june} |
july {july}
        </grammar>
        <nomatch>
            Sorry you have selected a wrong month
            <reprompt />
        </nomatch>
    </field>
    <block>
        You have chosen
        <value expr = "monthofyear" />
    </block>
</form>
```

Grammar with a Document-level Scope

```
<form id = "checkmonth" scope = "document">
    <field name = "monthofyear">
        <prompt>
            Please say the name of any month from march to july.
        </prompt>
        <grammar >
            march {march} | april {april} | may {may} | june {june} |
july {july}
        </grammar>
        <nomatch>
            Sorry you have selected a wrong month
            <reprompt />
        </nomatch>
    </field>
    <block>
```

```
            You have chosen
            <value expr = "monthofyear" />
        </block>
    </form>
```

If you define any grammar as having a document-level scope and the VoiceXML document containing that grammar is a root-level application document, then the grammar will remain active during the complete session of the application for all current sublevel documents. If you specify the document scope in both the <form> element and the <grammar> element, then the scope specified in the <grammar> element is active.

Menu Grammars

Menu grammars are also assigned the dialog-level scope by default and follow the same rules as form grammars. You can define menu grammars as having a document-level scope; in such cases, the menu grammars also follow the same rules as applicable to form grammars for activation. Example 5-5b illustrates the use of menu grammars.

Example 5-5b: *Using Menu Grammars (example5-5b.vxml)*

```
<?xml version = "1.0"?>
<vxml version = "1.0">
    <menu scope = "dialog">
        <prompt>
                Select red or blue.
        </prompt>
        <choice next = "#red" >
            <grammar mode = "voice" scope = "dialog">
                    red {red} |   reddish {red}
            </grammar>
            Red is good
        </choice>
        <choice next = "#blue">
                Blue is better
    <grammar>
                    blue {blue}
        </grammar>
        </choice>
        <noinput>
                Please say red or blue.
    </noinput>
    <nomatch>
                Please say red or blue.
    </nomatch>
```

```
        </menu>
        <form id = "red">
                <block>
                        You selected red, which is good.
                        <disconnect />
                </block>
        </form>
        <form id = "blue">
                <block>
                        You selected blue, which is better.
                        <disconnect />
                </block>
        </form>
</vxml>
```

While developing voice applications, you may need to create some forms containing more than one grammar with different scopes. In such cases, you need to define the scope of a grammar explicitly in every <grammar> element as shown in Example 5-6b.

Example 5-6b: *Defining Grammar Scope (example5-6b.vxml)*

```
<?xml version = "1.0"?>
<vxml version = "2.0">
     <form id = "check">
            <field name = "monthofyear">
                 <prompt>
                         Please say the name of any month from march to july.
</prompt>
                 <grammar mode = "voice" type = "application/grammar" scope =
"document">
                         march {march} | april {april} | may {may} | june {june} |
july {july}
                 </grammar>
                 <nomatch>
                         Sorry you have selected a wrong month
            <reprompt />
                 </nomatch>
            </field>
            <field name = "dayofweek">
                 <prompt>
                         Please say the name of any day from sunday to wednesday.
</prompt>
                 <grammar mode = "voice" type = "application/grammar" scope =
```

```
"dialog">
                         sunday {sunday} | monday {monday} | tuesday {tuesday} |
wednesday {wednesday}
                </grammar>
        <nomatch>
                Sorry you have selected a wrong day
                <reprompt />
        </nomatch>
        </field>
        <block>
            You have chosen
            <value expr = "monthofyear" />
            as the month and
            <value expr = "dayofweek" />
            as the day of your choice.
        </block>
    </form>
</vxml>
```

Here, we conclude our discussion on the scopes of grammars. Now, we shift the focus to the next important aspect of grammars—activation of grammars during execution of VoiceXML documents.

Grammar Activation Procedure

Once you have defined all the required grammars in your documents and the execution process of documents starts, the grammars are activated based on certain conditions. When the VoiceXML interpreter waits for a user utterance for the currently visited field item, the types of grammars become active according to their precedence, in the order listed here:

1. All grammars, including link grammars, defined for that particular field item become active.

2. All grammars, including link grammars, defined in the form containing that field item become active. If any root-level application document is currently loaded, all grammars defined in the root-level application document become active.

3. All grammars defined by the platform-specified event handlers such as the help event handler become active.

Suppose a user's utterance matches two currently active grammars that have the same precedence. In such a situation, the document order determines the grammar that will be used for matching the user input. If any of the form items containing the modal attribute is set to true, then all other grammars except the grammars at a form item's own level become inactive.

Preparing Grammars

In this section, we examine the speech recognition grammar format elements that are used to write grammars in VoiceXML. You use the following elements of the speech recognition grammar format to define a grammar:

- ► <rule>
- ► <ruleref>
- ► <one-of>
- ► <count>

The <rule> Element

The <rule> element defines a grammar rule for matching the user utterance with a particular filed item. The <rule> element has two attributes, described in Table 5-3.

The following code snippet illustrates the use of the <rule> element:

```
<?xml version="1.0"?>
<grammar type="application/grammar+xml" version="1.0">
    <rule id="red_green_blue" scope="public">
        <one-of>
            <item tag="red">red</item>
            <item tag="blue">blue</item>
            <item tag="green">green</item>
        </one-of>
    </rule>
</grammar>
```

The <ruleref> Element

Use the <ruleref> element to define the reference of a rule, even one existing in a separate grammar file. Table 5-4 describes the attributes of the <ruleref> element.

Attribute	Description	Optional
id	Used to define a unique ID for that particular rule. If the grammar file contains more than one rule, the ID is use to determine the rule distinctly.	No
scope	Used to define the scope of the rule as either local or public. If the local scope is defined, you can't access the rule from a different grammar file. With the public scope, the other grammar file can contain a reference to the rule. If not defined, the default value is private.	Yes

Table 5-3   *Attributes of the <rule> Element in VoiceXML 2.0*

Attribute	Description	Optional
tag	Used to store the value returned by the recognizer after the <ruleref> element is matched successfully.	Yes
uri	Used to define the location of the rule required to be matched.	Yes

Table 5-4   *Attributes of the <ruleref> Element in VoiceXML 2.0*

The following code snippet illustrates the use of the <ruleref> element:

```
<?xml version="1.0"?>
<grammar type="application/grammar+xml" version="1.0">
    <rule id="red_green_blue" scope="public">
       <one-of>
          <item>
             <ruleref uri="#red"/>
          </item>
          <item>
             <ruleref uri="#green"/>
          </item>
            <item  >
                        <ruleref uri = "blue" />
            </item>
       </one-of>
    </rule>
    <rule id="green" scope="private">
      <one-of>
          <item tag="green">green</item>
          <item tag="green">dark green</item>
          <item tag="green">light green</item>
          <item tag="green">bottle green</item>
      </one-of>
    </rule>
    <rule id="red" scope="private">
      <one-of>
          <item tag="red">red</item>
          <item tag="red">reddish</item>
          <item tag="red">light red</item>
          <item tag="red">dark red</item>
      </one-of>
    </rule>
<rule id="blue" scope="private">
      <one-of>
          <item tag="blue">blue</item>
          <item tag="blue">dark blue</item>
          <item tag="blue">light blue</item>
```

```
        <item tag="blue">sea blue</item>
      </one-of>
   </rule>
</grammar>
```

The <one-of> Element

The <one-of> element defines a set of alternatives for user utterance validation. The <one-of> element has only one attribute, as described in Table 5-5.

The following code snippet illustrates the use of the <one-of> element:

```
<?xml version = "1.0"?>
<grammar root = "maingrammar" version = "1.0" xml:lang = "en-US">
<rule id = "maingrammar" scope = "public">
<one-of>
        <item>
                <one-of tag="1">
                        <item>paris</item>
                        <item>cannes</item>
                <one-of>
        </item>
        <item>
                <one-of tag="2">
                        <item>london</item>
                        <item>edinburgh</item>
                        <item>glasgow</item>
                        <item>oxford</item>
                <one-of>
        </item>
        <item>
                <one-of tag="3">
                        <item>oslo</item>
                        <item>arendal</item>
                <one-of>
        </item>
</one-of>
</rule>
</grammar>
```

The <count> Element

The <count> element is used to define the value for the expression contained in the element that might be repeated by the user. The <count> element has only one attribute, as described in Table 5-6.

Attribute	Description	Optional
tag	Used to store the value returned by the recognizer after the <one-of> element is matched successfully to the user utterance.	Yes

Table 5-5   *Attribute of the <one-of> Element in VoiceXML 2.0*

Attribute	Description	Optional
number	Used to define the value as a string. The possible values are 0+, 1+, optional, and ? .	No

Table 5-6   *Attribute of the <count> Element in VoiceXML 2.0*

Summary

In this chapter, we discussed the grammars in VoiceXML. The chapter introduced the concept of grammars and their uses for the validation of user utterance. As a first step, we clarified the role of grammars and the two different formats used for writing the grammars. Next, you learned about the different types of grammars and their relation to each other. We also examined the activation and scooping rules meant for the different types of grammars found in VoiceXML. We concluded by describing the various elements used for preparing grammars in XML-based format.

CHAPTER 6

Developing a Voicemail System Using ASP and VoiceXML

I n this chapter, we show you how to develop a voicemail system using Active Server Pages (ASPs) and VoiceXML. Our example system will provide all the basic functionalities of a web-based mailing service over a telephony network. Through this system, users will be able to retrieve mail from their inboxes by using a simple telephony device.

Voicemail Application Design Considerations

The first step in the development cycle of a VoiceXML-based e-mail application is to decide what services you want the application to provide to the user. Following this, a design outline for the application needs to be sketched, laying down software and hardware requirements. The voice-based mailing system we envisage should allow the user to do the following:

▶ Read mail

▶ Compose mail

▶ Reply to incoming mail

We also provide a development and testing environment so as to test the application right on the desktop. For building such an application, the following software and hardware components are required:

▶ Motorola Application Development Kit (MADK) version 2.0 for testing the application in an environment that simulates the chosen terminal

▶ IPSWITCH IMail Server version 6.0 (http://www.ipswitch.com/)

▶ Diamac JMail component for accessing e-mail messages from ASP documents (http://www.dimac.net/)

You can also use any other mail server or VoiceXML simulator for writing the code, in which case you might need to change the code provided in this chapter according to the configuration used.

The Case for VoiceXML-based Mailing Services

Web-based mailing services have been available for about a decade, and millions of people are using them every minute. Then why go for a voice-based mailing service? Actually, a voice-based mailing service enables users to overcome some inherent deficiencies of web-based mailing services, some of which are listed here:

▶ Users can employ a web-based mailing service only through a computer or a similar device connected to the Internet. This affects the mobility of the mail service, because most computers aren't easily portable.

▶ Visually challenged people cannot use web-based mailing services, which rely on display devices such as monitors.

▶ In developing countries, the limited availability of computers makes it difficult for the masses to access web-based mailing services.

Now, let's see how a VoiceXML-based mailing application scores over its web-based counterpart:

▶ If a voice-based mailing application is deployed on a voice gateway connected to the Internet, a user can easily interact with the application through a telephony device such as a simple telephone or a cell phone. This substantially enhances the mobility of a VoiceXML-based mailing service over a web-based one.

▶ Visually challenged people can make use of VoiceXML-based mailing applications, as their interaction with such applications would be either through voice input or via the keypad of a telephony device.

▶ The number of telephone users is far greater than that of computer users in any part of the world. A voice-based mailing service would therefore be able to cater to a larger number of people, because it does not require access to computers.

Architecture of a VoiceXML-based Mailing Application

The following discussion gives you an idea of the architecture of a voice-based mailing application. In such an application, the user first logs on to the system using a unique ID and password, based on which application authenticates the user. After the authentication process, the application presents all available options to the user and waits for the user's response.

In the second phase, the user receives from the server a list of all mail messages found in his or her inbox. The user may select any message from the list and reply to the message if desired. A complete flowchart for this process is represented in Figure 6-1. The home page of the application works as the root-level document for the entire application, and all other documents work as sublevel documents.

Assumptions Made in Developing the Voicemail Application

To facilitate easy development for our application, we have made some assumptions:

▶ The user id and password are accepted only in the form of digits.

▶ The database design for storing mail on the server is not discussed here, as it is handled by the IMail server by default and no external database is used for this purpose.

▶ While replying to mail messages, the recorded audio is stored on the server and sent as an attachment with the outgoing mail.

▶ All the source code written for this application conforms to VoiceXML 1.0. The final specifications of the VoiceXML 2.0 framework were not available at the time of writing this book.

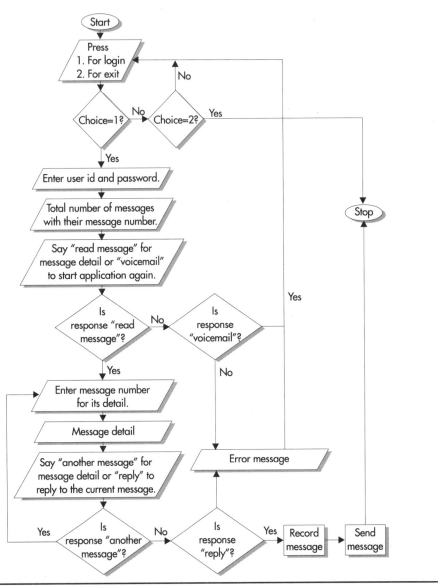

Figure 6-1   *Flowchart of the sample voicemail application*

Preparing the Home Page

Preparing the login section for the application is the first step towards developing a VoiceXML-based mailing application. When a user accesses the application, the home page provides two choices for the user—either log on to the system to proceed further with the application or terminate the session by choosing the exit option. Listing 6-1 shows the source code for voicemail.asp, which works as the home page of our application.

Listing 6-1: *Source Code for voicemail.asp*

```
<%@ Language=VBScript %>
<%
     Response.ContentType = "text/xml"
     Response.Write("<?xml version= ""1.0""?>")
%>
   <vxml version="1.0">
      <link next="http://jyotsna/voicemail/voicemail.asp">
      <grammar type="application/x-gsl">
            voicemail
      </grammar>
</link>
<menu>
     <prompt>
Please say or type any one of the following:
<enumerate/> or say help for further assistance
</prompt>
 <choice dtmf="1" next="http://jyotsna/voicemail/login.asp">login</choice>
 <choice dtmf="2" next="#exit">exit</choice>
<help>
            To start this application again say voicemail.
   </help>
     <noinput>
            I didn't hear anything please say login
      <enumerate/>
      </noinput>
     <nomatch>
I didn't get that, please say or type voicemail again
<enumerate/>
</nomatch>
     <catch event="nomatch noinput" count="4">
            <prompt>You have exceeded the limit of allowed retries. System
will now stop the
application.</prompt>
                  <throw event="telephone.disconnect.hangup"/>
     </catch>
     </menu>
<form id="exit">
     <catch event="exit">
            <throw event="telephone.disconnect.hangup"/>
     </catch>
</form>
 </vxml>
```

As you have seen in the Listing 6-1, in the very beginning of the code we have set the content type for the VoiceXML document using the Response.ContentType method:

```
<%@ Language=VBScript %>
<%
    Response.ContentType = "text/xml"
    Response.Write("<?xml version= ""1.0""?>")
%>
```

The content type setting may vary with different platforms. For more information regarding the content type accepted by your voice server, contact the system administrator or refer to the voice server manual.

After the VoiceXML version declaration, we define a <link> element for the home page. This is necessary because the home page works as a root-level document for the entire application, and users should be able to access it from anywhere in the application by just saying the hot word "voicemail."

```
<link next="http://jyotsna/voicemail/voicemail.asp">
    <grammar type="application/x-gsl">
            voicemail
    </grammar>
</link>
<menu>
```

The output of voicemail.asp is shown in Figure 6-2.

In the next step, we construct a menu-based interface for providing the available options to the user. Once the user selects an available option, the corresponding action will be performed on the server.

Preparing the Login Section

If the user selects the login option in the home page, the control is transferred to the login.asp file, which handles the login section of the application. The login section accepts the user id and password in the form of digits and transfers this information to the server for further processing. Listing 6-2 shows the code for the login.asp file that we use for accepting the user id and password in the login section.

Listing 6-2:	*Source Code for login.asp*

```
<%@ Language=VBScript %>
<%
    Response.ContentType = "text/xml"
    Response.Write("<?xml version= ""1.0""?>")
```

```
%>
<vxml version = "1.0" application = "http://192.168.1.100/voicemail.asp">
    <var name="uname"/>
    <var name="pwd"/>
      <form id="user">
            <field name="uname" type="digits">
              <prompt>Please enter your user id</prompt>
                  <filled>
                        <assign name="document.uname" expr="uname"/>
                        <goto next="#pass"/>
                  </filled>
            </field>
</form>
      <form id="pass">
                <field name="pwd" type="digits">
                <prompt> Please enter your password </prompt>
                  <filled>
                        <assign name="document.pwd" expr="pwd"/>
                  <goto next="#call_mail"/>
                  </filled>
                </field>
      </form>
      <form id="call_mail">
            <block>
                        <var name="loginname"  expr="document.uname"/>
                        <var name="password" expr="document.pwd"/>
                        <submit next="http://jyotsna/voicemail/receivemail.asp"
method="get" namelist="loginname password"/>
            </block>
      </form>
</vxml>
```

In this document, we have built two forms, one each for accepting the user id and the password. After collecting the user input, we call the third form to submit all the collected data to the server using the <submit> element, as shown here:

```
<form id="call_mail">
            <block>
                        <var name="loginname"  expr="document.uname"/>
                        <var name="password" expr="document.pwd"/>
                      <submit
next=http://jyotsna/voicemail/receivemail.aspmethod="get"
namelist="loginname
password"/>
            </block>
      </form>
```

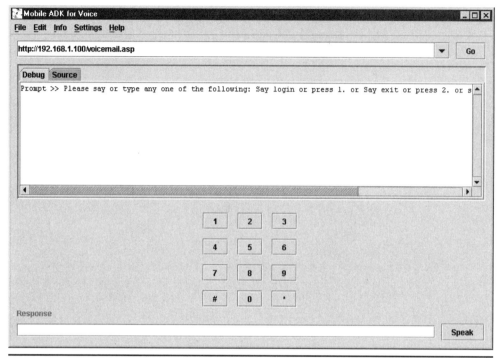

Figure 6-2 *Output of voicemail.asp*

As mentioned earlier, in this application, we accept both the user id and password in the form of digits. This has been done to avoid the task of preparing lengthy grammars for user names. The output of the login.asp is shown in Figures 6-3 and 6-4.

Accessing the Mailbox

Now, we proceed to the code for accessing the mailbox on the basis of the user id and password supplied by the user in the login section. For accessing the mailbox, we use the JMail component in conjunction with the IMail server. Listing 6-3 provides the source code of receivemail.asp, which is used for accessing the inbox and prompting the list for all messages found in the user inbox.

Listing 6-3: *Source Code for receivemail.asp*

```
<%@LANGUAGE=VBSCRIPT %>
<%
dim uname,pwd
uname = trim(Request.QueryString("loginname"))
```

```
pwd = trim(Request.QueryString("password"))
Response.ContentType = "text/xml"
Response.Write("<?xml version= ""1.0""?>")
%>
<vxml version = "1.0" application = "http://192.168.1.100/voicemail.asp">
<var name="msgno"/>
<var name="uname"/>
<var name="upass"/>
<form>
<block>
<%
Set pop3 = Server.CreateObject( "Jmail.POP3" )
on error resume next
pop3.Connect uname, pwd, "http://192.168.1.100"
     if (pop3.Count>0) then
     pop3.Logging = True
          message_count = 1%>
          Total number of messages is  <%=pop3.Count%>
          <%while (message_count<=pop3.Count)
               Set msgs = pop3.Messages.Item(message_count)
          %>
               Message number is <%=message_count %>
               Sender is <%=msgs.FromName%>
          Subject of the mail is      <%=msgs.Subject%>
               <%message_count = message_count + 1
          wend
     else%>
          You do not have mail in your mailbox.
     <%
     end if
     pop3.Disconnect
if(pop3.count>0) then%>
<goto next="#call"/>
<%
else%>
<goto next="http://jyotsna/voicemail/voicemail.asp"/>
<%end if
%>
</block>
</form>
<form id="call">
     <field name="check">
          <prompt> Say read message for the message details, or say voicemail to
return to application home. </prompt>
               <grammar type="application/x-gsl">
                    [  (read message)(voicemail)  ]
          </grammar>
               <filled>
                    <if cond="check=='read message'">
                    <goto next="#message"/>
                    <elseif cond="check=='voicemail'"/>
               <goto next="voicemail.asp"/>
               </if>
          </filled>
```

```
        </field>
</form>
<form id="message">
   <field name="msgno" type="digits">
        <prompt> Please say the message number for message details </prompt>
                    <filled>
                <assign name="document.msgno" expr="msgno"/>
                <goto next="#call_mail"/>
</filled>
   </field>
</form>
<form id="call_mail">
<block>
    <var name="messageno" expr="document.msgno"/>
    <var name="username" expr="<%=uname%>"/>
    <var name="password" expr="<%=pwd%>"/>
    <submit next="http://jyotsna/voicemail/receivemessage.asp" method="get"
namelist="messageno username password"/>
</block>
</form>
</vxml>
```

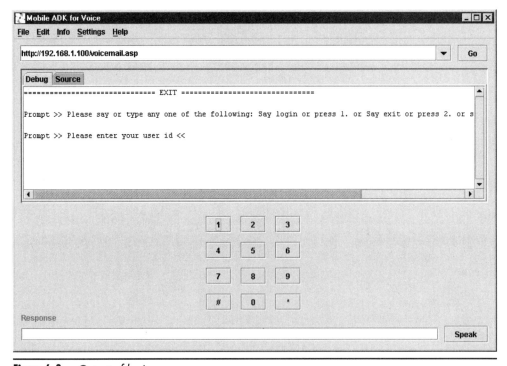

Figure 6-3 *Output of login.asp*

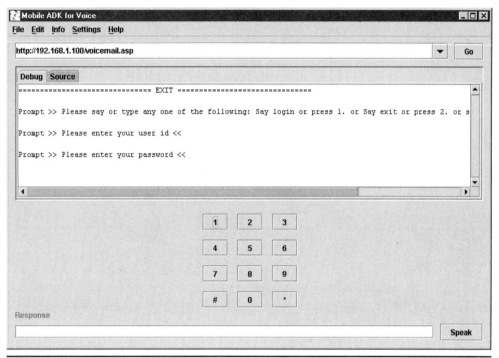

Figure 6-4   *Output of login.asp (continued)*

Let's take a closer look at the source code in Listing 6-3. As you have seen in the login section, first we access the values of the user id and password, which are contained in the query string. In the second step, we create an object on the server for connecting and receiving mail from the inbox. Thereafter, we start retrieving all mail messages and then provide a list containing the following details:

► Message number
► Sender of the message
► Subject of the message

This process is controlled by a looping condition that checks for the message count in the inbox and prompts for the details of all the messages found in the inbox, as shown in the following code snippet:

```
if (pop3.Count>0) then
     message_count = 1%>
     Total number of messages is  <%=pop3.Count%>
     <%while (message_count<=pop3.Count)
          Set msg = pop3.Messages.item(message_count)
```

```
        %>
                Message number is        <%=message_count %>
                Sender is       <%= msg.FromName %>
                Subject of the mail is        <%=msg.Subject%>
                <%message_count = message_count + 1
        wend
    else%>
        You do not have mail in your mailbox.
    <%
    end if
```

After getting the list of messages, the user has these two options:

▶ Read message

▶ Go back to home page

If the user chooses the read message option, we call the next form in the document and ask for the message number from the user. Once the user provides the message number, as shown in Figure 6-5, the received value is stored in a document-level variable, and the control is transferred to the next form.

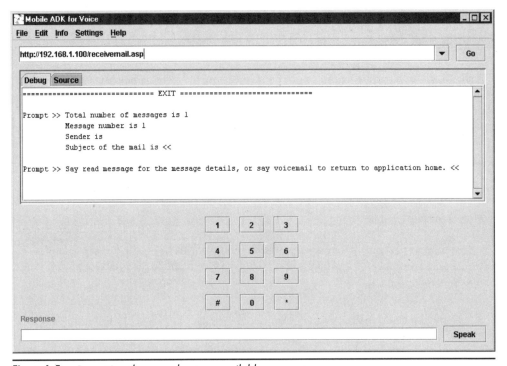

Figure 6-5   *Prompting the user about an available message*

In the next form, named call_mail, we first declare some variables and assign the corresponding values to them. In the last step, we transfer all the values to receivemessage.asp to receive a particular message from the inbox based on the values transferred.

```
<form id="call_mail">
<block>
    <var name="messageno" expr="document.msgno"/>
    <var name="username" expr="<%=uname%>"/>
    <var name="password" expr="<%=pwd%>"/>
    <submit next="http://jyotsna/voicemail/receivemessage.asp" method="get"
namelist="messageno username password"/>
</block>
</form>
```

In case there isn't any mail in the inbox, we inform the user of this with an appropriate message, as shown in Figure 6-6.

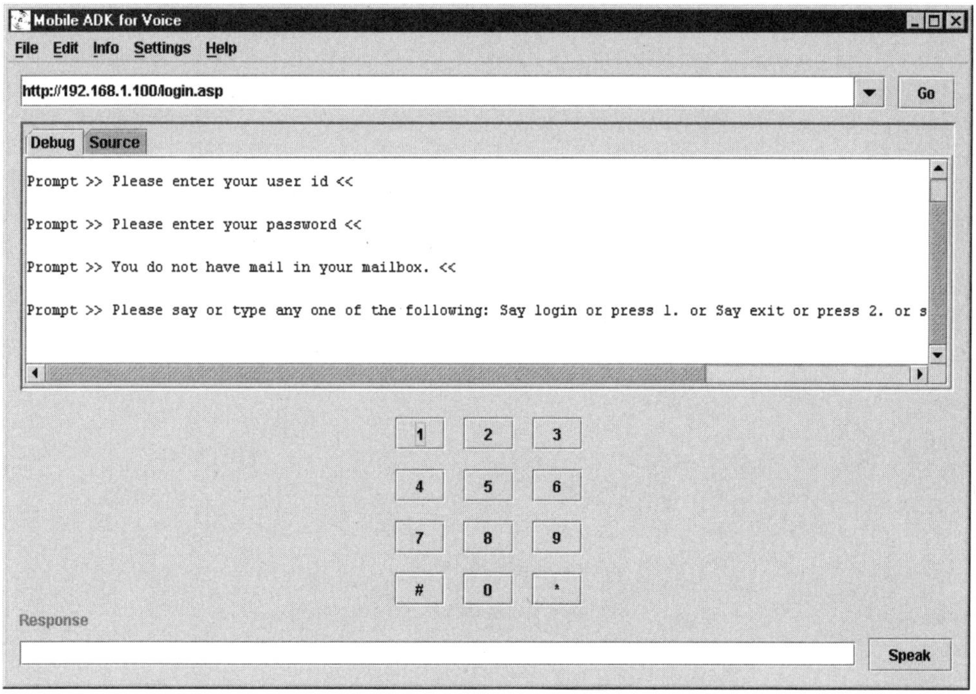

Figure 6-6   *Prompting the user about the nonavailability of messages*

Retrieving the Message

In this step, the message retrieved from the server is played back over the telephony device to the user. Listing 6-4 shows the source code of receivemessage.asp, which controls the retrieval process.

Listing 6-4: *Source Code for receivemessage.asp*

```
<%@LANGUAGE=VBSCRIPT %>
<%
uname = trim(Request.QueryString("username"))
pwd = trim(Request.QueryString("password"))
msgno = trim(Request.QueryString("messageno"))
Response.ContentType = "text/xml"
Response.Write("<?xml version= ""1.0""?>")
%>
<vxml version = "1.0" application = "http://192.168.1.100/voicemail.asp">
<var name="msgno"/>
<var name="uname"/>
<var name="upass"/>
<form>
<block>
<%
Set pop3 = Server.CreateObject( "Jmail.pop3" )
    on error resume next
    pop3.Connect uname, pwd, "http://192.168.1.100"
    Set msg = pop3.Messages.item(msgno) %>
            Message from <%=msg.From%> is
        <%=msg.Body%>
    <submit next="#call"/>
</block>
</form>
<form id="call">
    <field name="check">
        <prompt> Say another message for the details, or say reply to answer
this mail. </prompt>
                <grammar type="application/x-gsl">
                    [ (another message)(reply)  ]
                </grammar>
                <filled>
                    <if cond="check=='another message'">
                        <goto next="#anothermsg"/>
                    <elseif cond="check=='reply'"/>
                        <goto next="#replymail"/>
                </if>
                </filled>
    </field>
</form>
```

```
<form id="anothermsg">
    <field name="msgno" type="digits">
                <prompt> Please say the message number for message details
</prompt>
                        <filled>
                        <assign name="document.msgno" expr="msgno"/>
                        <goto next="#call_mail"/>
                        </filled>
    </field>
</form>
<form id="call_mail">
 <block>
    <var name="messageno" expr="document.msgno"/>
    <var name="username" expr="<%=uname%>"/>
    <var name="password" expr="<%=pwd%>"/>
    <submit next="http://jyotsna/voicemail/receivemessage.asp" method="get"
namelist="messageno username password"/>
 </block>
</form>
<form id="replymail">
    <block>
      <var name="messageno" expr="<%=msgno%>"/>
            <var name="username" expr="<%=uname%>"/>
            <var name="password" expr="<%=pwd%>"/>
            <submit next="http://jyotsna/voicemail/replymail.asp" method="get"
namelist="messageno username password"/>
      </block>
</form>
</vxml>
```

Now, let's examine the source code for receivemessage.asp in detail. The document in Listing 6-4 includes five forms for handling various tasks. The first form contains the code for connecting with the mail server and playing back a message over the telephony device.

In the next form, named call, we provide the user with two options: checking another message or going back to the home page of the application. If the user decides to check another message, the control is transferred to the next form in the document, which asks for the message number from the user. The form named call_mail is then called for retrieving the message, as shown in the following code:

```
<form id="anothermsg">
    <field name="msgno" type="digits">
                <prompt> Please say the message number for message details
</prompt>
                        <filled>
                        <assign name="document.msgno" expr="msgno"/>
                        <goto next="#call_mail"/>
                        </filled>
    </field>
</form>
```

The output of this process is shown in Figure 6-7.

The user can also reply to a message by just saying "reply" after listening to the message. If the user selects the reply option, we pass all the required information to replymail.asp by using the <submit> element in the form named reply_mail. Here is the information transferred to replaymail.asp:

- ▶ User id
- ▶ Password
- ▶ Message number

Replying to the Message

So far, we have discussed the procedure of retrieving mail messages from the inbox. After checking his or her mail, the user is also able to reply to messages by selecting the reply option. When the user chooses the reply option, the system will prompt the user with a series of messages and direct the user to record a message that will be sent as an attachment with the mail reply. The recorded message is stored on the server as an audio file, the format

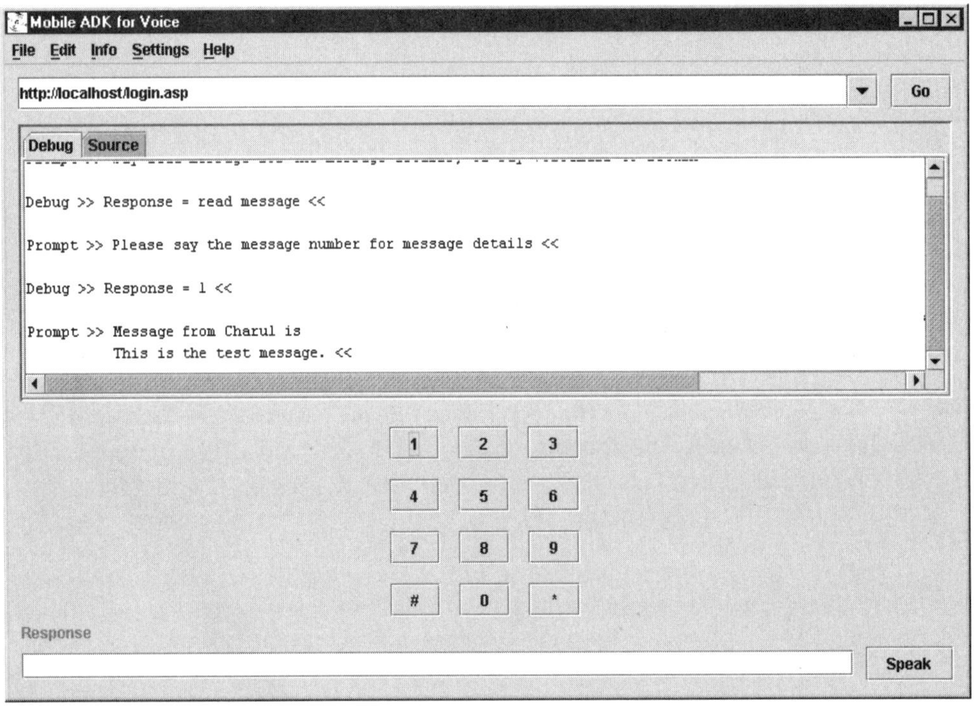

Figure 6-7 *Prompting the user to retrieve mail*

of which will vary with different platforms. Listing 6-5 provides the source code for replymail.asp, which is used for handling the complete process of replying to mail messages.

Listing 6-5: *Source Code for replymail.asp*

```
<%@LANGUAGE=VBSCRIPT %>
<%
uname = trim(Request.QueryString("username"))
pwd = trim(Request.QueryString("password"))
msgno = trim(Request.QueryString("messageno"))
Response.ContentType = "text/xml"
Response.Write("<?xml version= ""1.0""?>")
%>
<vxml version = "1.0" application = "http://192.168.1.100/voicemail.asp">
<var name="messageno"/>
<var name="username"/>
<var name="password"/>
<%
      Set pop3 = Server.CreateObject( "Jmail.pop3" )
      on error resume next
      pop3.Connect uname, pwd, "http://192.168.1.100"
      Set msg = pop3.Messages.item(msgno)
      set message = Server.CreateObject( "JMail.Message" )
      msgFrom = uname + "@developers.dreamtech.com"
      msgTo = msg.From
      subject = "RE:" + msg.subject
      message.From = msgFrom
      message.AddRecipient msgTo
     message.AddURLAttachment("http://192.168.1.100/voicemail/(msgno).wav")
      message.Subject = subject
    message.Send("192.168.1.100")
     message.Name = uname
        %>
<form>
<block>
      <submit next="#recordmsg"/>
</block>
</form>
<form id="recordmsg">
<record name="message" beep="true" maxtime="50s" dtmfterm="true" type="audio/wav">
      <prompt> At the tone, please say your message.</prompt>
      <noinput>I didn't hear anything, please try again.</noinput>
</record>
<field name="confirm" type="boolean">
      <prompt>Your message is <value expr="message"/>.</prompt>
      <prompt>To keep it, say yes. To discard it, say no.</prompt>
<filled>
<if cond="confirm">
          <submit enctype="multipart/form-data"
next="http://192.168.1.100/upload.asp" method="post" namelist="message"/>
</if>
      <clear/>
```

```
        </filled>
    </field>
    </form>
    </vxml>
```

Now, let's examine the source code in Listing 6-5 step by step to clarify it fully. As you might have noticed, in receivemessage.asp, we first access the user id and password variables passed by the previous file. In the next step, we create an object for the mail component on the server and then compose a new mail message by using the following lines of code:

```
<%
    Set pop3 = Server.CreateObject( "Jmail.pop3" )
    on error resume next
    pop3.Connect uname, pwd, "http://192.168.1.100"
    Set msg = pop3.Messages.item(msgno)
    set message = Server.CreateObject( "JMail.Message" )
    msgFrom = uname + "@developers.dreamtech.com"
    msgTo = msg.From
    subject = "RE:" + msg.subject
    message.From = msgFrom
    message.AddRecipient msgTo
    message.Subject = subject
    message.AddURLAttachment("http://192.168.1.100/voicemail/(msgno).wav")
    message.Send("192.168.1.100")
    message.Name = uname
        %>
```

At the time of composing the new mail, we add the URL of the saved audio file as an attachment so that the recipient of the mail is able to download the recorded message. After sending the mail, we prompt the user to record the message using the <record> element and submit all the received data to the server to save it as an audio file by using the following lines of code:

```
<record name="message" beep="true" maxtime="50s" dtmfterm="true" type="audio/wav">
    <prompt> At the tone, please say your message.</prompt>
    <noinput>I didn't hear anything, please try again.</noinput>
</record>
<field name="confirm" type="boolean">
<prompt>Your message is <value expr="message"/>.</prompt>
    <prompt>To keep it, say yes. To discard it, say no.</prompt>
<filled>
    <if cond="confirm">
            <submit enctype="multipart/form-data"
next="http://192.168.1.100/upload.asp"    method="post" namelist="message"/>
    </if>
    <clear/>
    </filled>
</field>
```

The complete mail reply process is shown in Figure 6-8.

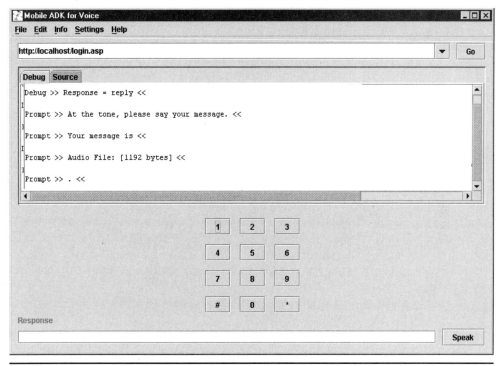

Figure 6-8   *Output of the mail reply process*

In the next step, we receive the user's response, which we have to save on the server in the audio format. For achieving this, we use the SoftArtisans FileUp component (available at http://www.softartisans.com/softartisans/saf.html), which uploads all the data on the server and then saves this data in the desired folder. The complete process is shown in Listing 6-6.

Listing 6-6:   *Source Code for upload.asp*

```
<%@LANGUAGE="VBscript"%>
<%
set oUpload = Server.CreateObject("SoftArtisans.FileUp")
oUpload.Path = "d:\main\voicemail"
oUpload.Save()
Response.ContentType = "text/xml"
Response.Write("<?xml version= ""1.0""?>")
%>
<vxml version = "1.0" application =
"http://192.168.1.100/voicemail.asp">
  <form>
```

```
      <block>
        Mail has been sent successfully.
        <submit next="voicemail.asp"/>
      </block>
  </form>
</vxml>
```

Summary

In this chapter, we discussed the technical scheme for developing a VoiceXML-based mailing application. We first decided what services would be provided by the application we envisaged. Following this, we identified the hardware and software requirements for developing the application and then depicted the working of the proposed application in a flowchart. We proceeded to work out strategies for preparing the home page, the login section, and so on. Finally, we showed you the code for enabling functionalities such as accessing the mailbox, retrieving and replying to messages, and the like, explaining aspects of the code in detail as we went along.

Using VoiceXML and JSPs for Movie Reservation Systems

I n this chapter, we use VoiceXML and Java Server Pages (JSPs) to develop a system that provides information regarding movie ticket reservations. The system enables users to reserve movie tickets by using a simple telephony device. It provides the user all the details regarding the status of ticket reservations for various movies being screened at various movie halls over the telephony network.

Application Requirements

The first step in developing the movie reservation application envisaged is to conceive a comprehensive outline of the design layout and to identify the requirements for developing and deploying the project. Because we intend to build a complete voice-based movie ticket reservation system, the following information needs to be provided to the user:

▶ The list of movie halls available for reserving tickets

▶ The list of movies running in each of the movie halls on the list

▶ Showtimes and number of tickets available for reservation for all movies running in the different movie halls

   The following software and hardware components are required for building the application and testing the code proposed for the application on the desktop.

▶ Motorola Application Development Kit version 2.0 (MADK) for testing the application in the simulated environment on your terminal

▶ Tomcat for running the JSPs (available at http://jakarta.apache.org/tomcat/)

▶ Java 2.0

▶ SQL Server for running the database on the server

Architecture of the Application

Let's examine the architecture of the application that we intend to develop. In this application, the user receives a list of the names of movie halls and the movies being screened in them, which are stored in a database on a server. The user can book the required number of tickets for any movie in any movie hall on any desired date depending on the availability, getting assistance from the system if required. On selecting a movie, the user is asked for the day of the week, for which details regarding the status of a reservation are required. On entering the day of the week, information regarding the showtimes and the number of tickets available for reservation for the day entered are presented to the user. At this stage, four different options are available:

▶ Reserve the required number of tickets for the movie chosen.

▶ Get details of showtimes and the number of tickets available for some other day of the week.

▶ Select some other movie from the list.

▶ Select some other movie hall from the list.

Upon selecting the first option, which is for booking tickets, the system asks the user for the showtime desired and the number of tickets to be reserved. If the number of tickets required is available for the showtime specified, the reservation is made. If the number of tickets required is more than what's available, the user is prompted to choose from the options that follow. The complete flowchart for this process is represented in Figures 7-1a, 7-1b, and 7-1c.

The home page of the application works as the root-level application document for the entire application, and all the other documents work as sublevel documents.

Assumptions Made in Developing the Movie Reservation Application

Before building the application, we made the following assumptions to facilitate development:

▶ The user can select the movie hall and the movie from the list using digits as well as voice input.

▶ Selection of the day of the week is accepted in the form of voice input only.

▶ The user can make the reservation for some other day, some other movie, or some movie hall in the list using digits as well as voice input.

▶ Selection of the showtime and the number of tickets to be booked are acceptable only in the form of voice input.

▶ All the source code written for this application is VoiceXML 1.0-compliant, as the final specifications of the VoiceXML 2.0 framework were not available at the time of writing this book.

Structure of the Database

Before getting into the details of the application, we'll first examine the database for this application. We have used SQL Server on the backend. Let's consider the table structures that exist in the database.

The table shown in Figure 7-2 is the Hall table, which contains details regarding the movie halls. The hall_id field is of numeric type and is the primary key of the table. The hall_name field contains the movie hall names; it is of varchar type and takes unique values (that is, two movie halls can't have the same name). Field address stores the address of the movie halls and is of varchar type.

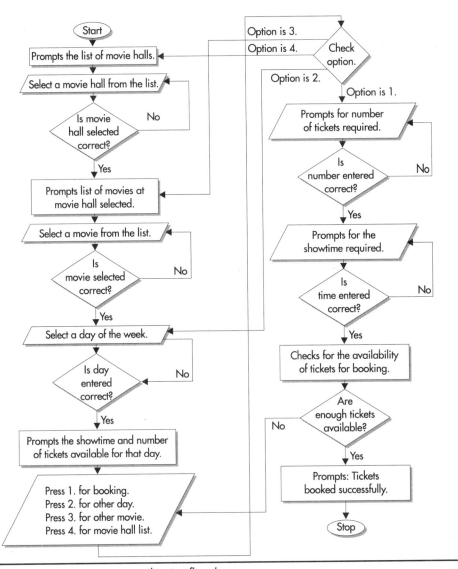

Figure 7-1 *Movie reservation application flowchart*

Figure 7-3 shows the Movie table, which stores details regarding the movies. The movie_id field is of numeric type and is the primary key of the table. The movie_name field contains the movie names; it is of varchar type and takes unique values (that is, two movies can't have the same name).

Figure 7-4 shows the Status table, which stores the movies running in the movie halls, showtimes, and the status of the tickets available for these movies. The hall_id field and the movie_id field are of numeric type, and the showtime field is of varchar type. These three

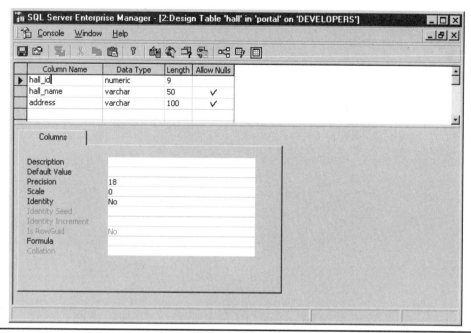

Figure 7-2   *The Hall table*

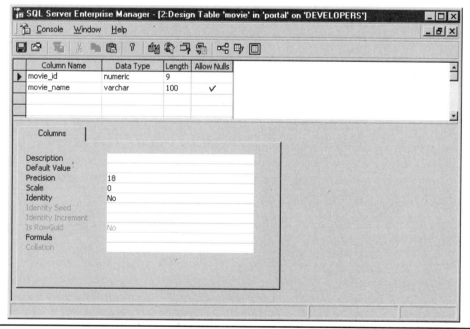

Figure 7-3   *The Movie table*

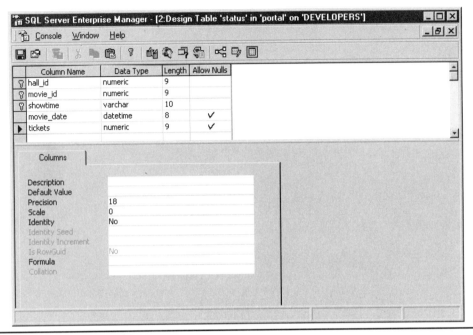

Figure 7-4   *The Status table*

fields form the primary key of the Status table. The hall_id field stores the id of the halls, movie_id stores the id of the movies, and showtime stores the showtime of the movies. The movie_date field stores the show dates of the movies and is of datetime type. The tickets field stores the number of tickets available for booking and is of numeric type.

Building the Home Page

The first task in developing the application is preparing the list of movie halls. When a user accesses the application, this list is presented first, and the user has to make a choice to proceed further with the application. Listing 7-1 contains the source code of hall.jsp, which serves as the home page of our application.

Listing 7-1:   *Source Code for hall.jsp*

```
<?xml version="1.0" ?>
<vxml version="1.0">
<link next="#exit">
            <grammar type="application/x-gsl">
            exit
            </grammar>
```

```
        </link>
<% Class.forName("sun.jdbc.odbc.JdbcOdbcDriver");%>
<% java.sql.Connection db =
java.sql.DriverManager.getConnection("jdbc:odbc:portal","sa","charul");  %>
<% java.sql.Statement st =
db.createStatement(java.sql.ResultSet.TYPE_SCROLL_INSENSITIVE,
java.sql.ResultSet.CONCUR_READ_ONLY); %>
<% java.sql.ResultSet rs ;   %>
<% String  id = "" ; %>
<% String name = "" ;  %>
<% String add = "" ;  %>
<% String urlName = "" ;  %>
<% String sqlStatement = "SELECT hall_id, hall_name, address  FROM hall ;"; %>
<% int r_count = 0 ;  %>
<% rs = st.executeQuery(sqlStatement); %>
        <% if (!rs.next()) %>
                <menu scope="document">
                <prompt><enumerate /> </prompt>
                <choice next="help"> No records exist. For assistance say
help</choice>
        <% else{ %>
        <menu scope="document">
                <% rs.beforeFirst(); %>
        <prompt><%= "Please select one of the following choices."%>
                <enumerate />
         </prompt>
                <% while (rs.next()) { %>
                        <% id = rs.getString("hall_id"); %>
                        <% name = rs.getString("hall_name");  %>
                        <% add = rs.getString("address");  %>
                        <choice <%= "dtmf=\"" +  id + "\"
                  next=\http://deepak:8080/examples/movieList.jsp?H_Id=
                  + id + "\">"  + name
%></choice>
                        <% }  %>
                <% }  %>
                <choice next="#exit">exit</choice>
                <noinput>I did not hear anything, please select any one of the
available choices.</noinput>
                <nomatch>The choice you have made is not available. Please select from
the available choices.</nomatch>
                </menu>
        <% rs.close(); %>
<form id = "exit" scope="document">
                <block  >
```

```
                        Thanks for using the application, now terminating.
                        <throw event = "telephone.disconnect.hangup" />
                </block>
        </form>
</vxml>
```

The output of hall.jsp is shown in Figure 7-5.

Let's take a closer look at this source code for clarification. In the beginning of the code, we establish connection with the database.

```
<% Class.forName("sun.jdbc.odbc.JdbcOdbcDriver");%>
<% java.sql.Connection db = java.sql.DriverManager.getConnection
("jdbc:odbc:portal","sa","charul");  %>
<% java.sql.Statement st = db.createStatement
(java.sql.ResultSet.TYPE_SCROLL_INSENSITIVE,
java.sql.ResultSet.CONCUR_READ_ONLY); %>
<% java.sql.ResultSet rs ;  %>
```

In the preceding code segment, we initialize and load the JDBC-ODBC driver to establish a database connection. An object of the DriverManager.getConnection() method connects to the portal database and returns an object of Connection class. The parameters passed to this

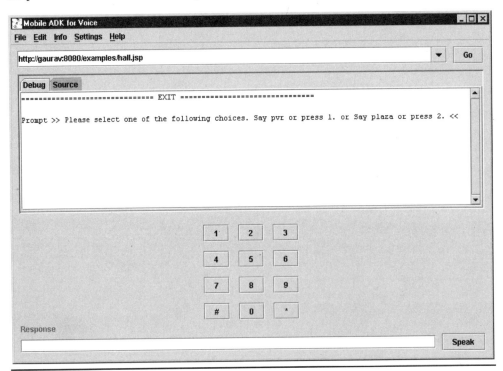

Figure 7-5   Output of hall.jsp

method are the URL of database, user id, and password of the database. An object of the Statement class is created to script a SQL query.

```
<% String sqlStatement = "SELECT hall_id, hall_name, address  FROM hall ;"; %>
<% rs = st.executeQuery(sqlStatement); %>
```

A SQL statement is declared, and data from the tables are accessed by executing this SQL statement. The executeQuery() method calls the DBMS to execute the SQL statements. The rs object of the ResultSet class stores the output of the statement executed. The Select statement is used to fetch the movie hall id, movie hall name, and address from the Hall table.

```
<% if (!rs.next()) %>
    <menu scope="document">
    <prompt><enumerate /> </prompt>
    <choice next="help"> No records exist. For assistance say help </choice>
<% else{ %>
```

The data is accessed through the methods defined in the ResultSet class. The next() method sets the position of the ResultSet cursor to the next row. Initially, the ResultSet cursor is positioned at the first row of ResultSet. These lines check for the existence of records in ResultSet. If no records exist, the application prompts "No records exist."

```
<% else{ %>
    <menu scope="document">
    <% rs.beforeFirst(); %>
    <prompt><%= "Please select one of the following choices."%><enumerate
/></prompt>
    <% while (rs.next()) { %>
        <% id = rs.getString("hall_id"); %>
        <% name = rs.getString("hall_name");  %>
        <% add = rs.getString("address");  %>
        <choice <%= "dtmf=\"" + id + "\" next=
\"http://deepak:8080/examples/movieList.jsp?H_Id=" +
id + "\">"  + name %></choice>
        <% } %>
<% } %>
```

In this code, the ResultSet value can be selected by specifying either the name or the number of the column. The beforeFirst() method takes the ResultSet cursor to the starting of ResultSet. The ResultSet object maintains a cursor to indicate the position of the current row.

The movie hall names are prompted to the user in the movie hall list. If some records exist in ResultSet, the user is prompted to select from ResultSet. The id of the movie hall selected is passed as a parameter to movieList.jsp.

Displaying the Movie List

Once the user selects a movie hall, the controls are transferred to movieList.jsp, which carries out the file handling for the movie list section of the application. In the next phase, we prompt the list of movies being screened in the movie hall selected by the user by calling movieList.jsp, shown in Listing 7-2. Once the user selects any of the available movies from the options, optionList.jsp will be called from the server.

Listing 7-2:   *Source Code for movieList.jsp*

```
<?xml version="1.0" ?>
<vxml version="1.0" application = "http://deepak:8080/examples/hall.jsp">
<% Class.forName("sun.jdbc.odbc.JdbcOdbcDriver");%>
<% java.sql.Connection db =
 java.sql.DriverManager.getConnection("jdbc:odbc:portal","sa","charul");  %>
<% java.sql.Statement st = db.createStatement
(java.sql.ResultSet.TYPE_SCROLL_INSENSITIVE,
 java.sql.ResultSet.CONCUR_READ_ONLY); %>
<% java.sql.ResultSet rs ;  %>
<% String hall_id = request.getParameter("H_Id"); %>
<% int id = 0 ;  %>
<% int r_count = 0 ;  %>
<% String mid = "" ;  %>
<% String name = "" ;  %>
<% String add = "" ;  %>
<% String urlName = "" ;  %>
<% String sqlStatement = "SELECT DISTINCT(status.movie_id),
movie.movie_name FROM movie, status WHERE status.movie_id=movie.movie_id
 and status.hall_id=" + hall_id + ";" ; %>
<% rs = st.executeQuery(sqlStatement); %>
        <% if (!rs.next()) %>
        <menu scope="document">
                <prompt><enumerate /> </prompt>
                <choice next="help"> No records exist. For assistance
say help</choice>
        <% else{%>
                <menu scope="document">
                <% rs.beforeFirst(); %>
                <prompt><%= "Please select one of the following choices."%>
<enumerate /></prompt>
                <% while (rs.next()) { %>
                    <% id = id + 1; %>
                    <% mid = rs.getString(1);  %>
                    <% name = rs.getString(2);  %>
                    <choice <%= "dtmf=\"" +  id + "\"
next=\"http://deepak:8080/examples/optionList.jsp?H_Id="
+ hall_id +  "&amp;M_Id=" + mid + "\">"  + name %></choice>
```

```
         <% } %>
     <% } %>
     <choice next="#exit">exit</choice>
     <noinput>I did not hear anything, please select any one of
the available choices.</noinput>
     <nomatch>The choice you have made is not available.
Please select from the available choices.</nomatch>
     <% rs.close(); %>
     </menu>
</vxml>
```

The output of movieList.jsp is shown in Figure 7-6.

In Listing 7-2, a SQL statement is declared and data in the tables are accessed by executing the SQL statement. The executeQuery() method calls the DBMS to perform the SQL statement. The rs object of the ResultSet class stores the result of the statement executed. The Select statement fetches the movie id and the movie name from the Movie table and Status table, respectively. The movie hall id is passed as an argument to movieList.jsp for the retrieval of records.

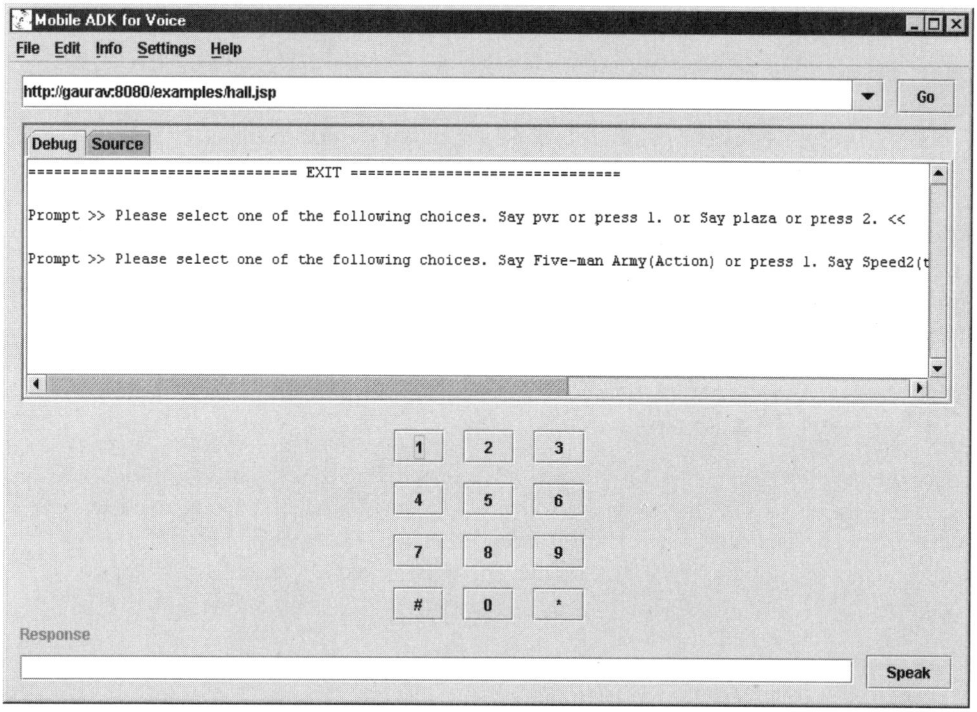

Figure 7-6   Output of movieList.jsp

```
<% if (!rs.next()) %>
        <menu scope="document">
        <prompt><enumerate /> </prompt>
        <choice next="help"> No records exist.
            For assistance say help</choice>
    <% else{%>
```

In the preceding code, data is accessed through the methods defined in the ResultSet class. The next() method sets the position of the ResultSet cursor to the next row. Initially the ResultSet cursor is positioned at the first row of ResultSet. These lines check for the existence of records in ResultSet. If no records exist, then the system prompts "No records exists."

```
<menu scope="document">
        <% rs.beforeFirst(); %>
        <prompt><%= "Please select one of the following choices."%>
         <enumerate />           </prompt>
        <% while (rs.next()) { %>
        <% id = id + 1; %>
        <% mid = rs.getString(1);  %>
        <% name = rs.getString(2);  %>
        <choice <%= "dtmf=\"" + id + "\" next=
\"http://deepak:8080/examples/optionList.jsp?H_Id=" + hall_id +
                amp;M_Id=" + mid + "\">"  + name %></choice>
    <% } %>
```

Here, the ResultSet value can be selected by specifying either the name or the number of the column. The beforeFirst() method takes the ResultSet cursor to the start of ResultSet. The ResultSet object maintains a cursor to indicate the position of the current row.

Movie names are presented to the user for selection in the movie list. If some records exist in ResultSet, the application prompts the user to select the movie from ResultSet. Once the user selects a movie and movie hall, the ids of the movie and the movie hall are passed as parameters to the next file, optionList.jsp.

Collecting the Input

Once the user selects a movie, the controls are transferred to the optionList.jsp file for accepting the movie day. In this phase, we accept the day for which the user seeks to reserve tickets. If the weekday the user indicates is incorrect, the system responds with an error message and asks the user for correct input. The source code for optionList.jsp appears in Listing 7-3.

Listing 7-3:   *Source Code for optionList.jsp*

```
<?xml version="1.0"?>
<vxml version="1.0" application = "http://deepak:8080/examples/hall.jsp">
```

```
<%@ page import = "java.util.*" %>
<% int day_id = 0 ;  %>
<% int diff = 0 ;   %>
<% String day = "";%>
<var name="hall_id" expr="<%= request.getParameter("H_Id") %>"/>
<var name="movie_id" expr="<%= request.getParameter("M_Id") %>"/>
<form id="daylist">
      <field name="day">
      <prompt><%= "Please say the name of the day."%></prompt>
          <grammar type="application/x-jsgf">
sunday | monday | tuesday | wednesday |thursday | friday | saturday</grammar>
<nomatch>Sorry, Please select a valid day</nomatch>
      </field>
      <filled >
      <var name="hall"  expr="document.hall_id"/>
      <var name="movie" expr="document.movie_id"/>
      <var name="wk_day" expr="day"/>
          <submit <%= " next=\http://deepak:8080/examples/displayList.jsp \
method=\"post\" namelist=\"hall movie wk_day\""  %> />
          </filled>
</form>
</vxml>
```

The output for this example is shown in Figure 7-7.

Let's examine the preceding code. In the starting lines, we declare these variables:

```
<var name="hall_id" expr="<%= request.getParameter("H_Id") %>"/>
<var name="movie_id" expr="<%= request.getParameter("M_Id") %>"/>
```

The hall_id and movie_id variables are initialized with the values passed from movieList.jsp.

```
<form id="daylist">
<field name="day">
          <prompt><%= "Please say the name of the day."%></prompt>
          <grammar type="application/x-jsgf">
sunday | monday | tuesday | wednesday | thursday | friday | saturday</grammar>
    <nomatch>Sorry, Please select a valid day</nomatch>
    </field>
```

The user is asked for a valid day of the week, which is accepted in the form of voice input only. If the user says an invalid day, the application responds with an error message and asks for valid input.

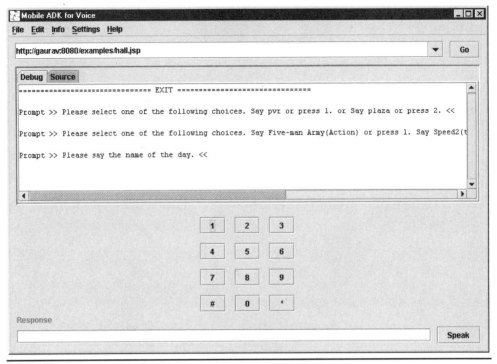

Figure 7-7   *Output of optionList.jsp*

```
<filled >
        <var name="hall"  expr="document.hall_id"/>
        <var name="movie" expr="document.movie_id"/>
        <var name="wk_day" expr="day"/>
        <submit <%= "
next=\"http://deepak:8080/examples/displayList.jsp
\" method= \"post\" namelist=\"hall movie wk_day\""  %> />

</filled>
```

The weekday selected by the user, the movie hall id, and the movie id are passed as parameters to the next file, displayList.jsp.

Displaying the Current Status

Once the user selects the weekday, the controls are transferred to the displayList.jsp file for generating the date of the movie. If the date generated is valid, the availability of records is checked. If the number of records is null, then the system responds "No records exist."

Otherwise, the user is informed of the current status (that is, the showtime and the number of tickets available) and is prompted with four different options for further selection:

▶ Reserve the required number of tickets for the movie chosen.

▶ Get details of showtimes and the number of tickets available for some other day of the week.

▶ Select some other movie from the list.

▶ Select some other movie hall from the list.

The complete source code of displayList.jsp is given in Listing 7-4.

Listing 7-4: *Source Code for displayList.jsp*

```
<?xml version="1.0"?>
<vxml version="1.0" application = "http://deepak:8080/examples/hall.jsp">
<%@ page import = "java.util.*" %>
<% int day_id = 0 ;  %>
<% int diff = 0 ;  %>
<% String hall_id     = request.getParameter("hall"); %>
<% String movie_id = request.getParameter("movie"); %>
<% String day           = request.getParameter("wk_day") ; %>
<% int day_no      =   0 ; %>
<% int m_date      =   0 ; %>
<% int m_month   =  0 ; %>
<% int m_year      =  0 ; %>
<% String mtime              =   ""; %>
<% String tickets       =   "";  %>
<% String movie_date       =   "" ; %>
<% String mov_date       =   "" ; %>
<menu  scope="dialog">
        <% if (day.equals("sunday")){ %>
        <% day_id = 1 ;  %>
        <% } else %>
        <% if (day.equals("monday")){ %>
        <% day_id = 2 ;   %>
        <% } else %>
        <% if (day.equals("tuesday")){ %>
        <% day_id = 3 ;   %>
        <% } else %>
        <% if (day.equals("wednesday")){ %>
        <% day_id = 4 ;   %>
        <% } else %>
        <% if (day.equals("thursday")){ %>
```

```
        <% day_id = 5 ;   %>
        <% } else %>
        <% if (day.equals("friday")){ %>
        <% day_id = 6 ;   %>
        <% } else %>
        <% if (day.equals("saturday")){ %>
        <% day_id = 7 ;   %>
        <% } %>
        <% Calendar now = Calendar.getInstance(); %>
        <% day_no  = now.get(Calendar.DAY_OF_WEEK) ; %>
        <% m_date  = now.get(Calendar.DAY_OF_MONTH); %>
        <% m_month = now.get(Calendar.MONTH) + 1; %>
        <% m_year  = now.get(Calendar.YEAR); %>
        <% diff = day_id - day_no;   %>
        <% if (diff >= 0 ) { %>
        <%    m_date = m_date + diff; %>
        <%    } else { %>
        <%     m_date = m_date - diff; %>
        <% } %>
        <% movie_date = String.valueOf(m_month); movie_date =
movie_date.concat("/");%>        <% movie_date =
movie_date.concat(String.valueOf(m_date));
movie_date = movie_date.concat("/");%>
        <% movie_date = movie_date.concat(String.valueOf(m_year));%>
        <% Class.forName("sun.jdbc.odbc.JdbcOdbcDriver");%>
        <% java.sql.Connection db = java.sql.DriverManager.getConnection
("jdbc:odbc:portal","sa","charul");   %>
        <% java.sql.Statement st = db.createStatement
(java.sql.ResultSet.TYPE_SCROLL_INSENSITIVE,
java.sql.ResultSet.CONCUR_READ_ONLY); %>
        <% java.sql.ResultSet rs ;   %>
        <% String sqlStatement = "select movie_date,showtime,tickets from
 status where status.hall_id=" + hall_id +
"and status.movie_id=" + movie_id + " and movie_date =" +
"'" + movie_date + "'" +";";%>
        <% rs = st.executeQuery(sqlStatement); %>
        <% if (!rs.next()) %>
            <prompt><enumerate /> </prompt>
            <choice next="help"> No records exist.
For assistance say help</choice>
        <% else{ %>
            <% rs.beforeFirst(); %>
            <% while (rs.next()) { %>
            <% mtime = rs.getString(2); %>
```

```
            <% tickets = rs.getString(3);   %>
                  <prompt> Showtime= <%= mtime  %>   </prompt>
            <prompt> Tickets= <%= tickets  %>  </prompt>
            <% } %>
            <prompt><%= "Please select one of the following choices......."%>
             <enumerate/>
             </prompt>
            <choice <%= "dtmf=\"" + 1 + "\" next=
\"http://deepak:8080/examples/booking.jsp?H_Id=" + hall_id +
"&amp;M_Id=" + movie_id + "&amp;M_date=" + m_date +
"&amp;M_month=" + m_month +"&amp;M_year=" + m_year + "\">"
+ "Booking" %></choice>
            <choice <%= "dtmf=\"" + 2 + "\"
next=\"http://deepak:8080/examples/optionList.jsp?H_Id=" + hall_id +
"&amp;M_Id=" + movie_id + "\">"  + "Other Day" %></choice>
       <choice <%= "dtmf=\"" + 3 + "\" next=
\"http://deepak:8080/examples/movieList.jsp?H_Id=" + hall_id + "\">"
+ "Other Movie" %></choice>
<choice <%= "dtmf=\"" + 4 + "\"
 next=\"http://deepak:8080/examples/hall.jsp \">"
  + "Hall List" %></choice> <noinput>
I did not hear anything, please select any one of the available choices.</noinput>
<nomatch>The choice you have made is not available. Please select from the
available choices.</nomatch>
       <% } %>
</menu>
<form id= "Booking" >
<block><%= "You selected choice " + 1 + "."%>
            <disconnect />
       </block>
</form>
<form id= "Other Day" >
     <block><%= "You selected choice " + 2 + "."%>
            <disconnect />
            </block>
</form>
<form id= "Other Movie" >
<block><%= "You selected choice " + 3 + "."%>
            <disconnect />
            </block>
</form>
<form id= "Hall List" >
<block><%= "You selected choice " + 4 + "."%>
            <disconnect />
            </block>
```

```
</form>
<% rs.close(); %>
</vxml>
```

The output of this example is shown in Figure 7-8.

As shown in Listing 7-4, the hall_id, movie_id, and day variables are declared and initialized with the values passed from optionList.jsp. The string variable, hall_id, is for the id of the movie hall chosen by the user; movie_id is for the id of the movie chosen by the user; and the string variable day is for the day of the week chosen by the user.

```
<% if (day.equals("sunday")){ %>
    <% day_id = 1 ; %>
    <% } else %>
    <% if (day.equals("monday")){ %>
    <% day_id = 2 ; %>
    <% } else %>
```

The value of day initializes the variable day_id with the day number. If the value of day is Sunday, day_id is initialized with 1, if day is Monday, it's initialized with 2, and so on.

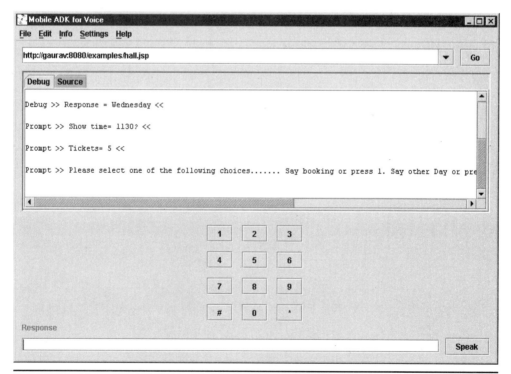

Figure 7-8   *Output of displayList.jsp*

```
<% Calendar now = Calendar.getInstance(); %>
      <% day_no  = now.get(Calendar.DAY_OF_WEEK) ; %>
      <% m_date  = now.get(Calendar.DAY_OF_MONTH); %>
      <% m_month = now.get(Calendar.MONTH) + 1; %>
      <% m_year  = now.get(Calendar.YEAR); %>
```

Now the object is initialized with the Calendar object. The getInstance() method of the Calendar class returns the current system date. The variable day_no is initialized with the value of the day number of the week corresponding to the current date.

The m_date variable is initialized with the value of the day of the month corresponding to the current date (that is, 1, 2, ... 23, ... 26, ...). The m_month variable is initialized with the value of the month number of the current date. We add value 1 to the month number as it returns values between 0 and 11 for the months January to December. The variable m_year is initialized with the year of the current date.

```
<% movie_date = String.valueOf(m_month); movie_date = movie_date.concat("/");%>
<% movie_date = movie_date.concat(String.valueOf(m_date)); movie_date =
movie_date.concat("/");%>
<% movie_date = movie_date.concat(String.valueOf(m_year));%>
```

The movie_date string is generated by concatenating the string value of the variables m_month, m_day, and m_year, initialized previously.

```
<% String sqlStatement = "select showtime,tickets from status where
status.hall_id=" + hall_id + "and status.movie_id=" + movie_id + " and
movie_date =" + "'" + movie_date + "'" +";";%>
<% rs = st.executeQuery(sqlStatement); %>
```

The SQL statement is declared to retrieve the records of the showtime, the number of tickets available according to the Status table of the movie hall, the movie running at the movie hall, and the date for reservation selected by the user. The executeQuery() method calls the DBMS to perform the SQL statements. The rs object of the ResultSet class stores the output of the statement executed.

```
<% if (!rs.next()) %>
      <prompt><enumerate /> </prompt>
      <choice next="help"> No records exist. For assistance say help</choice>
```

In the preceding code, data is accessed through the methods defined in the ResultSet class. The next() method sets the position of the ResultSet cursor to the next row. Initially, the ResultSet cursor is positioned at the first row of ResultSet. These lines check for the existence of records in ResultSet. If no records exist, the system replies "No records exist."

```
<% else{ %>
            <% rs.beforeFirst(); %>
            <% while (rs.next()) { %>
            <% mtime = rs.getString(1); %>
            <% tickets = rs.getString(2);  %>
            <prompt> show time= <%= mtime  %>   </prompt>
```

```
<prompt> Tickets= <%= tickets  %>  </prompt>
<% }  %>
```

Here, the ResultSet value can be selected by specifying either the name or the number of the column. The beforeFirst() method takes the ResultSet cursor to the start of ResultSet. The ResultSet object maintains a cursor to indicate the position of the current row.

The showtimes and the number of tickets available are presented to the user before the system reserves the tickets.

```
<prompt><%= "Please select one of the following choices......."%>
<enumerate/></prompt>
<choice <%= "dtmf=\"" + 1 + "\" next=
\"http://deepak:8080/examples/booking.jsp?H_Id=" + hall_id +
"&amp;M_Id=" + movie_id + "&amp;M_date=" + m_date + "&amp;M_month="
 + m_month +"&amp;M_year=" + m_year + "\">"
+ "Booking" %></choice>
        <choice <%= "dtmf=\"" + 2 + "\" next=
\"http://deepak:8080/examples/optionList.jsp?H_Id=" + hall_id +
"&amp;M_Id=" + movie_id + "\">"  + "Other Day" %></choice>
        <choice <%= "dtmf=\"" + 3 + "\" next=
\"http://deepak:8080/examples/movieList.jsp?H_Id=" + hall_id + "\">"
+ "Other Movie" %></choice><choice <%= "dtmf=\"" + 4 + "\"
next=\"http://deepak:8080/examples/hall.jsp\">"
+ "Hall List" %></choice>
```

The user is then prompted four different options for further selection:

▶ Reserve the tickets for the movies.

▶ Get details of showtimes and the number of tickets available some other day of the week.

▶ Select some other movie from the list.

▶ Select some other movie hall from the list.

Writing the Reservation Procedure

Once the user selects the booking option for reserving the tickets, the controls are transferred to booking.jsp, shown in Listing 7-5. The application asks the user for the number of tickets to be reserved and the preferred showtime. After the user selects the number of tickets and the showtime, control is transferred to the check_status.jsp file.

Listing 7-5: *Source code for booking.jsp*

```
<?xml version="1.0" ?>
<vxml version="1.0" application = "http://deepak:8080/examples/hall.jsp">
```

```
<%@ page import = "java.util.*" %>
<% int day_id = 0 ;  %>
<% int day_date = 0 ;  %>
<% int day_no = 0 ;  %>
<% int diff = 0 ;  %>
<% int tickets_req = 0 ;  %>
<% String day = "";%>
<% String show_time = "";%>
<% String stall = "" ;%>
<% int no_of_tickets = 0 ;%>
<% String mv = "/" ;%>
<% java.sql.ResultSet rs ;  %>
<var name="hall_id" expr="<%= request.getParameter("H_Id") %>"/>
<var name="movie_id" expr="<%= request.getParameter("M_Id") %>"/>
<var name="movie_date" expr="<%= request.getParameter("M_date") %>"/>
<var name="movie_month" expr="<%= request.getParameter("M_month") %>"/>
<var name="movie_year" expr="<%= request.getParameter("M_year") %>"/>
<form id="daylist" scope="document">
      <field name="no_of_tickets" type="number">
      <prompt><%= "Please say the number of tickets required."%></prompt>
 <nomatch>Sorry, please select a valid number</nomatch>
      </field>
      <field name="show_time" type="time">
            <prompt><%= "Please say the showtime."%></prompt>
      <nomatch>Sorry, please select a valid time</nomatch>
      </field>
      <filled>
            <var name="hall"  expr="document.hall_id"/>
            <var name="movie" expr="document.movie_id"/>
            <var name="m_date" expr="document.movie_date"/>
            <var name="m_month" expr="document.movie_month"/>
            <var name="m_year" expr="document.movie_year"/>
            <var name="tickets_req" expr="no_of_tickets"/>
            <var name="s_time" expr="show_time"/>
            <submit <%= " next=\http://deepak:8080/examples/check_status.jsp \
method=\"post\" namelist=\"hall movie m_date m_month m_year tickets_req s_time\""
  %> />
      </filled>
</form>
</vxml>
```

The output of booking.jsp is shown in Figures 7-9, 7-10, and 7-11.

As shown in Listing 7-5, the hall_id, movie_id, and day variables are declared and initialized with the values passed from displayList.jsp. The variable hall_id represents

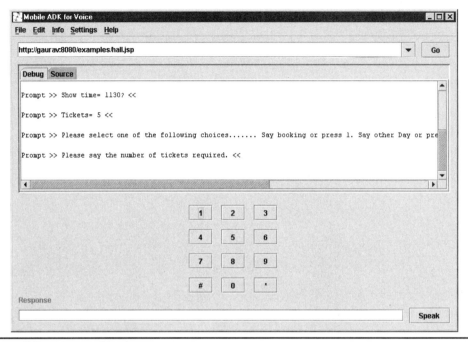

Figure 7-9   *Output of booking.jsp*

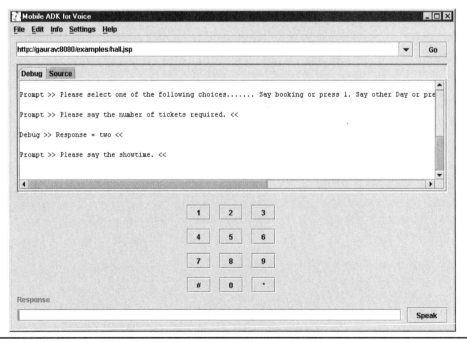

Figure 7-10   *Output of booking.jsp (continued)*

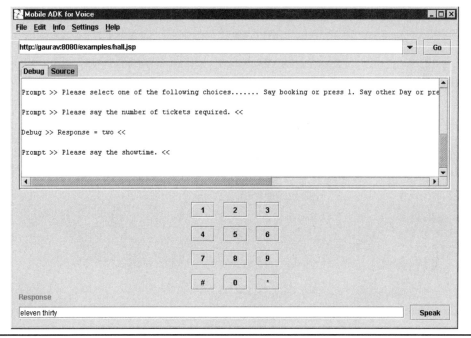

Figure 7-11 *Output of booking.jsp (continued)*

the id of the movie hall accepted by the user; movie_id represents the id of the movie, and the variables movie_date, movie_month, and movie_year are for the date, month, and year, respectively, of the reservation date.

```
<form id="daylist" scope="document">
     <field name="no_of_tickets" type="number">
          <prompt><%= "Please say the number of tickets required."%></prompt>
<nomatch>Sorry, please select a valid number</nomatch>
     </field>
```

The system asks the user how many tickets to reserve. If the user says an invalid number, the <nomatch> tag results in the system asking for a valid number.

```
<field name="show_time" type="time">
          <prompt><%= "Please say the showtime."%></prompt>
     <nomatch>Sorry, please select a valid time</nomatch>
     </field>
```

The system next asks the user for preferred showtimes. If the user gives an invalid input, the <nomatch> tag results in the system asking for a valid time.

```
<submit <%= " next=\http://deepak:8080/examples/check_status.jsp \
method=\"post\" namelist=\"hall movie m_date m_month m_year
     tickets_req s_time\"" %> />
```

Once the user selects the number of tickets and the showtime for the reservation, the controls are transferred to check_status.jsp using the <submit> element.

Final Episode

In this phase, check_status.jsp, shown in Listing 7-6, checks for the availability of tickets for the date and the showtimes desired. If no records are available, the application responds, "No records exist." If the number of tickets available is less than what's required, the system prompts, "Tickets not available"; otherwise, the tickets are booked and the user gets the prompt, "Tickets booked."

Listing 7-6: *Source Code for checkstatus.jsp*

```
<?xml version="1.0" ?>
<vxml version="1.0" application = "http://deepak:8080/examples/hall.jsp">
<%@ page import = "java.util.*" %>
<% Class.forName("sun.jdbc.odbc.JdbcOdbcDriver");%>
<% java.sql.Connection db =
java.sql.DriverManager.getConnection("jdbc:odbc:portal","sa","charul");  %>
<% java.sql.Statement st =
db.createStatement(java.sql.ResultSet.TYPE_SCROLL_INSENSITIVE,
 java.sql.ResultSet.CONCUR_READ_ONLY); %>
<% java.sql.ResultSet rs ;  %>
<% java.sql.Statement st1 =
db.createStatement(java.sql.ResultSet.TYPE_SCROLL_INSENSITIVE,
java.sql.ResultSet.CONCUR_READ_ONLY); %>

<% java.sql.ResultSet rs1 ;  %>
<% String sqlStatement1 = "" ; %>
<% String movie_date = "" ; %>
<% String hall_id = request.getParameter("hall"); %>
<% String movie_id = request.getParameter("movie"); %>
<% String movie_day = request.getParameter("m_date"); %>
<% String movie_month = request.getParameter("m_month"); %>
<% String movie_year = request.getParameter("m_year"); %>
<% String no_tickets = request.getParameter("tickets_req"); %>
<% String show_time = request.getParameter("s_time"); %>
<% String tickets = ""; %>
<% int i = Integer.parseInt(no_tickets); %>
<% int j = 0; %>
<menu      scope="document">
     <% movie_date = movie_month + "/" + movie_day + "/" + movie_year ;%>
     <% String sqlStatement = "select tickets from status where status.hall_id=
```

```
" + hall_id + "and status.movie_id=" + movie_id +
" and movie_date =" + "'" + movie_date + "'" + " and showtime="
 + "'" + show_time +   "' ;";%>
<% rs = st.executeQuery(sqlStatement); %>
<% if (!rs.next()) %>
            <choice next="help"> No records exist. For assistance say
 help</choice>
      <% else{ %>
            <prompt>very good </prompt>
            <% rs.beforeFirst(); %>
            <% while (rs.next()) { %>
            <% tickets = rs.getString(1);  %>
      <% }  %>
      <% j = Integer.parseInt(tickets); %>
      <prompt><%= j %></prompt>
      <% if ( i < j ) { %>
            <prompt><%= i %></prompt>
            <% String balance = String.valueOf(j-i); %>
            <prompt><%= balance %></prompt>
            <% sqlStatement1 = "update status set tickets=" + balance +
" where status.hall_id=" + hall_id +
"and status.movie_id=" + movie_id + "
                  and movie_date =" + "'" + movie_date + "'" +
" and showtime=" + "'" +  show_time +   "' ;";%>
            <% st1.executeUpdate(sqlStatement1); %>
            <prompt><%= "Tickets booked . Thank you. "%></prompt>
      <% } else { %>
            <prompt><%= j %></prompt>
            <prompt><%= "Sorry, tickets not available.
  You can't book more than "%></prompt>
            <prompt><%= j %></prompt>
            <prompt><%= "Tickets.   "%></prompt>
      <% }  %>
            <prompt><%= "Please select one of the following choices......."%>
<enumerate /></prompt>
            <choice <%= "dtmf=\"" + 1 + "\"
 next=\"http://deepak:8080/examples/booking.jsp?H_Id="
+ hall_id +  "&amp;M_Id=" + movie_id + "&amp;M_date=" + movie_day +
 "&amp;M_month=" + movie_month +"&amp;M_year=" + movie_year + "\">"
  + "Booking" %></choice>
            <choice <%= "dtmf=\"" + 2 + "\"
 next=\"http://deepak:8080/examples/optionList.jsp?H_Id=" +
hall_id + "&amp;M_Id=" + movie_id + "\">"  + "Other Day" %></choice>
            <choice <%= "dtmf=\"" + 3 + "\"
next=\"http://deepak:8080/examples/movieList.jsp?H_Id=" +
```

```
hall_id + "\">"  + "Other Movie" %></choice>
            <choice <%= "dtmf=\"" + 4 + "\"
 next=\"http://deepak:8080/examples/hall.jsp  \">"  +
"Hall List" %></choice>
            <noinput>I did not hear anything, please select any one of the
 available choices.</noinput>
            <nomatch>The choice you have made is not available. Please select from
 the available choices.</nomatch>
</menu>
<form id= "Booking" >
<block><%= "You selected the choice " + 1 + "."%>
            <disconnect />
            </block>
</form>
<form id= "Other Day" >
<block><%= "You selected the choice " + 2 + "."%>
            <disconnect />
            </block>
</form>
<form id= "Other Movie" >
<block><%= "You selected the choice " + 3 + "."%>
            <disconnect />
            </block>
</form>
<form id= "Hall List" >
<block><%= "You selected the choice " + 4 + "."%>
            <disconnect />
            </block>
</form>
<% rs.close(); %>
</vxml>
```

The output of check_status.jsp is shown in Figure 7-12.

Now let's take a closer look at this code. In the first phase, the variable movie_date is initialized with the concatenated value of the variables movie_month, movie_day, and movie_year, as shown here, followed by the SQL statement:

```
<menu       scope="document">
    <% movie_date = movie_month + "/" + movie_day + "/" + movie_year ;%>
<% String sqlStatement = "select tickets from status where status.hall_id="
 + hall_id + "and status.movie_id=" + movie_id +
" and movie_date =" + "'" + movie_date + "'" +
" and showtime=" + "'" + show_time +  "' ;";%>
    <% rs = st.executeQuery(sqlStatement); %>
```

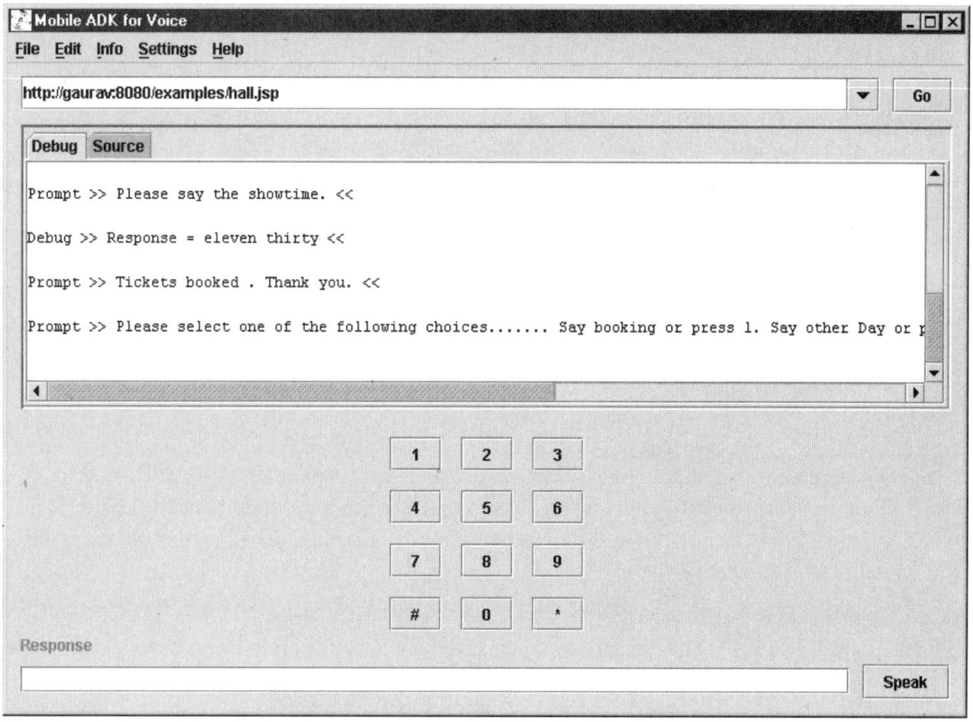

Figure 7-12   Output of check_status.jsp

The SQL statement is declared and data from the tables are accessed by executing the SQL statement. The executeQuery() method calls the DBMS to execute the SQL statements. The rs object of the ResultSet class stores the result of the statement executed. The select statement fetches the number of tickets available from the Status table. The variables hall_id, movie_id, movie_date, and show_time are passed as arguments for the retrieval of records.

```
<% if (!rs.next()) %>
          <choice next="help"> No records exist.
For assistance say help</choice>
```

In the preceding code, the data is accessed through the methods defined in the ResultSet class. The next() method sets the position of the ResultSet cursor to the next row. Initially, the ResultSet cursor is positioned at the first row of ResultSet. These lines check for the existence of records in ResultSet. If no records exist, the application prompts, "No records exist."

```
<% else{ %>
          <% rs.beforeFirst(); %>
          <% while (rs.next()) { %>
```

```
        <% tickets = rs.getString(1);  %>
   <% }  %>
```

The beforeFirst() method takes the ResultSet cursor to the start of ResultSet. In the preceding code, the ResultSet value can be selected by specifying either the name or the number of the column. The ResultSet object maintains a cursor to indicate the position of the current row.

```
<% sqlStatement1 = "update status set tickets=" + balance +
" where status.hall_id=" + hall_id + "and status.movie_id="
+  movie_id + "          and movie_date =" + "'" + movie_date
+ "'" + " and showtime=" + "'" + show_time +  "' ;";%>
<% st1.executeUpdate(sqlStatement1); %>
<prompt><%= "Tickets booked . Thank you. "%></prompt>
```

A SQL statement is declared and the tables are updated by executing the SQL statement. The executeUpdate() method calls the DBMS to execute the SQL statement. If the number of tickets available is more than or equal to the number of tickets asked for by the user, the system responds, "Tickets booked."

```
<% } else { %>
<prompt><%= "Sorry,  tickets not available.  You can't book more than "%>
```

If the number of tickets available for booking is less than what's required, the tickets aren't booked and the user receives the prompt, "Tickets not available."

```
<choice <%= "dtmf=\"" + 1 + "\"
next=\"http://deepak:8080/examples/booking.jsp?H_Id=" + hall_id +
"&amp;M_Id=" + movie_id + "&amp;M_date=" + movie_day +
"&amp;M_month=" + movie_month +"&amp;M_year=" + movie_year + "\">"
 + "Booking" %></choice> <choice <%= "dtmf=\"" + 2 + "\"
next=\"http://deepak:8080/examples/optionList.jsp?H_Id=" + hall_id +   "&amp;M_Id="
+ movie_id + "\">"  + "Other Day" %></choice>
<choice <%= "dtmf=\"" + 3 + "\"
next=\"http://deepak:8080/examples/movieList.jsp?H_Id=" + hall_id + "\">"  +
"Other Movie" %></choice>
<choice <%= "dtmf=\"" + 4 + "\" next=\"http://deepak:8080/examples/hall.jsp
\">"  + "Hall List" %></choice>
```

After prompting the message, the system provides the user with the option to book more tickets, select some other day or movie, or return to the home page of the application. If the user chooses the exit option anywhere in the application, the system terminates the application and informs the user about the status, as shown in the Figure 7-13.

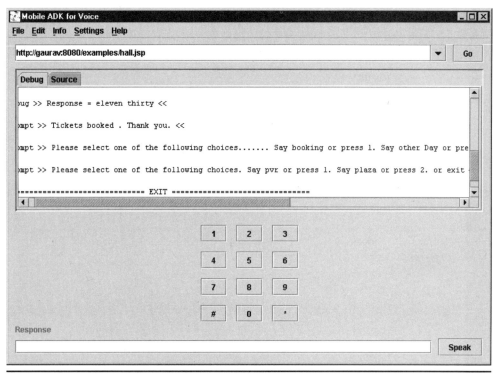

Figure 7-13   *Terminating the application*

Summary

In this chapter, we discussed the procedure of developing a VoiceXML-based movie ticket reservation system. The chapter first identifies the services the application would provide, followed by the hardware and software requirements for developing it. In the next phase, we focused on the architecture and the database design of the application. Finally, we explored the code used to provide all of the initially identified services in a detailed manner.

Developing a Voice-based Banking System

IN THIS CHAPTER:

I n this chapter, we discuss the various aspects of developing a voice-based banking service system by combining the technologies of VoiceXML and ColdFusion. Users can employ this system to facilitate some of the usual banking transactions over a telephony network.

Architecture of the Voice Banking Application

Let's plan the general architecture of the voice banking application we seek to develop. In this application, the user first logs on to the system by furnishing the assigned customer identification number and personal identification number. Based on the information provided, the system first authenticates the user, and if the user's credentials are verified successfully, the application starts by prompting the first four options to the user and waits for the user to respond.

The user may select any one of the four options to proceed further. Figure 8-1 shows a flowchart of the process up to this point.

The first four options are as follows:

► Inquiry

► Transfer money

► Order new chequebook or account statement

► Exit

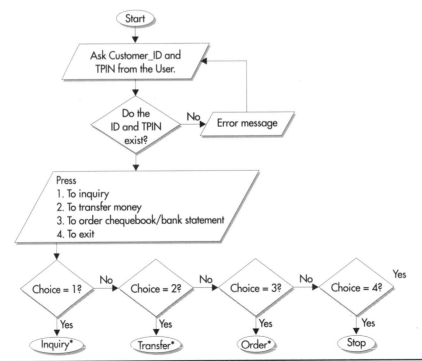

Figure 8-1 *Flowchart of the voice banking application home page*

Further processing depends on the option selected by the user. The system will proceed by executing that section of the application relevant to the user input. If the user selects the inquiry option from the home page, the application starts the execution process of the inquiry module, informs the user of the services offered under the inquiry section of the application, and waits for user response to proceed further. The procedural layout of this section is represented by the flowchart in Figure 8-2.

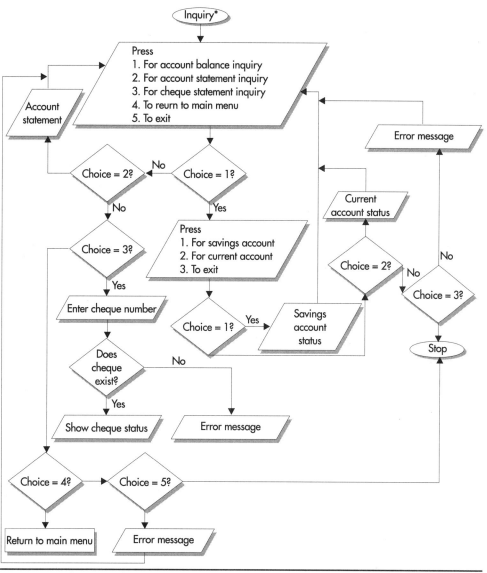

Figure 8-2 *Flowchart of the inquiry section*

If the user selects the second option, to transfer money, from the home page, the execution of the associated module starts. By means of this section of the application, the user can transfer money across accounts by providing the required information. Figure 8-3 shows a graphical representation of the architecture of the money transfer section.

If the user selects the option to order a chequebook or account statement, the system will execute the events corresponding to the associated section. This module aids the user in ordering new chequebooks and obtaining account statements over the telephone. A flowchart depicting the architecture of this module appears in Figure 8-4.

If the user selects the exit option at any stage while interacting with the system, the application will be terminated. The user can also terminate the application anytime during the transaction just by saying the "exit" hot word.

Database Structure for the Application

Let's examine the database structure we use for this application. We elected to use Microsoft Access 2000 to generate our database. The various types of data required to build the

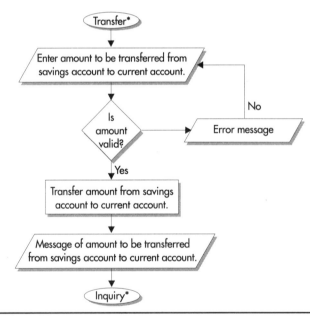

Figure 8-3   *Flowchart of the money transfer section*

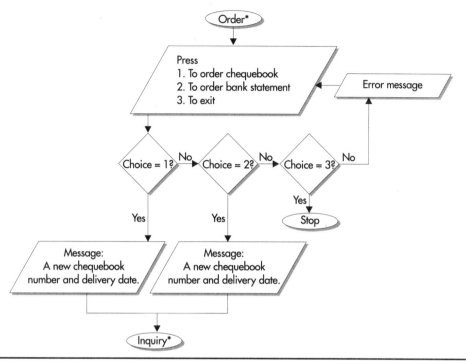

Figure 8-4   *Flowchart of the order chequebooks and account statement section*

application have been stored in nine tables. These tables are listed in Table 8-1. Following is a brief description of each of the tables along with a representation of its schema.

Table Name	Table Description
customer	Stores the personal information of customers
account_statement	Stores the account statement information of all users
cheque_status	Stores information regarding cheques
current_account	Stores information related to current accounts
order_bank	Stores information related to users' requests for the issue of new chequebooks or account statements
saving_account	Stores information regarding savings accounts
transfer	Stores all the information regarding cash transfers conducted by users

Table 8-1   *Banking Services Application Tables*

Customer Table

This table stores all the personal information regarding customers that the application needs, as follows:

▶   Telephone identification number

▶   Customer identification number

▶   Name of the customer

▶   Address of the customer

Figure 8-5 shows the schema adopted for this table.

Account_statement Table

This table stores all the information used to generate the account statement for the user such as debit and credit balance of the user. Specifically, the account_statement table contains the following:

▶   Customer identification number

▶   Savings account number

▶   Debit balance

▶   Credit balance

▶   Transaction date

▶   Closing balance

Figure 8-6 shows the schema adopted for this table.

Cheque_status Table

This table stores information regarding the status of cheques, as listed here:

▶   Customer identification number

▶   Savings account number

▶   Cheque number

▶   Status

Figure 8-7 shows the data types used by the various fields of this table.

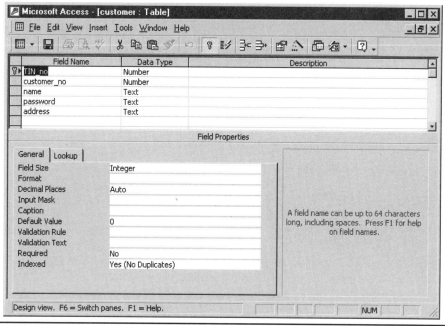

Figure 8-5   *The schema for the customer table*

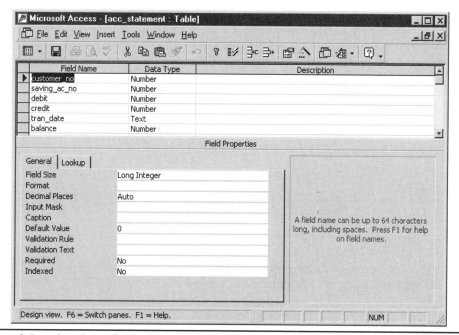

Figure 8-6   *The schema for the account_statement table*

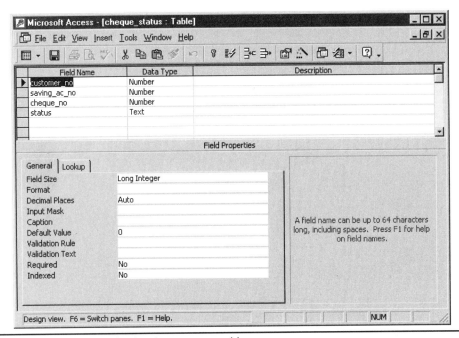

Figure 8-7   *The schema for the cheque_status table*

Current_account Table

This table stores the information related to the current accounts, such as the balance of account. In particular, the current_account table contains the following:

▶ Customer identification number

▶ Current account number

▶ Balance

▶ Modified date

Figure 8-8 shows the schema adopted for this table.

Order_bank Table

This table stores all the information needed for the application to respond to user requests for new chequebooks or account statements, as listed here:

▶ Customer identification number

▶ Chequebook number

► Bank statement

► Order date

Figure 8-9 shows the data type schema of the order_bank table.

Saving_Account Table

The saving_account table stores data regarding savings accounts. The following fields are used to store the data:

► Customer identification number

► Savings account number

► Balance

► Modified date

Figure 8-10 shows the data type schema for the various fields of the saving_account table.

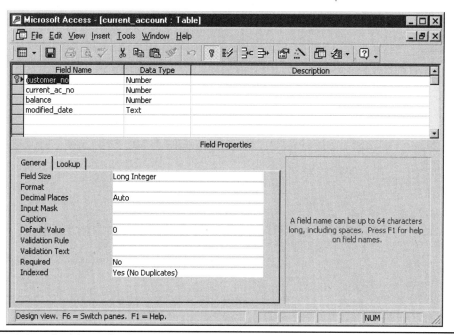

Figure 8-8   *The schema for the current_account table*

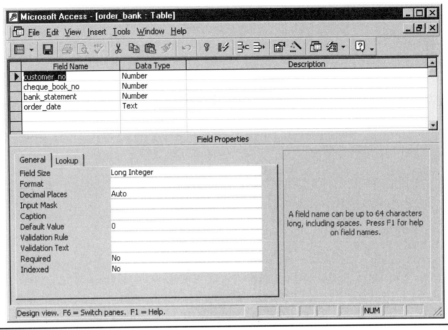

Figure 8-9   *The schema for the order_bank table*

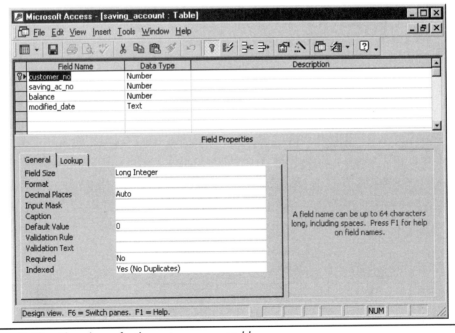

Figure 8-10   *The schema for the saving_account table*

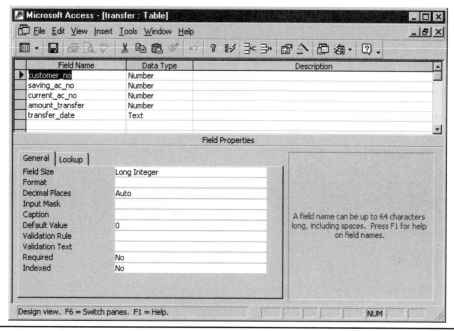

Figure 8-11   *The schema for the transfer table*

Transfer Table

The transfer table stores information regarding money transfer transactions conducted by users in the following fields:

▶ Customer identification number

▶ Savings account number

▶ Current account number

▶ Amount transfer

▶ Transfer date

Figure 8-11 shows the data type schema of the various fields of the transfer table.

Preparing the Login Section

In this section, we discuss the process of developing the home page section of our application. This process may be further divided into two parts:

▶ Login and authentication process

▶ Prompting of the home page

First, we look at the login and authentication process, which works as the gateway for the application. Every time a user accesses the application, the system will ask for his or her customer identification number and telephone identification number to authenticate the user.

Collecting the Customer Identification Number

Here, the system first asks for the customer identification number and authenticates it against what is stored in the database. This process is controlled by two files, telebank.cfm and custlogin.cfm. Listing 8-1 shows the source code for the telebank.cfm file.

Listing 8-1:   *Source Code for telebank.cfm*

```
<cfcontent type = "text/xml">
</cfcontent>
<vxml version="1.0">
    <var name="custno"/>
<form id="user">
      <field name="custno" type="digits">
  <prompt>Please enter your customer ID</prompt>
            <filled>
                  <assign name="document.custno" expr="custno"/>
                  <goto next="#call_login"/>
            </filled>
      </field>
</form>
<form id="call_login">
 <block>
    <var name="custnumber"  expr="document.custno"/>
    <submit next="custlogin.cfm" method="get" namelist="custnumber"/>
 </block>
</form>
 </vxml>
```

Now, let's examine the source code of telebank.cfm. In the very first line of the document, we declare the content type using the ColdFusion tag <CFCONTENT>.

```
<cfcontent type = "text/xml"></cfcontent>
```

We declare the content type as text/xml. The content type may also be defined as text/vxml or any other custom content type supported by the voice server. In the next phase, we write the

VoiceXML code and build a form to collect the customer identification number from the user as digits. Later in the document, we assign the input value to a variable and submit the value to the server for the authentication process by using the following lines of code:

```
<form id="call_login">
 <block>
    <var name="custnumber"  expr="document.custno"/>
    <submit next="custlogin.cfm" method="get" namelist="custnumber"/>
 </block>
</form>
```

The output of the complete process is shown in Figure 8-12.

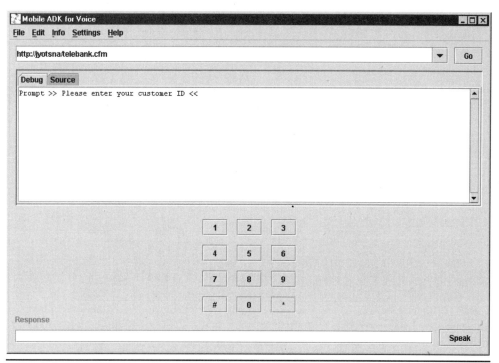

Figure 8-12   *Output of telebank.cfm*

Authenticating the Customer Identification Number

In the second phase, we construct the code for the authentication process of the customer identification number value that we collected from the user in the previous document. For this purpose, we use the file named custlogin.cfm. Listing 8-2 presents the code of this file.

Listing 8-2:   *Source Code for custlogin.cfm*

```
<CFAPPLICATION NAME="TELEBANKING" SESSIONMANAGEMENT="yES">
</CFAPPLICATION>
<CFQUERY NAME="cust" DATASOURCE="teleDSN" DBTYPE="ODBC">
     SELECT customer_no FROM CUSTOMER WHERE customer_no = #url.custnumber#
</CFQUERY>
<CFSET SESSION.custnum = url.custnumber></CFSET>
<CFSET CUSTNO = cust.recordCount></CFSET>
<cfcontent type = "text/xml"></cfcontent>
<vxml version="2.0">
<form>
<block>
         <cfif CUSTNO is 0>
              <CFOUTPUT>This customer number does not exist. Please try
again</CFOUTPUT>
              <goto next="telebank.cfm"/>
         <cfelse>
              <CFOUTPUT><goto next="login.cfm"/></CFOUTPUT>
         </cfif>
     </block>
</form>
</vxml>
```

In the code for custlogin.cfm, we first write a query named cust to select the customer identification number from the customer table, based on the value collected in the previous file, using the <CFQUERY> tag. After executing the query, we store the customer identification number in a session variable named SESSION.custnum. At the time of query execution, if any record successfully matches the criteria of selection, the ColdFusion server assigns an integer value to the variable named cust.recordcount, which is greater than zero. If no records are found, the system assigns zero to the cust.recordcount variable. After the query execution, we store cust.recordcount in a variable named CUSTNO.

In the latter part of the document, we include the VoiceXML code for informing the user about the result of the authentication process we just performed. In this section of the document, we use the <CFIF> tag to check the value of variable CUSTNO. A CUSTNO value of zero indicates that no record matching the value of the customer identification number entered by the user exists in the database, and we redirect the user to the previous document.

A CUSTNO value greater than zero indicates the existence of some matching record in our database. In such cases, we call the next file, named login.cfm, to continue the authentication process. This file uses a combination of VoiceXML <goto> and ColdFusion <CFOUTPUT> elements. The source code that controls this entire process is shown here:

```
<cfif CUSTNO is 0>
        <CFOUTPUT>This customer number does not exist. Please try
again</CFOUTPUT>
        <goto next="telebank.cfm"/>
<cfelse>
        <CFOUTPUT><goto next="login.cfm"/></CFOUTPUT>
</cfif>
```

Figures 8-13 and 8-14 demonstrate the output of this process. Figure 8-13 shows the nonexistence of the record, if the customer identification number provided by the user is not found in the database. If the record is found, the application will ask for the password, as shown in Figure 8-14.

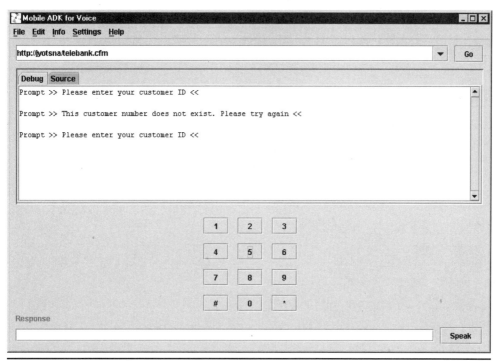

Figure 8-13   *Output of custlogin.cfm in case of a nonexisting record*

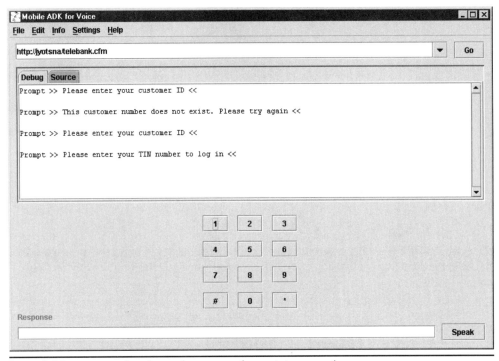

Figure 8-14 *Output of custlogin.cfm in case of an existing record*

Collecting the Telephone Identification Number

In this section, the system asks for the telephone identification number of the user and authenticates the input provided. For controlling this process, we use two files, login.cfm and telelogin.cfm. Listing 8-3 shows the code of login.cfm.

Listing 8-3: *Source Code for login.cfm*

```
<cfcontent type = "text/xml">
</cfcontent>
<vxml version="2.0">
    <var name="tinno"/>
<form id="user">
<field name="tinno" type="digits">
        <prompt>Please enter your TIN number to log in</prompt>
            <filled>
```

```
                    <assign name="document.tinno" expr="tinno"/>
             <goto next="#call_login"/>
        </filled>
        </field>
</form>
<form id="call_login">
 <block>
    <var name="tinnumber"  expr="document.tinno"/>
    <submit next="telelogin.cfm" method="get" namelist="tinnumber"/>
 </block>
</form>
 </vxml>
```

The code for login.cfm is quite similar to that for telebank.cfm, except we collect the telephone identification number instead of the customer identification number. On obtaining this input from the user, we call the next file in the queue, telelogin.cfm, for authenticating the data collected. The output of login.cfm is shown in Figure 8-15.

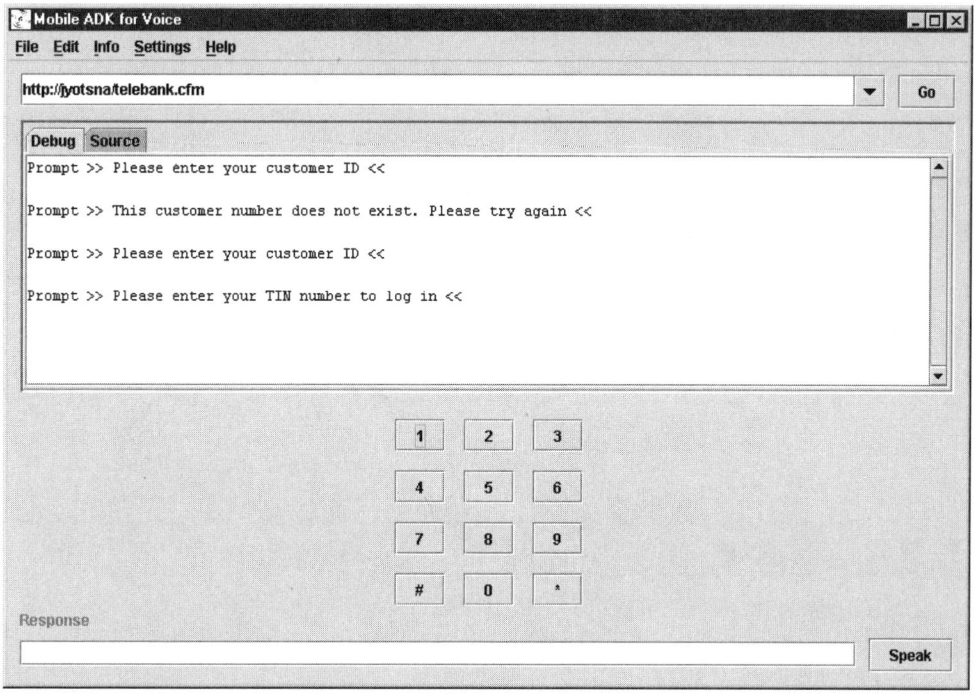

Figure 8-15   *Output of login.cfm*

Authenticating the Telephone Identification Number

As evident in the code for authenticating the telephone identification number (Listing 8-3), we are following the same process as the one for authenticating the customer identification number.

If no file in the datebase matches the user input, we inform the user of the failure of authentication through a process similar to the one described in the section "Authenticating the Customer Identification Number."

If the database contains a record that matches the user input, we move on to the main menu of the application. The source code controlling the whole process is given in Listing 8-4.

Listing 8-4: *Source Code for telelogin.cfm*

```
<CFQUERY NAME="tin" DATASOURCE="teleDSN" DBTYPE="ODBC">
      SELECT TIN_no FROM CUSTOMER WHERE TIN_no = #url.tinnumber#
</CFQUERY>
<CFSET TINNO = tin.recordCount></CFSET>
<cfcontent type = "text/xml"></cfcontent>
<vxml version="2.0">
<form>
      <block>
            <cfif TINNO is 0>
                  <CFOUTPUT>This TIN number does not exist. Please try
again</CFOUTPUT>
                  <goto next="login.cfm"/>
            <cfelse>
                  <CFOUTPUT><goto next="menu.cfm"/></CFOUTPUT>
            </cfif>
      </block>
</form>
</vxml>
```

Figure 8-16 depicts the output of the process if the authentication fails.

Building the Main Menu of the Application

Here, we detail the main menu section of the banking services application. Once the credentials of the user are successfully authenticated, the main menu section is loaded and becomes the home page for the rest of the application life cycle. This menu prompts all the

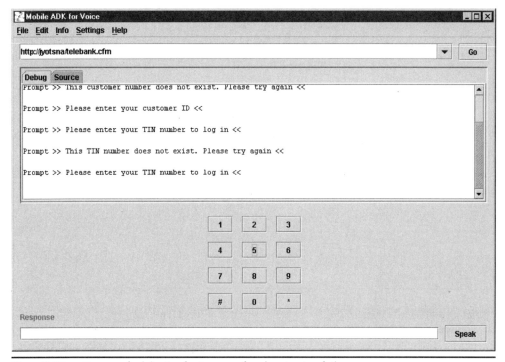

Figure 8-16   *Output of telelogin.cfm in case of authentication failure*

available options to the user for proceeding further. The complete source code of menu.cfm is given in Listing 8-5.

Listing 8-5:   *Source Code for menu.cfm*

```
<cfcontent type = "text/xml"></cfcontent>
<vxml version="1.0">
<link next="http://jyotsna/telebanking/menu.cfm">
        <grammar type="application/x-gsl">
        Home
        </grammar>
</link>
    <menu>
        <prompt>Please choose any one of the following:<enumerate/></prompt>
        <choice dtmf="1" next="enquiry.cfm">Inquiry</choice>
        <choice dtmf="2" next="transfer_money.cfm">Transfer money</choice>
        <choice dtmf="3" next="order.cfm">Order chequebook or bank
statement</choice>
        <choice dtmf="4" next="#exit">Exit</choice>
```

```
        <help>
                Press 1 for inquiry
                Press 2 to transfer money
                Press 3 to order chequebook or bank statement
                Press 4 to exit from the application
        </help>
        <noinput>I didn't detect anything, please enter<enumerate/></noinput>
    <nomatch> I didn't get that, <enumerate/></nomatch>
        <catch event="nomatch noinput" count="4">
            <prompt>You have exceeded the number of allowed retries. System
will now stop
the application.</prompt>
                <throw event="telephone.disconnect.hangup"/>
        </catch>
    </menu>
    <form id="exit">
        <catch event="exit">
            <throw event="telephone.disconnect.hangup"/>
        </catch>
    </form>
 </vxml>
```

Let's examine the code in detail. At the beginning of the document, we first set the content type using the <CFCONTENT> tag. After setting the content type for the document, we use the following lines of code to build a menu-based structure that represents all the available options to the user:

```
<menu>
        <prompt>Please choose any one of the following:<enumerate/></prompt>
<choice dtmf="1" next="enquiry.cfm">Inquiry</choice>
        <choice dtmf="2" next="transfer_money.cfm">Transfer money</choice>
        <choice dtmf="3" next="order.cfm">Order chequebook or bank
statement</choice>
        <choice dtmf="4" next="#exit">Exit</choice>
    <help>
        Press 1 for inquiry
        Press 2 to transfer money
        Press 3 to order chequebook or bank statement
        Press 4 to exit from the application
    </help>
        <noinput>I didn't detect anything, please enter<enumerate/></noinput>
    <nomatch> I didn't get that, <enumerate/></nomatch>
        <catch event="nomatch noinput" count="4">
            <prompt>You have exceeded the number of allowed retries. System
will now stop
the application.</prompt>
                <throw event="telephone.disconnect.hangup"/>
        </catch>
    </menu>
```

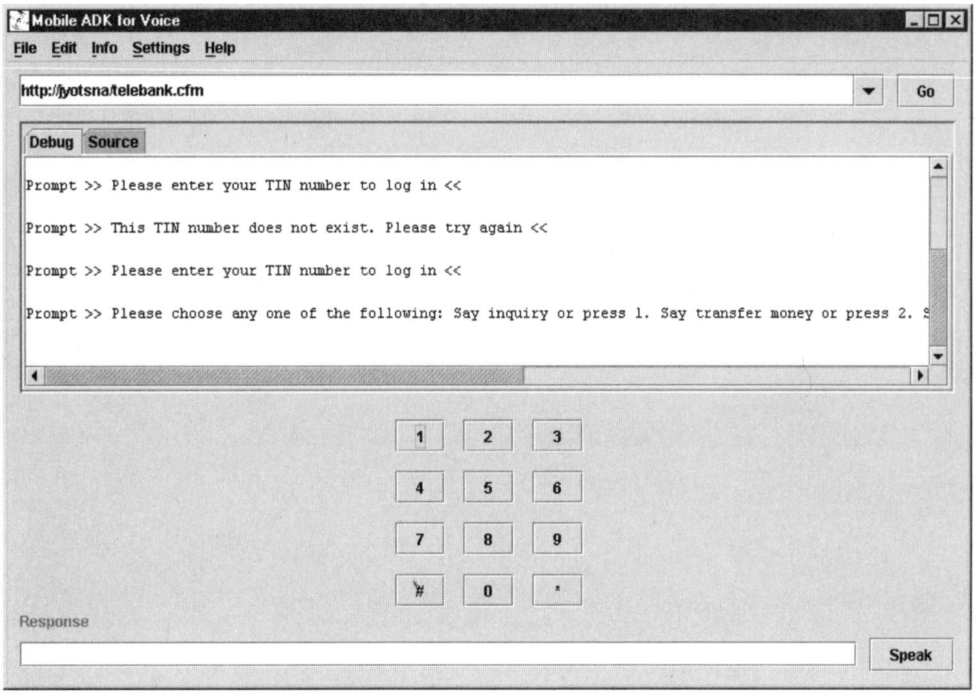

Figure 8-17   *Output of menu.cfm*

The user may choose any of the available options to proceed further with the application as required. The output of the menu.cfm is represented in Figure 8-17.

Designing the Inquiry Module Main Page

If the user selects the inquiry option in the home page, the system starts the execution of the inquiry module of the application and loads enquiry.cfm to present to the user all the options available in the inquiry module. Listing 8-6 contains the source code for enquiry.cfm.

Listing 8-6:   *Source Code for enquiry.cfm*

```
<cfcontent type = "text/xml"></cfcontent>
<vxml version="2.0">
<link next="http://jyotsna/telebanking/login.cfm">
        <grammar type="application/x-gsl">
        Telebanking
        </grammar>
    </link>
```

```
<menu>
<prompt>Please choose any one of the following:<enumerate/></prompt>
<choice dtmf="1" next="balance_enquiry.cfm">account balance inquiry</choice>
 <choice dtmf="2" next="statement.cfm">account statement inquiry</choice>
<choice dtmf="3" next="cheque_state.cfm">cheque statement inquiry</choice>
<choice dtmf="4" next="menu.cfm">return to menu</choice>
 <choice dtmf="5" next="#exit">exit</choice>
<help>
        Press 1 for account balance inquiry
        Press 2 for account statement inquiry
        Press 3 for cheque statement inquiry
        Press 4 to return to the main menu
        Press 5 to exit from the application
</help>
            <noinput>I didn't detect anything, please choose<enumerate/></noinput>
<nomatch> I didn't get that, <enumerate/></nomatch>
        <catch event="nomatch noinput" count="4">
        <prompt>You have exceeded the number of allowed retries. System will
now stop the
application.</prompt>
        <throw event="telephone.disconnect.hangup"/>
    </catch>
</menu>
    <form id="exit">
    <catch event="exit">
        <throw event="telephone.disconnect.hangup"/>
    </catch>
</form>
</vxml>
```

In Listing 8-6, we first build a menu to provide all the available options to the user. Further processing is done based on the option selected by the user. In addition to the ubiquitous exit option, the following options are available:

- ▶ Account balance inquiry
- ▶ Account statement inquiry
- ▶ Cheque statement inquiry
- ▶ Return to main menu

Figure 8-18 shows the output of enquiry.cfm.

Building the Account Balance Inquiry Section

In this section, we discuss how we built the account balance inquiry module. This section provides the user the capability of checking the account balance using any telephony device. This section is subdivided into two parts, one for handling savings accounts and one for

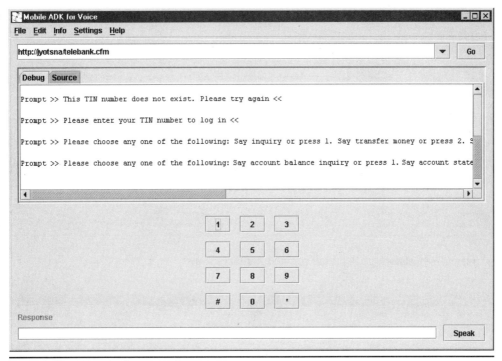

Figure 8-18   *Output of enquiry.cfm*

handling current accounts. The code of balance_enquiry.cfm, shown in Listing 8-7, provides the balance inquiry functionality for both savings accounts and current accounts.

Listing 8-7:   *Source Code for balance_enquiry.cfm*

```
<cfcontent type = "text/xml"></cfcontent>
<vxml version="2.0">
     <link next="http://jyotsna/telebanking/login.cfm">
          <grammar type="application/x-gsl">
          Telebanking
          </grammar>
     </link>
<menu>
     <prompt>Please choose any one of the following:<enumerate/></prompt>
     <choice dtmf="1" next="saving_enquiry.cfm">savings account balance
inquiry</choice>
          <choice dtmf="2" next="current_enquiry.cfm">current account balance
inquiry</choice>
          <choice dtmf="3" next="#exit">Exit</choice>
     <help>
          Press 1 for savings account balance inquiry
          Press 2 for current account balance inquiry
```

```
          Press 3 to exit from the application
          </help>
          <noinput>I didn't detect anything, please choose<enumerate/></noinput>
          <nomatch> I didn't get that, <enumerate/></nomatch>
          <catch event="nomatch noinput" count="4">
                <prompt>You have exceeded the number of allowed retries. System
will now stop
the application.</prompt>
                      <throw event="telephone.disconnect.hangup"/>
      </catch>
</menu>
      <form id="exit">
      <catch event="exit">
            <throw event="telephone.disconnect.hangup"/>
      </catch>
      </form>
 </vxml>
```

Figure 8-19 shows the output of balance_enquiry.cfm.

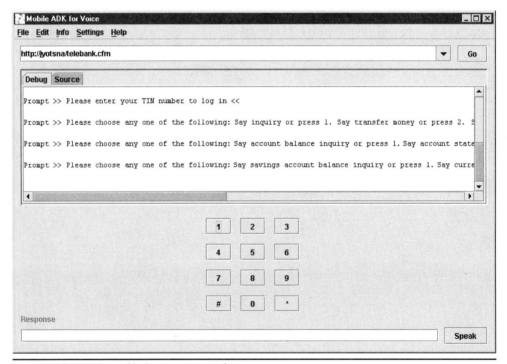

Figure 8-19   *Output of balance_enquiry.cfm*

Savings Account Inquiry

In this section, we look at the code for checking the balance of a savings account. Listing 8-8 shows the source code of saving_enquiry.cfm, which is used for this purpose.

Listing 8-8: *Source Code for saving_enquiry.cfm*

```
<CFAPPLICATION NAME="TELEBANKING" SESSIONMANAGEMENT="yES">
</CFAPPLICATION>
<CFQUERY NAME="saving" DATASOURCE="teleDSN" DBTYPE="ODBC">
     SELECT saving_ac_no,balance FROM saving_account WHERE customer_no =
#SESSION.custnum#
</CFQUERY>
<cfcontent type = "text/xml"></cfcontent>
<vxml version="2.0">
<form>
<block>
     <CFOUTPUT QUERY="saving">
          Your savings account number is #saving_ac_no#
          Your savings account balance is #balance#
     </CFOUTPUT>
     <goto next="enquiry.cfm"/>
</block>
</form>
</vxml>
```

Here, we write a SQL query to fetch the balance information from the database using the <CFQUERY> tag. In this query, we use the customer number to retrieve the balance information for the particular customer using the statement in the following code snippet. After querying the database, we prompt the result to the user later in the document through the <CFOUTPUT> tag.

```
<CFQUERY NAME="saving" DATASOURCE="teleDSN" DBTYPE="ODBC">
     SELECT saving_ac_no,balance FROM saving_account WHERE customer_no =
#SESSION.custnum#
</CFQUERY>
```

Figure 8-20 shows the output of Listing 8-8.

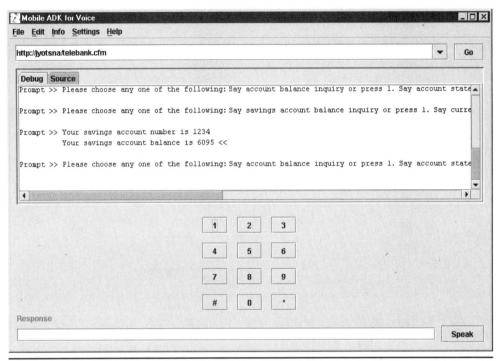

Figure 8-20   Output of saving_enquiry.cfm

Current Account Inquiry

Listing 8-9 shows the source code listed for the file named current_enquiry.cfm, which provides the functionality of checking the balance in the current account.

Listing 8-9:   Source Code for current_enquiry.cfm

```
<CFAPPLICATION NAME="TELEBANKING" SESSIONMANAGEMENT="yES">
</CFAPPLICATION>
<CFQUERY NAME="saving" DATASOURCE="teleDSN" DBTYPE="ODBC">
      SELECT current_ac_no,balance FROM current_account WHERE customer_no =
#SESSION.custnum#
</CFQUERY>
<cfcontent type = "text/xml"></cfcontent>
```

```
<vxml version="1.0">
<form>
     <block>
          <CFOUTPUT QUERY="saving">
               Your current account number is #current_ac_no#
               Your current account balance is #balance#
          </CFOUTPUT>
          <goto next="enquiry.cfm"/>
     </block>
</form>
</vxml>
```

Figure 8-21 shows the output for this source code.

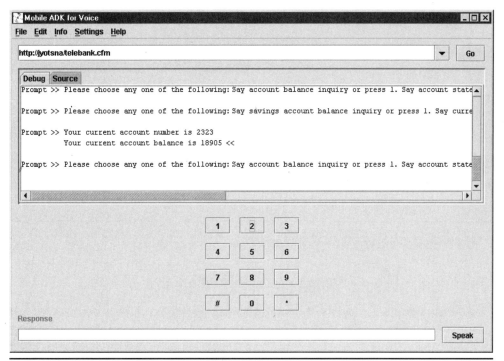

Figure 8-21   *Output of current_enquiry.cfm*

Building the Account Statement Inquiry Module

If the user selects the account statement inquiry option for obtaining his or her account statement over the telephone, the control is transferred to statement.cfm for generating the required information. In our application, account statements are generated only for savings accounts. The source code of statement.cfm appears in Listing 8-10.

Listing 8-10: *Source Code for statement.cfm*

```
<CFAPPLICATION NAME="TELEBANKING" SESSIONMANAGEMENT="yES">
</CFAPPLICATION>
<CFQUERY NAME="saving" DATASOURCE="teleDSN" DBTYPE="ODBC">
    SELECT saving_ac_no,debit,credit,balance,tran_date FROM acc_statement WHERE
customer_no = #SESSION.custnum#
</CFQUERY>
<CFSET ACCNO = saving.saving_ac_no></CFSET>
<cfcontent type = "text/xml"></cfcontent>
<vxml version="2.0">
<form>
    <block>
            <CFOUTPUT>Your savings account number is #ACCNO#</CFOUTPUT>
        <CFLOOP QUERY="saving">
            <CFOUTPUT>
                    Credit on #tran_date# is #credit#
                    Debit on #tran_date# is #debit#
                    Closing balance on #tran_date# is #balance#
            </CFOUTPUT>
        </CFLOOP>
        <goto next="enquiry.cfm"/>
    </block>
</form>
</vxml>
```

Figure 8-22 shows the output of statement.cfm.

Building the Cheque Statement Inquiry Module

This section provides the facility of checking the status of various cheques issued by the user. Once the user selects this option from the menu, the system asks the user to specify the cheque (by cheque number) for which he or she wants the status. On receiving this information, the file cheque_state.cfm is called to query the database for retrieving the required information before

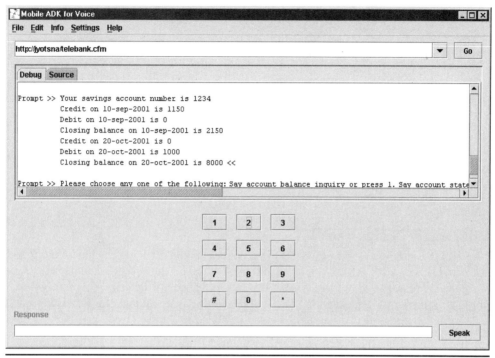

Figure 8-22   *Output of statement.cfm*

prompting the status to the user. The process is controlled by the cheque_state.cfm, the source code of which is shown in Listing 8-11.

Listing 8-11:   *Source Code for cheque_state.cfm*

```
<cfcontent type = "text/xml">
</cfcontent>
<vxml version="2.0">
    <var name="chequeno"/>
<form id="user">
      <field name="chequeno" type="digits">
  <prompt>Please specify the cheque number to find out its status</prompt>
            <filled>
                  <assign name="document.chequeno" expr="chequeno"/>
```

```
                  <goto next="#call_cheque"/>
              </filled>
          </field>
</form>
<form id="call_cheque">
 <block>
     <var name="chequenumber"  expr="document.chequeno"/>
     <submit next="cheque.cfm" method="get" namelist="chequenumber"/>
 </block>
</form>
 </vxml>
```

Figure 8-23 shows the output of this code.

Prompting the Cheque Status

The way this module works is quite simple. Once the user provides a cheque number, the system queries the database, fetches the status of the cheque specified, and presents the result to the user. We have already seen the code of cheque_state.cfm, which provides for this functionality. The cheque_state.cfm file in turn uses cheque.cfm for bringing about this functionality. Listing 8-12 shows the code for cheque.cfm.

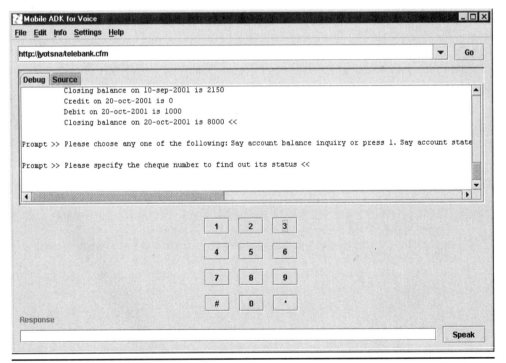

Figure 8-23   Output of cheque_state.cfm

Listing 8-12:   *Source Code for cheque.cfm*

```
<CFAPPLICATION NAME="TELEBANKING" SESSIONMANAGEMENT="yES">
</CFAPPLICATION>
<CFQUERY NAME="cheque" DATASOURCE="teleDSN" DBTYPE="ODBC">
     SELECT saving_ac_no,status FROM cheque_status WHERE customer_no =
#SESSION.custnum# AND cheque_no = #url.chequenumber#</CFQUERY>
<CFSET CHEQUENO = cheque.recordCount></CFSET>
<cfcontent type = "text/xml"></cfcontent>
<vxml version="2.0">
<form>
     <block>
          <cfif CHEQUENO is 0>
          <CFOUTPUT>This cheque number does not exist. Please try
again</CFOUTPUT>
          <cfelse>
          <CFOUTPUT QUERY="cheque">
               Your savings account number is #saving_ac_no#
     Status of this cheque is #status#
          </CFOUTPUT>
     </cfif>
     <goto next="enquiry.cfm"/>
     </block>
</form>
</vxml>
```

In the code for cheque.cfm, we include the following SQL query for obtaining the status of the specified cheque based on the customer identification number (customer_no) and the savings account number. This information is retrieved from the cheque_status table.

```
<CFQUERY NAME="cheque" DATASOURCE="teleDSN" DBTYPE="ODBC">
     SELECT saving_ac_no,status FROM cheque_status WHERE customer_no =
#SESSION.custnum# AND cheque_no = #url.chequenumber#</CFQUERY>
```

In the next step, we inform the user of the status of the cheque specified by prompting the result. The <CFIF> tag is used to denote the different possible conditions, as shown here:

```
          <cfif CHEQUENO is 0>
               <CFOUTPUT>This cheque number does not exist. Please try
again</CFOUTPUT>
          <cfelse>
               <CFOUTPUT QUERY="cheque">
                    Your savings account number is #saving_ac_no#
Status of this cheque is #status#
               </CFOUTPUT>
          </cfif>
```

Figure 8-24 shows the output of cheque.cfm.

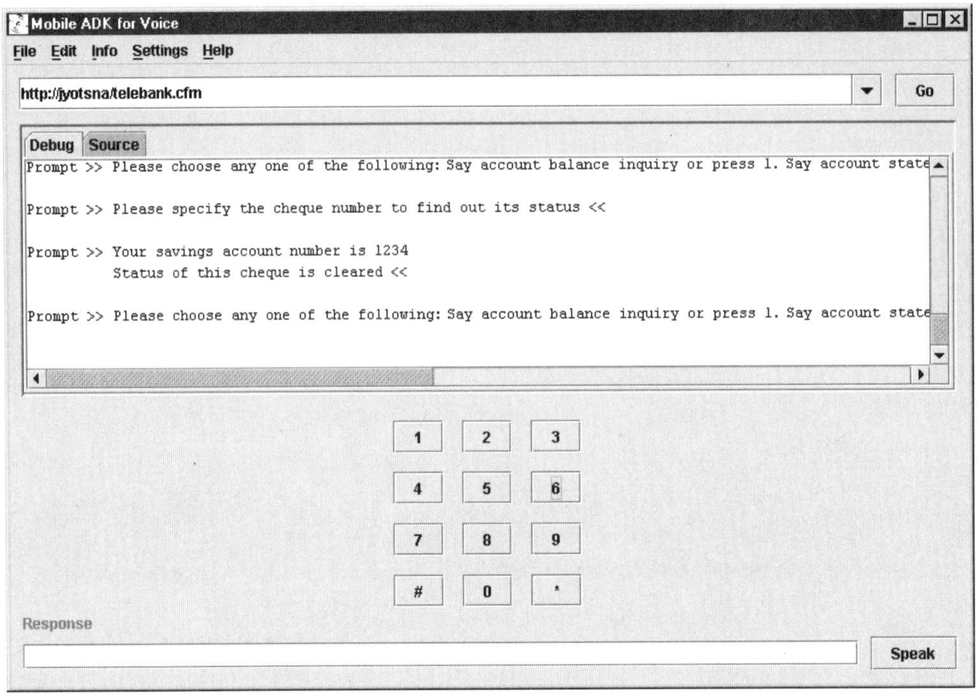

Figure 8-24 Output of cheque.cfm

Designing the Transfer Money Module

In this section, we explain how we created the transfer money module of our application. This module provides the capability of transferring cash from a savings account to the current account if the required details are provided. This process is controlled by two files, transfer_money.cfm and transfer.cfm. Of these, transfer_money.cfm collects the required information from the user and submits it to the server for further processing. The source code of transfer_money.cfm is provided in Listing 8-13.

Listing 8-13: *Source Code for transfer_money.cfm*

```
<cfcontent type = "text/xml">
</cfcontent>
<vxml version="2.0">
<var name="amount"/>
<form id="user">
<field name="amount" type="digits">
        <prompt>Please enter the amount to be transferred from savings account to
```

```
current account</prompt>
      <filled>
            <assign name="document.amount" expr="amount"/>
                <goto next="#call_transfer"/>
            </filled>
      </field>
</form>
<form id="call_transfer">
<block>
    <var name="amounttransfer"  expr="document.amount"/>
    <submit next="transfer.cfm" method="get" namelist="amounttransfer"/>
 </block>
</form>
</vxml>
```

As should be evident, we use the code in Listing 8-13 for collecting details regarding the user who wishes to transfer money from a savings account to the current account and the amount to be transferred. The user input is then submitted to the server for further processing using the <submit> element.

Figure 8-25 shows the output of transfer_money.cfm.

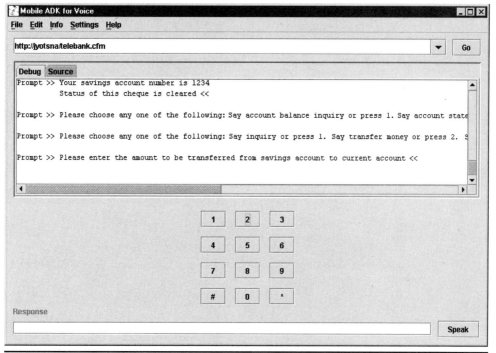

Figure 8-25   *Output of transfer_money.cfm*

Writing Code for Transferring Money

Once the data is collected from the user and submitted to the server as described in the previous section, transfer.cfm is used for transferring the required amount from the savings account to the current account. The source code of transfer.cfm appears in Listing 8-14.

Listing 8-14: *Source Code for transfer.cfm*

```
<CFAPPLICATION NAME="TELEBANKING" SESSIONMANAGEMENT="YES">
</CFAPPLICATION>
<CFQUERY NAME="saving" DATASOURCE="teleDSN" DBTYPE="ODBC">
     SELECT saving_ac_no,balance FROM saving_account WHERE customer_no =
#SESSION.custnum#
</CFQUERY>
<CFQUERY NAME="current" DATASOURCE="teleDSN" DBTYPE="ODBC">
     SELECT current_ac_no,balance FROM current_account WHERE customer_no =
#SESSION.custnum#
</CFQUERY>
<CFSET transferamount = url.amounttransfer></CFSET>
<CFSET currentbalance = (current.balance) + (transferamount)></CFSET>
<CFSET validamount = (saving.balance) - (transferamount)></CFSET>
<CFSET today = Now()></CFSET>
<cfcontent type = "text/xml"></cfcontent>
<vxml version="2.0">
<form>
     <block>
          <cfif validamount LT 1000>
               <CFOUTPUT>You have only #saving.balance# balance in your savings
account. Please try again</CFOUTPUT>
          <cfelse>
               <CFQUERY NAME="update_current" DATASOURCE="teleDSN"
 DBTYPE="ODBC">
                    UPDATE current_account SET balance =
#currentbalance#, modified_date = #today#  WHERE customer_no =
#SESSION.custnum# </CFQUERY>
               <CFQUERY NAME="update_saving" DATASOURCE="teleDSN"
 DBTYPE="ODBC">
                    UPDATE saving_account SET balance =
(#saving.balance#) - (#transferamount#), modified_date =
#today# WHERE customer_no = #SESSION.custnum#</CFQUERY>
               <CFQUERY NAME="insert_transfer"
DATASOURCE="teleDSN" DBTYPE="ODBC">
                    INSERT INTO transfer
(customer_no,saving_ac_no,current_ac_no,amount_transfer,
transfer_date) VALUES(#SESSION.custnum#,#saving.saving_ac_no#,
#current.current_ac_no#,#transferamount#,#today#)
               </CFQUERY>
```

```
            <CFOUTPUT>Amount has been transferred from savings to
current account.</CFOUTPUT>
            </cfif>
            <goto next="menu.cfm"/>
      </block>
</form>
</vxml>
```

Let's discuss this code step by step. This code includes many queries, the first of which, named saving, is shown here:

```
<CFQUERY NAME="saving" DATASOURCE="teleDSN" DBTYPE="ODBC">
      SELECT saving_ac_no,balance FROM saving_account WHERE customer_no =
#SESSION.custnum#
</CFQUERY>
```

In this query, we retrieve the current balance and the savings account number from the savings account table of the user based on the customer identification number. After this, we obtain the current account number and the balance in the current account of the user using the query named current, shown here:

```
<CFQUERY NAME="current" DATASOURCE="teleDSN" DBTYPE="ODBC">
      SELECT current_ac_no,balance FROM current_account WHERE
customer_no = #SESSION.custnum#
</CFQUERY>
```

In the next phase, we include the code for transferring the money based on certain conditions. We start with a <CFIF> tag to check the first condition. Here, we ensure that if the specified amount is transferred to the current account, the balance in the savings account doesn't fall below the required minimum to be retained. If this happens, no transfer takes place, and the user is informed accordingly. The following code handles this situation:

```
            <cfif validamount LT 1000>
                  <CFOUTPUT>You have only #saving.balance# balance in
your savings account. Please try again</CFOUTPUT>
```

If the amount specified is available for transfer, we start the process of transferring money into the current account of the user via a series of SQL queries. In the first query for this series, update_current, we update the balance and modify the date in the current_account table as follows:

```
            <CFQUERY NAME="update_current" DATASOURCE="teleDSN"
DBTYPE="ODBC">
                  UPDATE current_account SET balance = #currentbalance#,
modified_date = #today#  WHERE customer_no = #SESSION.custnum#
            </CFQUERY>
```

In the next phase, we update the savings account balance by deducting the transferred amount from it and also enter the date of modification, as shown in the following query:

```
<CFQUERY NAME="update_saving" DATASOURCE="teleDSN"
DBTYPE="ODBC">
               UPDATE saving_account SET balance = (#saving.balance#) -
(#transferamount#), modified_date = #today# WHERE customer_no = #SESSION.custnum#
</CFQUERY>
```

In the last query, insert_transfer, we insert all the details in the transfer table and complete the transferring process, as shown in the following code.

```
<CFQUERY NAME="insert_transfer" DATASOURCE
="teleDSN" DBTYPE="ODBC">
               INSERT INTO transfer customer_no,saving_ac_no,
current_ac_no,amount_transfer,transfer_date)
VALUES(#SESSION.custnum#,#saving.saving_ac_no#,
#current.current_ac_no#,#transferamount#,#today#)
               </CFQUERY>
```

Figure 8-26 shows the output of this code.

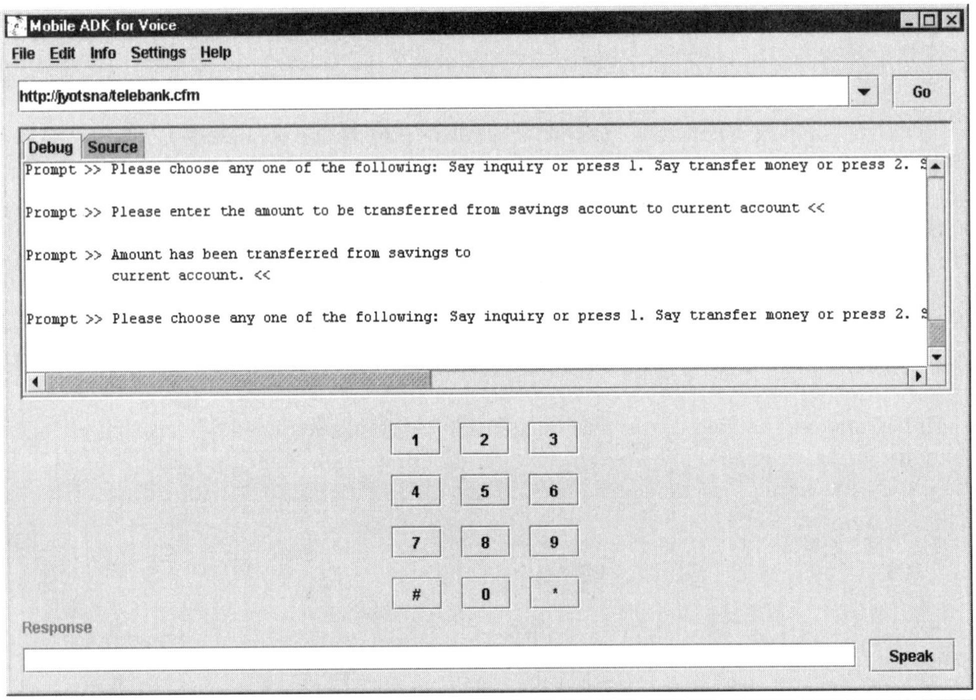

Figure 8-26   Output of transfer.cfm

Designing the Order Chequebook and Bank Statement Module

This section provides the capability of ordering chequebooks and obtaining bank statements. Just as with all the modules discussed so far, this module is also subdivided into two parts, order.cfm and order_chequebook.cfm, each handling a separate task.

Listing 8-15 provides the source code of order.cfm, which employs a menu-based approach for providing the options available to the user.

Listing 8-15:   *Source Code for order.cfm*

```
<cfcontent type = "text/xml"></cfcontent>
<vxml version="2.0">
     <link next="http://jyotsna/telebanking/login.cfm">
          <grammar type="application/x-gsl">
                    Telebanking
          </grammar>
     </link>
     <menu>
     <prompt>Please choose any one of the following<enumerate/></prompt>
          <choice dtmf="1" next="order_chequebook.cfm">order new
chequebook</choice>
          <choice dtmf="2" next="order_bankstatement.cfm">order a bank
statement</choice>
          <choice dtmf="3" next="#exit">exit</choice>
     <help>
          Press 1 to order new chequebook
          Press 2 to order a bank statement and
          Press 3 to exit from the application
     </help>
          <noinput>I didn't detect anything please choose<enumerate/></noinput>
     <nomatch> I didn't get that, <enumerate/></nomatch>
          <catch event="nomatch noinput" count="4">
               <prompt>You have exceeded the number of allowed retries. System
will now stop
the application.</prompt>
               <throw event="telephone.disconnect.hangup"/>
          </catch>
     </menu>
     <form id="exit">
          <catch event="exit">
               <throw event="telephone.disconnect.hangup"/>
          </catch>
     </form>
 </vxml>
```

Figure 8-27 shows the output of this source code.

Building the Order Chequebook Module

If the user selects the order chequebook option, order.cfm transfers the control to order_chequebook.cfm. Let's examine in detail the procedure for issuing a new chequebook to the user. The source code responsible for this task is given in Listing 8-16.

Listing 8-16: *Source Code for order_chequebook.cfm*

```
<CFAPPLICATION NAME="TELEBANKING" SESSIONMANAGEMENT="yES">
</CFAPPLICATION>
<CFQUERY NAME="chequebook" DATASOURCE="teleDSN" DBTYPE="ODBC">
     SELECT cheque_book_no FROM order_bank
</CFQUERY>
<CFQUERY NAME="adr" DATASOURCE="teleDSN" DBTYPE="ODBC">
     SELECT address FROM customer WHERE customer_no = #SESSION.custnum#
</CFQUERY>
<CFSET chequebookno = chequebook.cheque_book_no></CFSET>
<CFSET today = Now()></CFSET>
<CFLOOP query = "chequebook">
  <cfif chequebook.cheque_book_no GT chequebookno>
     <CFSET chequebookno = chequebook.cheque_book_no>
  </cfif>
</CFLOOP>
<CFSET chequebookno = chequebookno + 1>
<cfcontent type = "text/xml"></cfcontent>
<vxml version="2.0">
<form>
     <block>
          <CFOUTPUT>A new chequebook with number #chequebookno#
 will be sent to address #adr.address# within fifteen days</CFOUTPUT>
          <CFQUERY NAME="insert_order" DATASOURCE="teleDSN"
DBTYPE="ODBC">INSERT INTO order_bank (customer_no,cheque_book_no,
bank_statement,order_date)
VALUES(#SESSION.custnum#,#chequebookno#,0,#today#)
          </CFQUERY>
          <goto next="enquiry.cfm"/>
     </block>
</form>
</vxml>
```

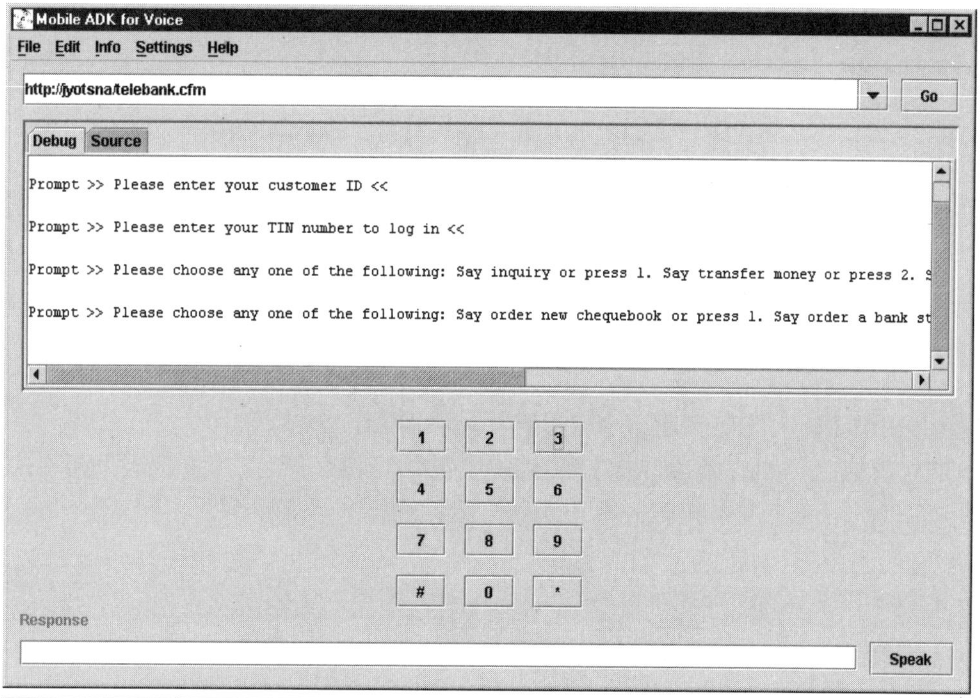

Figure 8-27   *Output of order.cfm*

In this source code, we start with the SQL queries. The first query, named chequebook, selects a chequebook number from the order_bank table before moving to the next query, named adr. Using the second query, we retrieve the address of the user, based on the customer identification number, from the customer table for later use in the document, as shown here:

```
<CFQUERY NAME="chequebook" DATASOURCE="teleDSN" DBTYPE="ODBC">
     SELECT cheque_book_no FROM order_bank
</CFQUERY>
<CFQUERY NAME="adr" DATASOURCE="teleDSN" DBTYPE="ODBC">
     SELECT address FROM customer WHERE customer_no = #SESSION.custnum#
</CFQUERY>
```

In the next step, we build a looping construct using the <CFLOOP> tag to get the latest issued chequebook number so that we assign the correct number to the chequebook we are about to issue. Following this, we insert the VoiceXML code for informing the user of the serial number of the chequebook issued.

While informing the user, we also update our records using the <CFQUERY> tag and complete the transaction as follows:

```
<CFOUTPUT>A new chequebook with number #chequebookno#
will be sent to address #adr.address# within fifteen days</CFOUTPUT>
            <CFQUERY NAME="insert_order" DATASOURCE="teleDSN"
DBTYPE="ODBC">INSERT INTO order_bank (customer_no,
cheque_book_no,bank_statement,order_date)
VALUES(#SESSION.custnum#,#chequebookno#,0,#today#)
            </CFQUERY>
```

Figure 8-28 shows the output of order_chequebook.cfm.

Building the Order Bank Statement Module

The last module of this application is the bank statement order module. The source code in Listing 8-17 is from the file named order_bankstatement.cfm, which controls this process.

Listing 8-17: *Source Code for order_bankstatement.cfm*

```
<CFAPPLICATION NAME="TELEBANKING" SESSIONMANAGEMENT="yES">
</CFAPPLICATION>
<CFQUERY NAME="adr" DATASOURCE="teleDSN" DBTYPE="ODBC">
     SELECT address FROM customer WHERE customer_no = #SESSION.custnum#
</CFQUERY>
<CFSET today = Now()></CFSET>
<cfcontent type = "text/xml"></cfcontent>
<vxml version="2.0">
<form>
     <block>
            <CFOUTPUT>Bank statement will be sent to address
#adr.address# within fifteen days</CFOUTPUT>
            <CFQUERY NAME="insert_order" DATASOURCE="teleDSN"
DBTYPE="ODBC"> INSERT INTO order_bank
(customer_no,cheque_book_no,bank_statement,order_date)
VALUES(#SESSION.custnum#,0,1,#today#)
            </CFQUERY>
            <goto next="enquiry.cfm"/>
     </block>
</form>
</vxml>
```

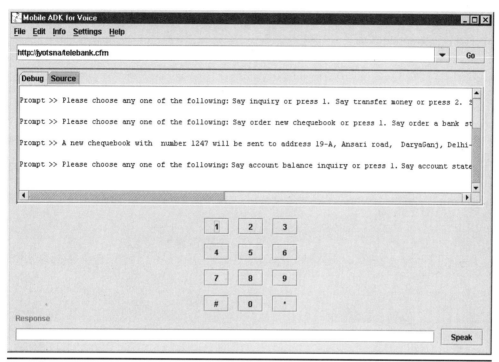

Figure 8-28   *Output of order_chequebook.cfm*

Here, we first select the address of the customer from the customer table based on the customer identification number. After this, we inform the user as well as insert in the order_bank table the date of issue of the statement using the following code below:

```
<CFOUTPUT>Bank statement will be sent to address #adr.address# within fifteen
 days</CFOUTPUT>
           <CFQUERY NAME="insert_order" DATASOURCE="teleDSN" DBTYPE="ODBC">
 INSERT INTO order_bank (customer_no,cheque_book_no,
bank_statement,order_date) VALUES(#SESSION.custnum#,0,1,#today#)
           </CFQUERY>
```

Figure 8-29 shows the output of this code.

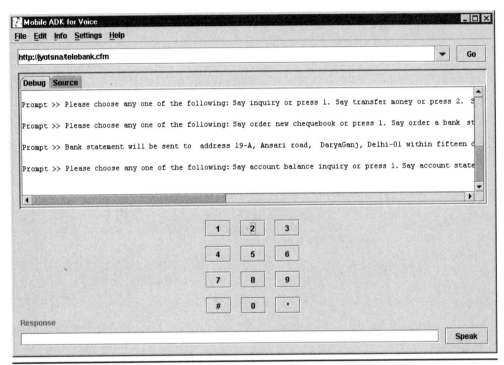

Figure 8-29   *Output of order_bankstatement.cfm*

Summary

In this chapter, we developed a voice-based banking system by combining the technologies of VoiceXML and ColdFusion. We discussed all aspects involved in developing the application. To begin with, we outlined the general architecture of the application. We examined the general database structure of the application before delving into the finer details. We then discussed the home page of the application at length, referring to each of the modules separately. We showed you the workings of each module, with detailed code description and figures wherever relevant for better understanding. This chapter served to illustrate the flexibility of VoiceXML technology by presenting a server-side voice application that integrates the technologies of VoiceXML and ColdFusion.

Integrating CCXML with VoiceXML Applications

IN THIS CHAPTER:

This chapter is devoted to Call Control Extensible Markup Language (CCXML), which was designed by W3C and represents the latest addition to the framework of voice applications. We analyze the early specifications of CCXML, examine the present day trends of the language, and discuss in what direction the language is poised to evolve. The chapter covers the following topics:

▶ Introduction to CCXML

▶ Event processing and call management

▶ Document flow and execution process in CCXML

▶ Working with variables in CCXML

▶ Event handling in CCXML

▶ Call management in CCXML

▶ Conferences management in CCXML

Introduction to Call Control Extensible Markup Language

CCXML represents a recent advance proposed by WC3 in the framework used for creating voice applications. This language was introduced primarily to extend the scope of VoiceXML so that it would support advanced telephony-related features in voice applications. CCXML's forte is that it can be associated with any dialog implementation language such as VoiceXML or with traditional IVR systems.

Before going into detail regarding CCXML, it would be relevant to clarify why a separate language is needed for supporting advanced telephony features in voice applications and why VoiceXML itself cannot be used for this purpose. Here are some of the major areas where VoiceXML is wanting:

▶ VoiceXML was developed on the basis of certain presumptions as to what would be required of a voice application. The language was not equipped to cater to demands beyond these presumptions.

▶ Functionally, VoiceXML serves to develop the user interface for voice applications. The support it derives from various other languages such as SSML is what accounts for most of its functionalities.

▶ Although VoiceXML does offer effective methods for controlling telephony features such as disconnecting and transferring calls, it offers no means for enabling or controlling such necessary features as conferencing and multiparty call handling.

In these regards, CCMXL has some definite advantages over VoiceXML in addition to its support of advanced telephony features:

▶ CCXML supports a large number of telephony-related events that aren't supported by the event-processing faculty of VoiceXML applications.

▶ CCXML facilitates building applications that can handle elaborate multiparty conferencing and similar processes by incorporating specific provisions.

▶ CCXML provides more sophisticated call handling compared to VoiceXML, such as facilitating making outgoing calls as well as creating conversation sessions between two different users of an application.

Event Processing Requirements

In a large voice application, a number of synchronous and asynchronous events occur during user interaction. The basic limitation of the VoiceXML language is that, being an event-processing model designed basically for user interface implementation, it can handle only synchronous events.

CCXML, on the other hand, is capable of handling asynchronous events that could occur during a session. Thus, within an application, you could combine a VoiceXML program with a CCXML program, each running as a separate thread, so that synchronous events such as nomatch or noinput are taken care of by the VoiceXML program and asynchronous ones are handled by the CCXML program.

In such applications, whenever an asynchronous event occurs, it is appended to the queue of the associated CCXML document for processing while the VoiceXML document proceeds with processing within its scope, keeping the interaction alive. The CCXML program picks events from the queue in turn, and after processing removes each event from the queue. Thus, the task of event processing is carried out by the CCXML part, whereas the VoiceXML part takes care of the user interaction.

Conferencing Requirements

Though VoiceXML offers the option of creating a single-party conversation between two nodes by providing the <transfer> element, it doesn't offer any option for creating multiparty conferences that include more than two callers at the same time, nor does it give the user the capability to join an ongoing conference. CCXML offers the following for managing conferencing:

▶ Options for organizing as well as for maintaining conferences, such as that for receiving more than one audio stream from different callers and relaying them as a single audio stream to all the connected users.

▶ Options that allow VoiceXML interpreters to create and control conferences by employing moderators for an ongoing conference.

▶ Options that allow splitting the single audio stream received into various streams and relaying them to all connected users.

▶ Most of the conferencing features of CCXML are specific to the implementation platform, so this platform may be maneuvered to extend the conferencing features of an application that employs CCXML.

Call Management Requirements

Although VoiceXML supports some of the features related to telephony, it doesn't provide for efficient control over the events related to these features. The following are some of the requirements of a large-scale voice application that aren't provided by VoiceXML:

▶ Ability to place outbound calls

▶ Selective call answering facility

▶ Access to phone network signaling and error criteria

These requirements may be met by incorporating a CCXML program in the application.

Document Flow and Execution Process in CCXML

In this section, we discuss the document flow and the execution process of a CCXML document. Before going into the details of these topics, however, an understanding of the various CCXML elements will give you a better appreciation of the discussion that follows. Take a look at Table 9-1, which lists some of the main elements of CCXML along with a brief description of each.

Element	Description
\<accept\>	Specifies an incoming phone call be accepted.
\<assign\>	Assigns a value to a previously declared variable.
\<authenticate\>	Authenticates a CCXML script in the document.
\<ccxml\>	Represents the top-level element. All the CCXML-based documents start with this tag.
\<createcall\>	Places an outbound call.
\<createccxml\>	Creates a new CCXML document.
\<createconference\>	Creates a multiparty audio conference in CCXML.
\<destroyconference\>	Destroys a multiparty audio conference in CCXML.
\<dialogstart.	Starts the execution of a VoiceXML document.
\<dialogterminate\>	Terminates the execution of a VoiceXML document.
\<disconnect\>	Disconnects an ongoing phone connection.
\<else\>	Works with the \<if\> element.

Table 9-1 *Important CCXML Elements*

Element	Description
<elseif>	Works with the <if> element.
<eventhandler>	Builds a block of event processing statements.
<if>	Builds logical conditions in documents.
<join>	Specifies a connection to audio streams.
<reject>	Specifies incoming phone call be rejected.
<transition>	Builds a block containing single-event processing.
<unjoin>	Disconnects audio streams.
<var>	Declares a variable in a CCXML document.

Table 9-1   *Important CCXML Elements* (continued)

The execution of a CCXML document starts from the top-level element, <ccxml>. The rest of the elements are processed sequentially according to their order in the document. The flow of execution may be changed later in the document by using the <if>, <else>, <elseif>, <goto>, and <submit> elements.

A CCXML document conducts most of the processing by using its event handlers. CCXML documents can also control the execution of VoiceXML documents up to a certain level. For example, to stop the execution of an ongoing VoiceXML document, a CCXML document may be used.

The CCXML program can also start the execution process of a new VoiceXML document. Also, at the time of starting a new session of a VoiceXML document, a CCXML document can be used to specify the mode of launching the new session. The following two modes are possible:

▶ CCXML may launch a new interpreter session by freezing the current ongoing interpreter session.

▶ CCXML may launch a new interpreter session by destroying the current ongoing interpreter session.

If a new session is started after freezing the ongoing session, the previous session is resumed after completing the new session. If a new session is started after destroying the previous session, the previous session isn't resumed.

Let's consider these two situations in detail. Suppose three VoiceXML interpreters are currently active and the user is interacting with the top-level interpreter. Now starting a new session by freezing the current one works much like pushing an interpreter into the stack. If you start the new session by destroying the current session, the top-level interpreter is replaced by the new session.

The CCXML document starts the VoiceXML interpreter session by using the <dialogstart> element. Once a new interpreter session starts, it will be terminated if any of the following three events occurs:

▶ CCXML terminates the session explicitly by using the <dialogterminate> element.

▶ The session receives a telephone.disconnect event as a result of execution of the <disconnect> element or because the user hangs up the call.

▶ The VoiceXML interpreter encounters the <exit> element in the VoiceXML document while executing the document.

If the CCXML document starts the execution of a VoiceXML document for collecting some information from the user, that VoiceXML document can send the collected information back to the CCXML interpreter by using the namelist attribute of the <exit> element. You can use the namelist attribute to define the name of the variables containing the information to be sent back to the CCXML interpreter.

The <ccxml> Element

This is the topmost element for all CCXML documents. All other elements reside under this element. The <CCXML> element has only one attribute, as shown here.

Attribute	Description
version	Defines the version of the current CCXML document, the default value being 1.0.

The <dialogstart> Element

The <dialogstart> element is used to launch a new VoiceXML document session by associating it with a call leg (real-world telephone connection). This document is launched in a separate process while the CCXML documents continue the handling of events. Attributes of the <dialogstart> element are listed in Table 9-2.

The execution of the CCXML documents continues in a separate thread, whereas the document launched by the <dialogstart> element is processed in a different thread. If the dialog isn't started for any reason, the interpreter throws a dialog.nostarted event. Once the processing of dialog is completed, the CCXML interpreter receives a dialog.exit event, which is queued and processed in sequential order.

Attribute	Description
src	Contains the URL of the document to be executed.
type	Defines the MIME type of the document. If omitted, the default value "application/xml+vxml" is assigned. The CCXML interpreter can also guess the correct MIME type on the basis of the filename extension.
name	Defines the name of the ECMAScript variable that will hold the value of session-name. This can be used later such as while terminating the dialog by using the <dialogterminate> element.
callid	Defines the call leg object associated with the newly executed dialog.

Table 9-2   *Attributes of the <dialogstart> Element*

The <dialogterminate> Element

In CCXML, it is possible to stop the execution of an ongoing dialog instance by using the <dialogterminate> element. If the CCXML interpreter encounters a <dialogterminate> element while executing the CCXML document, it sends the event to the VoiceXML interpreter. On receiving this event, the VoiceXML interpreter reacts as if it encountered an <exit/> element in the document and terminates the execution of the document. The <dialogterminate> element has only one attribute associated with it, described here.

Attribute	Description
sessionid	Defines the name of the session for the termination procedure. This sessionid was generated by the <dialogstart> element at the time of launching a new dialog.

The <if> Element

The <if> element is use to set a logical condition. You may include the <else> and <elseif> elements to enhance the functionality of the <if> element while building the logical condition. Both the <if> and the <elseif> elements contain a single attribute, described here. The <else> element doesn't have any attributes.

Attribute	Description
cond	Provides a Boolean condition that can be checked to see whether it is true or false.

The <goto> and <fetch> Elements

In a multidocument VoiceXML application, you can use the <goto> element for the purpose of navigation. However, there is one drawback associated with the <goto> element. If the <goto> element is used as it is in the VoiceXML scheme, the execution process is blocked when the interpreter encounters this element. Only after the defined document has been successfully located will the process be resumed.

This happens in a multidocument-based CCXML application also if the <goto> element is used in the same manner. However, in this case the situation can be avoided by placing the <fetch> element before the <goto> element. With this, the CCXML interpreter will first locate the defined CCXML document and parse and store it in memory if it is successfully located. If the defined document could not be processed successfully for some reason, notification to this end is served. Since the <goto> element is used in the next step, control is transferred to the defined document only here. If the processing of the defined document fails, you can skip the <goto> element. As a result of this, the application can continue processing all incoming events uninterruptedly. Both the <goto> and <fetch> elements contain a single attribute, as shown here.

Attribute	Description
next	Defines the URL of document to be loaded.

The <createccxml> Element

The <createccxml> element is used to create new CCXML instances. Once created, such instances do not retain any relationship with their parent instances. The <createccxml> element contains the single attribute described here.

Attribute	Description
src	Defines the URI of the CCXML document for execution.

Working with Variables

Variable handling in CCXML is exactly the same as in VoiceXML. Variables can be declared explicitly by using the <var> element or implicitly by using the <assign> element as shown here:

```
<var name="instanceid" />
<assign name="status" expr="hangsup"/>
```

You can assign values to the variables already declared by using the <assign> element. Both the <var> and the <assign> elements contain two attributes, described here.

Attribute	Description
name	Defines the name of variable being declared.
expr	Defines the new value the variable now contains.

Event Handling in CCXML

Event handling is one of the primary jobs the CCXML part of an application has to perform. In this section, we focus on the procedures for event handling in CCXML. We have already discussed events such as the <nomatch> event with regard to VoiceXML. The events in VoiceXML are always generated by some action performed by the user or by the system. Contrary to this, in CCXML, the interpreter may receive various kinds of events at any given time from various sources, such as the events generated by the telephony network. The event model in CCXML is telephony related and takes after the Java Telephony API (JTAPI) and Javasoft JCP event models.

Events in CCXML are handled by the <eventhandler> elements. Each ongoing CCXML interpreter session has a queue of events sorted according to their order of arrival and processed according to the principle of First In, First Out (FIFO).

In CCXML, the <eventhandler> elements of a system are processed according to a scheme known as event handler interpretation algorithm (EHIA). In processing events, the uppermost event from the stacked queue is removed. After this, it is determined whether any of the set of <transition> elements accepts this event. If one such set is found, the instructions of that set are processed in sequential order of the documents.

If none of the <transition> element set accepts the event, the event is dropped, the uppermost of the events still in the queue is selected, and this event undergoes the same process. If the queue is found empty, the execution process is paused until an event gets placed in the queue.

The <eventhandler> element can also declare a variable known as a *state variable,* the scope of which is limited to the <eventhandler> and its elements. The <eventhandler> element contains the two attributes described here.

Attribute	Description
id	Defines the name of the event handler.
statevariable	Defines the name for the <eventhandler> statevariable.

The attributes of the <transition> element are described here.

Attribute	Description
state	Defines the current possible state of the event handler.
event	Defines a dot-separated string that represents the matching event type.
cond	Provides a Boolean condition that can be checked against to see whether it is true or false. Becomes TRUE when transition is selected.
name	Defines the name of the variable set for receiving events and their associated variables

Standard Events in CCXML

CCXML includes a set of predefined events called *standard events*. These standard events mainly fall into one of the following two categories:

▶ Telephony-related events

▶ Language-related events

Telephony-related Events

The telephony-related events in CCXML constitute a model that is based on the Javasoft JCC call model. In CCXML, this model employs three basic classes for releasing events, listed here and discussed in the sections that follow:

▶ Call class

▶ Connection class

▶ Provider class

Call Class   The Call class releases three basic events, which are shown here. These events are used by the CCXML application for determining the status of calls.

Event	Description
call.CALL_CREATED	Moves the call into IDLE state, which is the initial state for all the calls.
call.CALL_ACTIVE	Moves the call to the ACTIVE state. All the calls of an ongoing session are represented by this state.
call.CALL_INVALID	Moves the call into INVALID state. Disconnected calls or those having no connections are represented by this state.

Connection Class   The Connection class releases seven basic events, which are listed and described in Table 9-3. These events are used by the CCXML application for determining the status of connections.

Provider Class   The Provider class releases three basic events, as listed in Table 9-4. These events are used by the CCXML application for determining the status of the provider.

Event	Description
connection.CONNECTION_ALERTING	Represents the address at which an incoming call is to be notified.
connection.CONNECTION_CONNECTED	Represents that an address is actively taking part in the call and the connection is established.
connection.CONNECTION_CREATED	Represents the state of all the new connections as the IDLE state.
connection.CONNECTION_DISCONNECTED	Represents that the call is disconnected and no ongoing connection is present.
connection.CONNECTION_FAILED	Represents that the call has failed due to some reason and a connection isn't established successfully.
connection.CONNECTION_INPROGRESS	Represents that a connection is in progress and the call is connected to both parties.
connection.CONNECTION_UNKNOWN	If generated, indicates the current state of the connection is unknown.

Table 9-3   *Connection Class Events*

Event	Description
provider.PROVIDER_IN_SERVICE	Represents that the provider is currently alive and is available for making and receiving calls.
provider.PROVIDER_OUT_OF_SERVICE	Represents that the provider is currently out of service and is temporarily not available for making and receiving calls.
provider.PROVIDER_SHUTDOWN	Represents that the service provider is currently shut down and will no longer be available for making and receiving calls.

Table 9-4   *Connection Class Events*

Language-related Events

The language-related events fall under the second category of CCXML events. Both CCXML and VoiceXML interpreters generate such events. Table 9-5 lists the standard language-related events. More of such events are likely to be added in future versions of CCXML.

Event	Description
dialog.exit	Occurs at the end of document execution. This event is sent to the CCXML interpreter by the VoiceXML interpreter.
dialog.disconnect	Occurs when a <disconnect> element is found by the VoiceXML interpreter, which in turn sends this event to the CCXML interpreter.
dialog.transfer	Occurs when a transfer operation has been performed by the VoiceXML interpreter after encountering the <transfer> element. The VoiceXML interpreter then sends this event to the CCXML interpreter.
ccxml.fetch.done	Occurs when a fetch operation conducted by the CCXML interpreter is completed.
ccxml.joined	Occurs when a join operation conducted by the CCXML interpreter is completed.
ccxml.authenticated	Occurs when an authenticate operation conducted by the CCXML interpreter is completed.

Table 9-5   *Language-related Events*

Call Management in CCXML

The desire for efficient call management was in fact what prompted the very invention of the CCXML language. CCXML offers developers close control over complex telephony-related features such as multiparty conferencing. Call management represents an area where CCXML has definitely outclassed VoiceXML. In this section, we discuss the provisions in CCXML for controlling operations related to incoming and outgoing calls.

Incoming Call-related Operations

In CCXML, two basic elements are available for accepting and rejecting an incoming call: the <accept> and <reject> elements, respectively. In a CCXML document, the transition block is used for accepting or rejecting an incoming call. Whatever action the transition block takes, the platform will notify the telephony network by a signaling process. The <accept> element is used to accept incoming calls, and it contains a single attribute, described here.

Attribute	Description
callid	Indicates the id for signaling an incoming call being accepted. This is an optional attribute and can be omitted. If this attribute is omitted, the interpreter will accept the call using the id of the event currently being processed. The acceptance of an incoming call will cause the generation of a connection.CONNECTION_ CONNECTED event.

The <reject> element is used to reject an incoming call. The attribute of the <reject> element is described here.

Attribute	Description
callid	Indicates the id for signaling an incoming call being rejected. This is an optional attribute and can be omitted. If the attribute is omitted, the interpreter will reject the call using the id of the event currently being processed.

Outgoing Call-related Operations

You can also place outgoing calls in CCXML documents by using the <createcall> element. This element may be employed to instruct the platform to place a call to a specified destination. When the call is placed, the CCXML interpreter receives asynchronous events that can be used later for effecting sufficient call control in the application. The execution of the <createcall> element doesn't interfere with the execution of the program. The CCXML document continues the work of interacting with other callers and handling conferences. The <createcall> element contains two attributes, which are described here.

Attribute	Description
dest	Defines the destination URI in the form of a valid telephone number.
name	Defines the name of the variable that receives the callid of the outgoing call.

Conference Management in CCXML

The availability of features for creating and handling conferences is one of the most significant advantages of CCXML. You can create and destroy conferences by using the <createconference> and <destroyconference> elements, respectively. You can also allow users to join or leave ongoing conferences by using the <join> and <unjoin> elements, respectively. When any of these events occur, the corresponding asynchronous events are generated on the server and subsequently sent to the interpreter for processing. The <createconference> element contains a single attribute, which is shown here. The other elements for managing conferences are discussed in the sections that follow.

Attribute	Description
name	Defines the name of a variable in the form of a valid URI that receives the conference identifier. This conference identifier should always be unique so that the conference can be referenced later.

The <destroyconference> Element

The <destroyconference> element is used to destroy an ongoing conference session on the server. The <destroyconference> element contains the single attribute described here.

Attribute	Description
conferenceid	Defines the id of an ongoing conference that is to be destroyed.

The <join> Element

The <join> element provides users the functionality for joining an ongoing conference. While using the <join> element for adding the users in conference, two audio endpoints are defined. If both the audio points defined are call legs, the system bridges the two call legs. If one of the endpoints is a call leg and the other is a conference, the user is added to the defined ongoing conference. The two possible modes for conferences are half duplex and full duplex. In half-duplex mode, User A is able to listen to the audio stream coming from User B, while User B isn't able to listen to the audio stream coming from User A. In full-duplex mode, both User A and User B are able to listen to the audio streams coming from the other user at the same time.

This table describes the attributes of the <join> element.

Attribute	Description
sessionid1	Defines the first of the two audio endpoints.
sessionid2	Defines the second of the two audio endpoints.
duplex	Defines the mode of conference. The possible values are "HALF" and "FULL."

The <unjoin> Element

The <unjoin> element allows users to leave an ongoing conference on the server. This element contains the two attributes described in this table.

Attribute	Description
sessionid1	Defines the first of the two audio endpoints you need to separate to disconnect the user from the conference.
sessionid2	Defines the second of the two audio endpoints you need to separate to disconnect the user from the conference.

Disconnecting Calls in CCXML

In CCXML applications, the <disconnect> element is used to disconnect a call leg. This table describes the lone attribute of this element.

Attribute	Description
callid	Indicates the id of the call leg that should be disconnected. This attribute is optional. If omitted, the interpreter uses the id of the current event being processed.

The disconnection of a call generates the connection.CONNECTION_DISCONNECTED event on the server.

Summary

In this chapter, we described the various features offered by Call Control Extensible Markup Language, the newest addition to the voice browser framework. We discussed some of the salient features of this language and its scope, and how it integrates with VoiceXML to build telephony applications with enhanced functionalities such as better call control, provision for conferencing, and so on. We described the various processes such as document flow and event handling involved in CCXML-based applications. The concepts of call management and conferencing were analyzed in detail, so as to enable you to understand the basic principles of CCXML.

Introduction to the Microsoft Web Telephony Engine

I n this chapter, we detail one of the latest technologies for building full-fledged, autonomous voice applications—the Microsoft Web Telephony Engine, or WTE as it is often called. It was introduced by Microsoft Corporation and represents a unique technology for developing voice-enabled web sites that can also work on voice-based browsers such as telephones. Although at the first blush this technology might appear similar to VoiceXML, it radically differs from the latter in that it doesn't call for any specific language for developing voice-based applications. WTE just expands the limits of HTML by introducing a few extensions and adopts a new architecture for the deployment of voice-enabled web sites. This chapter should equip you with enough know-how of the Microsoft Web Telephony Engine to provide you with a platform for developing applications using this technology.

Introduction to the Web Telephony Engine

The Web Telephony Engine is a system-level component that runs as a service once installed and configured in Windows 2000 Server version. The Web Telephony Engine provides the facility to use conventional web sites over the telephone network by rendering HTML code in audible format. Using this technology, you can also develop web sites that can be accessed from both voice browsers and conventional web browsers. Developing such dual-accessible web sites using Web Telephony is much easier than developing them using a conventional IVR system.

Advantages of WTE

With regard to developing and deploying voice-enabled web applications, the Web Telephony Engine offers some unique advantages that similar technologies available in the market don't:

▶ If a web application already exists, developing a Web Telephony application using the Web Telephony Engine is quite easy, because the entire architecture of such an application would be based on HTML extensions. On the other hand, with the conventional IVR system, developing a Web Telephony application involving an existing web application is quite an involved process, as it requires that the developer handle complicated languages.

▶ For building dual-access applications, the Web Telephony Engine is more suitable than IVR systems, because a single Web Telephony application, if designed for dual access, can access both voice browsers and conventional browsers. With IVR systems, you have to create a separate infrastructure for accessing each of these browsers.

▶ Since the Web Telephony Engine is characteristically a server-side technology, you can install a telephony engine at a location other than where your documents are stored and connect it with the local web server using the HTTP protocol.

Features of WTE

The Web Telephony Engine uses standard HTML elements for rendering information in the audible form and communicating over a telephone network. For achieving this, WTE employs some extensions of HTML elements such as call handling. As WTE uses HTML, albeit with some extensions, building multilevel applications that contain nested menus and links is much easier with WTE than with conventional IVR systems.

In addition, because WTE uses the Internet Explorer component to access an application over the HTTP protocol, it also supports scripting facilities within an application, making the application more powerful and endowing it with enhanced features. To integrate complex operations in the application, you can use ActiveX components or Java applets, thus simplifying the process. WTE also enables you to employ scripting technologies such as VBScript and JScript, as well as other Microsoft products, such as IIS or SQL Server, to easily render your application more flexible and sharp.

Installing and Configuring WTE

Before starting to develop an application using WTE, you have to install and configure WTE correctly. The minimum system requirements for developing an application using WTE are as follows:

- ▶ Windows 2000 Server operating system
- ▶ Microsoft SAPI 4.0a-compliant speech recognition engines
- ▶ Microsoft text-to-speech engine
- ▶ Windows 2000-supported voice board or voice modem

After ensuring that the minimum requirements have been provided, run the WTE setup according to the instructions of the Setup Wizard, making sure to provide all the required information. After successful installation, the Web Telephony Engine runs as a service in Windows 2000.

Here is an important item to note with regard to the setup process: During setup, a Service Configuration dialog box will appear asking for a domain name, username, and password. The domain user must have administrator rights on the computer. If you choose to set up WTE in local system mode, the following limitations will be imposed:

- ▶ If you run WTE in local system mode, facilities available through the NTLM authentication will not be available.

- ▶ WTE running in local system mode will not be able to open the HKLM_ CURRENT_USER registry key. Since WTE uses the Internet Explorer controls and options to access applications, any change made to the Internet Explorer will be ineffective on the Web Telephony Engine and is liable to cause several problems at the time of deployment.

Overview of Web Telephony Applications

A Web Telephony application is a simple IVR system as far as the users of such an application are concerned. It uses various menus and listings for providing the requested information. From the developer's point of view, a Web Telephony application is a web site that provides information through the telephones of users by rendering information in audible form by means of the Web Telephony Engine.

As mentioned earlier, a Web Telephony application can also work as a dual-accessible application—that is, the users can avail the application by using both visual and voice browsers. Like all web applications, a Web Telephony application must have a home page from where the user can start navigating the application, and can contain a post-call page. The post-call page is most often the last page in the application, and WTE usually navigates the post-call page after the call session with a user has ended.

All Web Telephony applications consist of a group of pages containing HTML code with some extensions; these applications may also contain some server-side language pages, such as ASPs and JSPs, that developers might have used to generate the HTML pages that are to be rendered in audible format by the WTE after completing some operations.

The WTE uses a telephony service provider (TSP) to communicate with the telephone system attached to it. The engine communicates with the TSP with the help of Microsoft TAPI 3.0. All Web Telephony applications use TSP functionalities through the ITBasicCallControl object exposed by the TAPI 3.0 Call object.

Call Handling in Web Telephony Applications

In this section, we discuss the call handling techniques of WTE, such as answering a call, transferring calls between applications, and disconnecting calls.

Answering a Call

When a TAPI line receives a call from a user, it informs the WTE about the call. On receiving the notification from the TAPI line, the WTE creates a session object and starts answering the call by rendering the application home page in audible format. This process occurs automatically. You may also configure the WTE so as to leave the call answering process to the application.

If your application is configured to answer the call, some preprocessing tasks need to be completed before answering the call. In such a case, the user may be provided some aural indication to inform him or her that some processing is under way until the call is answered by the application.

If the call is to be answered by the application, WTE creates a session object as soon as it receives notification of an incoming call (from TAPI) and starts searching the home page of the application. The home page of the application always contains a script pertaining to call handling, and this script serves to answer the call or to transfer the call to another application. For this purpose, it uses the methods of the TAPI call object.

To abandon a call, the External object available in WTE is used, as shown here:

```
SCRIPT Language=VBS>
If CallAbandonstate=1 Then
 Window.external.Abandon
Else
 Window.external.ITBasicCallControl.Answer
End If
</SCRIPT>
```

Transferring the Call

In WTE, it is possible to transfer a call from one application to another or to any other reachable telephone number by using the method for transferring exposed by the TAPI call object. However, if your engine is playing an audio file on the same line that needs to be transferred, the transfer operation is likely to fail. To avert this, use the code shown in Listing 10-1. This code detects all the active media streams, stops the audio stream if it is found to be active, and then performs the call transfer operation.

Listing 10-1:   *Call Transfer Operation Using VBScript*

```
<script language=vbscript>
sub stopstream
    DIM CallToBeTransfer
    DIM myDispMapper
    DIM StreamControl
    DIM pITStream
    Set CallToBeTransfer=external.itbasiccallcontrol
    Set myDispMapper =
CreateObject("DispatchMapper.DispatchMapper.1")
    Set StreamControl =
myDispMapper.QueryDispatchInterface(_"{EE3BD604-3868-11D2-
A045-00C04FB6809F}",CallToBeTransfer)
    For Each pITStream in StreamControl.Streams
        lMediaType = pITStream.MediaType
        if lMediaType = 8 Then
            pITStream.StopStream
        End If
    Next
    CallToBeTransfer.blindTransfer "3243077"
end sub
</script>
```

In the preceding code, we collect information regarding all the active media streams on the line and then, using a FOR condition, we check for active audio streams. If the lMediaType variable with the value 8 is found, we stop the stream and then transfer the call using the blind transfer method. The value 8 is specified for audio type streams in the TAPI3.H file that expose the TAPI call object in TAPI version 3.0.

Disconnecting the Call

While a user interacts with a WTE application, various events generated by the user as well as the server side are liable to disconnect the call. The following are some of the events capable of causing disconnection:

▶ If the user hangs up the telephone, the call is disconnected and TAPI serves notification to the WTE for performing the next specified task.

▶ If a call is transferred to another location via the transfer method of the ITBasicCallControl object, the original call might be disconnected. The call is transferred by the user by pressing the key specified for the assistant operator.

▶ If an error is encountered in the rendering process, which causes the termination of the application, the call is invariably disconnected.

▶ Whenever the Web Telephony Engine navigates a page that contains the script for the call disconnection, the call is disconnected by the disconnect method of the ITBasicCallControl method.

▶ If in the rendering process the WTE reaches the end of the HTML content and finds no further link for navigation, the call is disconnected.

As the WTE relies completely on the TAPI call object for all telephony-related activities, we consider the ins and outs of TAPI version 3.0 at length in Chapter 11.

Prompts in WTE

In this section, we discuss the prompting techniques in WTE. The two available options are playing prerecorded audio files to the user and using a text-to-speech (TTS) engine to render the available text content on the HTML page. As the speech generated by TTS engines is a bit unnatural, it's preferable to use Wave files for the fixed dialogs of an application. However, while using the dynamic data generated by any server-side processing language, you cannot employ Wave files to speak out to your customers, and in such cases, you should use TTS engines for rendering the data.

To disable the TTS engine for any specific application, set the Render TTS property of the WTEApplication object to false, as shown in the following code:

```
window.external.configuration.RenderTTS=false
```

The value of this property can be changed any time during the session to true to enable the TTS engine of the application, as shown here:

```
window.external.configuration.RenderTTS=true
```

Using the Wave Files for Prompting

For associating Wave files with HTML elements, use the VOICEFILE attribute. If WTE encounters the VOICEFILE attribute at the time of rendering the application, it plays the associated Wave file and ignores any kind of attached text in the element. The code snippet given here clarifies this:

```
<A HREF="help.html"
VOICEFILE="http://www.dreamtechsoftware.com/wte/help.wav"
ACCESSKEY=2>Help section</A>
```

When WTE encounters the link, it plays the help.wav file and ignores the text associated with the link. In the case of a web browser, the user can identify the page containing the link for the help section, because it is displayed in blue.

Using the Text-to-Speech Engine

If the TTS engine is used to render the content of an application, WTE will employ the TTS engine named SAM, which is available by default, to render the content. To change this default engine, you can install other TTS engines available from the Microsoft site and then configure them using the WTE administration tool. Now look at the previous code snippet reproduced here without the VOICEFILE attribute:

```
<A HREF="help.html" ACCESSKEY=2>Help section</A>
```

In this case, WTE renders the associated text of the element together with information regarding the specified access key for activating the options, such as "Press 2 for Help section." While using the TTS engine, you can control the output by using some of the aural CSS properties defined by the W3C, such as those for controlling the volume and pitch of spoken text.

Collecting Caller Input

In a WTE application, input regarding various events need to be collected from users for processing and proceeding with the session. User input can be collected in the following two formats:

► Spoken input from the caller
► DTMF-based caller input

First, let's take a look at the technique for collecting spoken input from the caller. This process is entirely dependent on speech recognition engines. Any speech recognition engine that is SAPI 4.0a compliant may be used. By using speech recognition facilities in the application, you provide a natural way of interacting between the application and users.

Before using a speech recognition engine, you need to configure it by setting the WTEApplication.UseSR property to true, as shown here:

```
window.external.configuration.UseSR=true
```

The following are the two basic modes in which speech recognition engines may be used in WTE:

▶   Free dictation mode

▶   Menu mode

Using the Free Dictation Mode

The free dictation mode is used when the user provides no information regarding name, address, and so on in advance. The user can speak for any field item to be created using the <textarea> or the <input> element. Subsequently, the speech recognition engine translates the spoken input into text, and WTE enters the text in the corresponding field. While collecting spoken input from the user, you can also use grammars for enhanced accuracy and better control over the spoken input.

When choices available to the user are limited, the menu mode is preferable. In this mode, after the user says his or her choice, the system will try to match the user input with a list of available menu items. This mode provides a higher amount of accuracy because the choices are limited, and therefore users are less likely to make mistakes while making selections.

In the sections that follow, we discuss the use of grammars in free dictation mode and in menu mode.

Using Grammars

Whenever we refer to a collection of spoken input from the user, grammars are associated with it. In Chapter 5, you read about the grammars in VoiceXML. Here, we discuss the grammars in WTE and the procedure for using these grammars.

Before you start working with these grammars, keep in mind that WTE currently uses SAPI version 4.0a, the grammar format which is based on the context-free grammar (CFG) format of SAPI4.0a. Microsoft later changed the grammar format in SAPI version 5.0 to XML format-based grammar so that developers may write their grammars in XML format and use a grammar compiler to convert them into native CFG format, which the SAPI engines use. However, WTE still uses the CFG format for grammars.

In WTE, you can use the GRAMMAR attribute with the elements that create menus for presenting options and entry fields for entering text. In defining menu items, the GRAMMAR attribute defines a set of words or phrases. The user can select any of these by speaking, as shown in this example:

```
<p>
Select one of the following options
</p>
```

```
<SELECT NAME="store=10 ">
    <OPTION GRAMMAR="'toys' 'doll' 'children toys' 'plaything'" VALUE="Toys"
VOICEFILE="http://www.dreamtechsoftware.com/wte/toys.wav">Toys </OPTION>
    <OPTION GRAMMAR="'automobiles' 'cars' 'bikes'" VALUE="Automobiles"
VOICEFILE="http://www.dreamtechsoftware.com/wte/automobiles.wav">Automobiles
</OPTION>
    <OPTION GRAMMAR="'books' 'novels' 'stories'" VALUE="books"
VOICEFILE="http://www.dreamtechsoftware.com/wte/books.wav">Books</OPTION>
    <OPTION GRAMMAR="'food' 'coke' 'pizza'" VALUE="food"
VOICEFILE="http://www.dreamtechsoftware.com/wte/food.wav">Food </OPTION>
</SELECT>
```

In free dictation mode, after getting input from the user, the application can save it as a Wave file on the server for later use. The recording process is controlled by using the VOICEFILE attribute in conjunction with the <textarea> or the <input> element. The VOICEFILE attribute specifies the name and the location of the Wave file on the server. If the VOICEFILE attribute specifies the file location using the HTTP protocol, the file is uploaded to the given path.

Using the Menu Mode

As mentioned previously, the menu mode is another mode of collecting input from users. This mode employs a menu containing a list of items, with every item associated with some location in the application. The menu mode is usually used to build the navigation system of an application, wherein WTE navigates the location within the application that is associated with the option selected by the user from a menu. The following HTML elements can be used to build a menu-based interface in a WTE application:

▶ A series of <a> elements, including the HREF attribute

▶ A series of radio controls (input type= "RADIO"), each of which has the same value in the NAME attribute

▶ The <option> elements used along with the <select> element

Assigning DTMF Values to Menu Items

WTE automatically assigns a specific DTMF value to the menu item that the user selects by pressing the corresponding DTMF key. The DTMF values assigned to the menu items will depend on the number of items in the menu. If the number of items in the menu is less than 10, the WTE will assign a single-digit number to each item of the menu starting from 0 to 9 depending on the availability. If the number of items is more than 10, the WTE will assign a double-digit number to each menu item.

While assigning values to the DTMF keys, WTE takes into account all previous assignments. For example, if Key 1 is assigned to the home page and Key 2 to the back link, at the time of assignment, WTE starts numbering the keys starting from Key 3. The DTMF keys may also be defined using the ACCESSKEY attribute in the menu items.

Representing the Menus

While rendering the menu item, the WTE combines the associated text with the Wave file, if any, specified by the VOICEFILE attribute using the cue, cue-after, and cue-before CSS properties. If CSS properties are found in the elements, WTE will process the elements in the following order:

1. The cue-before property

2. The cue property

3. The text or the VOICEFILE associated with the element

4. The cue-after property

You can use either a text string or a Wave file with the previously mentioned CSS properties to specify the location of the Wave file and to provide the URL of the Wave file, as shown here:

```
cue-before:URL(http://www.dreamtechsoftware.com/wte/menustart.wav)".
```

To see how these CSS properties work, look at the following code snippet:

```
<P>Please select one of the following sections. </P>
<SELECT NAME="store" SIZE="10" >
    <OPTION VALUE="Flowers" STYLE="cue-before:'For'; cue-after:' press
1,'">Flowers section
    <OPTION VALUE="books" STYLE="cue-before:'for'; cue-after:' press 2,'">Books
section
    <OPTION VALUE="Toys" STYLE="cue-before:'or press 3 for'; ">Toys
section
</SELECT>
```

When WTE renders this code, it produces the following output:

```
Please select one of the following sections. For Flowers section press 1, for
Books section press 2, or press 3 for toys section.
```

It is possible to have more than one menu on a single page. In such cases, a menu can provide the link to another menu or a specific menu item by referencing the NAME or ID attribute.

Terminating the Input

In WTE, for terminating user input we use the InputTerminator property along with all the entry fields created using the <textarea> and <input> elements. The InputTerminator property specifies a string for the termination of the input collection process after the user is through with the data entering process. For example, if you assign the asterisk (*) symbol as an input terminator, once the user finishes the process of entering the data in any entry field, he or she may press the * key on his or her telephone keypad to terminate the input process and let the application proceed to the processing phase.

You can also use the MAXLENGTH attribute to specify the maximum number of characters for a Text type <input> element. In such a case, user input will be terminated by the application when it reaches the specified limit. The use of this attribute is preferred when the user input has a fixed length, such as with telephone numbers. Even if the MAXLENGTH attribute has been used, the user can press the input terminator to terminate the input before it reaches the limit.

If neither the InputTerminator nor the MAXLENGTH attribute is defined, you have to use the script to terminate the user input. If an empty string exists in the InputTerminator property, WTE will generate a warning log.

Navigation in WTE

In WTE, two basic types of navigation are used: *automatic navigation* and *application driven navigation*. In this section, we discuss both these navigation processes, considering the navigation operations and announcements in detail.

Automatic Navigation in WTE

When a new call arrives, the WTE automatically navigates to the specified home page of the application. In the home page, the behavior of the application may be controlled by setting various variables, or by performing some preprocessing tasks before starting the rendering of the application.

If the user disconnects the call, or if the user makes too many mistakes and as a result the system disconnects the call, the WTE automatically navigates to the post-call page, if one has been defined, to perform post-call processing such as handling the data collected from the user.

Application-Driven Navigation in WTE

As we discussed in the previous section, in WTE applications navigation is accomplished by using menus. A menu represents a set of options for the user to select from. Once the user selects any one of the available choices, WTE navigates to the location associated with that particular menu item. In case of the <a> element, WTE navigates to the location specified by the HREF attribute. You can also use the script to call the available navigation methods, such as window.navigate, to navigate to any location in the application.

Navigation Operations in WTE

In WTE, the three basic navigation operations—home, back, and operator—are supported. By using the home navigation operation, the user can access the home page of the application anytime during the call. Back navigation allows the user to navigate backwards in the application. Operator navigation enables the user to transfer the call to the operator for assistance and may be used if some problem is encountered while interacting with the application. You can assign DTMF keys to these operations by using the HomeKey, BackKey, and OperatorKey properties in your application or via the WTE administration tool.

While assigning the DTMF keys to the home, back, and operator operations, check whether these keys have already been assigned to some other properties. In WTE, the navigation operations are often ignored while collecting data from the user in entry fields. If the application ignores the navigation operations while collecting data from the user, the user is allowed to enter input using those keys that have been specified for navigation operations. To make the application ignore navigation operations when the user provides input, set the IgnoreNavigationKeysTillTermination property to true, as shown in the following code. This property affects only the entry fields created using the <input> and <textarea> elements.

```
WTEApplication.IgnoreNavigationKeysTillTermination  = True
```

Navigation Announcements in WTE

Every time you navigate from one location to another in a WTE application, some time is needed to start rendering the content of the new location. For example, if you are navigating to an ASP page that will query the database, some idle time is involved. You can use the NavigationAnnouncement property to play back a specified text string or a Wave file during this time. This serves to apprise the user of data processing as well as to entertain the user. You can set this property in an application either by using the WTE administration tool or programmatically, as shown here:

```
WTEApplication.NavigationAnnouncement = "Please wait, while the
system is processing"
WTEApplication.NavigationAnnouncement =
"http://www.dreamtechsoftware.com/wte/wait.wave"
```

Once the NavigationAnnouncement property is set during navigation, the WTE starts rendering the specified string or playing back the specific Wave file repeatedly until a requested location returns with some content.

Using HTML Elements in WTE

In this section, we discuss the WTE functionality of rendering HTML elements such as the process of rendering buttons and forms.

Forms in WTE

For almost a decade, HTML forms have been used for collecting data from users. Forms collect a series of interlinked data. In HTML forms, the browser first collects all the data and then sends out a single HTTP request to the server along with the collected data. In WTE, an application can send an HTTP request by using elements in a form or by using these elements without a form. This is possible because WTE renders each element in sequential order and waits for user input after rendering an element before processing the next element in the document.

Buttons in WTE

In all WTE applications, buttons are used to provide a Boolean type menu-based scheme to the user. You may create a button by using the <button> element or via the <input> element that has the button type. Also, CSS properties may be used with a button for its introduction, as shown in this example:

```
<BUTTON STYLE = "cue-before: 'For'; cue-after: 'Press 1, To skip this  press 9'"
OnClick="buttonclicked()">Toys</BUTTON>
```

The WTEApplication object model offers two properties to specify keys the user can use for clicking and skipping a button. The ClickButtonKey property enables you to specify the DTMF key that the user may press to click a particular button. The SkipButtonKey property specifies the DTMF key that the user may press to skip a button while interacting with the application.

If speech recognition is enabled in your application, you can also define some words or phrases to specify the clicking and skipping of a button through the ClickButtonPhrases and SkipButtonPhrases properties. While using CSS properties with the <button> element, you can also use the VOICEFILE attribute to play back a Wave file.

Check Boxes in WTE

In WTE, you can also use check boxes for building Boolean type menu-based interfaces. As you know, a check box can have two possible values after it is visited. If any of the values are checked by the user, this represents positive user response, and if the values are left clear, this represents negative user response.

You can build a check box menu by using the <input> element for defining its type as follows:

```
<INPUT TYPE="checkbox" NAME="yesno">
```

The WTEApplication object exposes two properties that specify the DTMF keys for the caller to enter his or her response or to clear the check box. The SelectCheckBoxKey property defines the DTMF key that the user should press to indicate a positive response, whereas the ClearCheckBoxKey property defines the DTMF key for a negative response.

If speech recognition is enabled in the application, you can use the SelectCheckBoxPhrases property to define a set of words or a phrase to be spoken to indicate a positive response. For defining a set of words or a phrase for indicating a negative response, you can use the ClearCheckBoxPhrases property. If you are providing the set of words and phrases by using any one of these properties, you should ensure that the properties don't contain an empty string.

Frames in WTE

Frames have become a usual component of HTML-based web sites nowadays. WTE also supports the uses of frames in an application by virtue of the <frameset> element. You can thus create pages containing fixed menus and content and also replace the menus on a page depending on actions performed by the user. WTE lays down certain rules for rendering frames that you need to observe while developing applications containing frames:

▶ During the rendering process, when WTE encounters the first <frameset> element, it starts the rendering from the top-level frame set collection and proceeds in the order in which the frames are specified in the <frameset>element.

▶ If any of the top-level pages contain an additional <frameset> element, that element is rendered following the same pattern as for rendering the top-level <frameset> element.

▶ While interacting with the application, if the user selects a link from a static menu and you specify the resulting document be loaded in another frame, that frame is rendered first. After completing the rendering process of that frame, the rendering continues per the rules.

▶ If any document in the collection contains links and intrinsic controls, the index of this document is declared as the static menu index, and it will not change even if the document itself changes.

▶ The static menu and current index are stored only for those pages that have a direct link between the top level and the current level. If the user selects to navigate a page that doesn't have a direct link between the current level and the top level and later returns to that <frameset>, the <frameset> is rendered as a new <frameset> because the index isn't stored.

List Boxes in WTE

In WTE applications, list boxes are used to build non-Boolean menu-based interfaces. You can create list boxes by using the <option> element under the <select> element. WTE renders the list boxes as menu items, so it prompts all the available options to the user and waits for the user to select any one of the options by pressing an option-associated key or by speaking a specified set of words or phrase.

WTE also supports multiselection list boxes. You can include the MULTIPLE attribute under the <select> element to create a multiselection list box. In a multiselection list box, if the user selects one choice, rendering starts from the item next to the selected item.

Using Labels in WTE

In WTE, labels contain strings created using the <label> element. Labels associate text with controls that don't have any scope or that can't sum up text, such as controls created using the <button> or the <input> element. You can associate labels with controls by using the FOR attribute.

When WTE renders a control, it also renders the associated <label> element. If any of the <label> elements aren't associated with a control, those elements will be rendered when encountered in the application.

Using Tables in WTE

In WTE, you can also represent data in tabular format by using the WTEApplication .RenderTablesAsTabularData property. If the value of this property is set to false, WTE renders the table data as the simple text data, arranged top to bottom and left to right. If the value of this property is true, WTE renders the data as a tabular data.

At the time of rendering data in tabular format, WTE uses some of the rules listed here for making the connection between the header and data cells in the table:

- ▶ The HEADER attribute is used to provide a listing of relevant header information regarding any data cell. All the header cells are named by using the ID attribute, and any element with the HEADERS attribute and ID outside the table, if found, is ignored and a warning log generated on the server.
- ▶ For providing the Abbreviated header, use the ABBR attribute.
- ▶ All the cells that have a HIDDEN attribute are ignored by WTE and will not be rendered.
- ▶ If the header information isn't found, all table data cells containing the AXIS attribute are rendered as header information, as the current version of WTE doesn't support the AXIS attribute.
- ▶ If header information is missing, row headers are inserted as they are encountered in the document from left to right in the case of a left-to-right table.
- ▶ If header information is missing, column headers are inserted after the row headers from top to bottom as they are encountered in the document.

WTE will render the tables in the following order:

- ▶ The process starts with the rendering of a summary of the tables and will then proceed to the rendering of captions for the tables.
- ▶ In the next phase, all data cells are processed with their headers per the rules, the rendering of data cells being done row after row.

If any of the tables in your application contain menu items, all these menu items are collected at the time of parsing the table and are prompted to the user at the end of the table. All the menu items that reside inside a table are collected only once; it is possible that the cell containing the menu item is visited more than once, but the menu items are collected only once during the process.

Working with Events in WTE

Two types of events are available to users, standard web browser events and WTE events. Standard web browser events are fired by the Internet Explorer and can be used with WTE. WTE-specific events are fired by WTE, and these can be used only with WTE, not with Internet Explorer.

How the Event Handler Works

An event handler is an application that retrieves information regarding events when called by WTE or Internet Explorer. An event handler works as a dual-accessible application. If Internet Explorer calls the event handler, the event handler will use the standard IE event object to retrieve information associated with the event; if the event handler is called by the WTE, the event handler will use the event object provided by the WTE extended object model to retrieve information regarding the event.

Standard Web Browser Events

The WTE application is able to automatically receive all the events fired by Internet Explorer. For example, in a WTE application you can write code to associate some action with the onload event.

You should ensure that your application doesn't use the standard events related to the user interface of a graphical web browser. For example, don't use the onmouseover event in an application you develop in the WTE environment.

WTE-specific Events

In the WTE environment, the onselectionerror, onselectiontimeout, onkeypress, and onchange events are fired only by WTE; none of these events is fired by Internet Explorer.

We discuss some of the important events in a WTE application, in the following sections:

▶   onchange

▶   onclick

▶   onkeypress

▶   onselectionerror

▶   onselectiontimeout

The onchange Event

If the value of an intrinsic control is changed during interaction between the user and the application, the onchange event is fired. You can use this event in your application in the following manner:

- ▶ While using inline mode
- ▶ With the FOR and EVENT attributes
- ▶ With any scripting language such as Microsoft Visual Basic Scripting Edition

The onclick Event

If the user selects a menu item, clicks a button, or selects a check box, or if a button is automatically clicked in the application, the onclick event is fired.

The onkeypress Event

When a user interacts with the application and starts entering data in entry fields (created by the <textarea> or <input> element and having the Text type) by using the keypad of a telephony device, the onkeypress event is fired. In WTE applications, this event is fired every time a user presses a DTMF key while entering data.

By using this event, you can determine the value of the key pressed by the user before this value is entered in an entry field. For example, if the user is entering data for the telephone number field, by using the onkeypress event you determine the value of the key the user presses, and in case of a nondigit key such as the * key, you can interrupt the process and inform the user that the input is invalid.

The onselectionerror Event

While selecting a menu item, if the user presses a nonvalid DTMF key (that is, one that isn't destined for the selection of that particular menu item), the onselectionerror event is fired by WTE. This event can be used in an application in the following manner:

- ▶ While using inline mode
- ▶ With the FOR and EVENT attributes
- ▶ With any scripting language such as Microsoft Visual Basic Scripting Edition

The onselectiontimeout Event

If the user takes too much time selecting a menu item or an intrinsic control and exceeds the time limit specified for the timeout, the onselectiontimeout event is fired by WTE. By using this event, you can inform the user about the timeout operation and prompt for entering data in accordance. You can use this event in your application in the following manner:

- ▶ While in inline mode
- ▶ With the FOR and EVENT attributes
- ▶ With any scripting language such as Microsoft Visual Basic Scripting Edition

Working with CSS Properties in WTE

In this section, we discuss the CSS properties that you can use in your WTE application when prompting the user. The following CSS properties are available for use in WTE applications:

- ► cue, cue-before, and cue-after properties
- ► cut-through property
- ► media property
- ► display property
- ► volume property
- ► pitch property
- ► speak-header cell property
- ► speech-rate property

The cue, cue-before, and cue-after Properties

In WTE applications, you can use the cue, cue-before, and cue-after properties to arrange the order of audio items available for playing while speaking to the user. The cue property enables playing of the text of a Wave file before and after rendering a specified element's text or Wave file defined using the VOICEFILE attribute.

The cue-before property plays the specified audio before WTE starts rendering the content of the associated element, whereas the cue-after property plays the specified audio after completion of rendering the audio content of the associated element.

When using the cue, cue-before, and cue-after properties, you may specify text or may use a particular Wave file by providing its URL for the rendering process. If the associated element contains a VOICEFILE attribute, the audio specified by the cue-after property is played after rendering all the audio content associated with the element and its children.

The cut-through Property

If you wish to provide the user with the capability of interrupting audio and starting input, use the cut-through property. If the value of this property is set to yes, the user is capable of interrupting the rendering of audio and starting input. If the value of this property is set to no, the user isn't able to interrupt the audio played by WTE and can start giving input only after rendering of the audio is completed.

This property may be provided as a menu option so that users familiar with the application need not wait for the rendering process of menu items to be completed before selecting their desired option. If WTE encounters an element that contains the cut-through property set to the value no, WTE clears all the previously collected and unused user inputs. The cut-through property works only if the installed voice board supports duplex operations.

The media Property

The media property is used to specify the media type of the targeted device on which the output is rendered. The possible values are listed in Table 10-1.

Value	Description
all	Indicates the output of the rendering process is intended for all types of devices.
aural	Indicates the output of the rendering process is intended only for aural browsers.
print	Indicates the output of the rendering process is intended for printed matter or for documents viewed onscreen in print preview mode.
screen	Indicates the output of the rendering process is intended for computer display terminals.

Table 10-1   *Values of the media Property*

The display Property

This property controls the appearance of an element, when it is rendered on the graphical browser, by using the different values listed in Table 10-2.

The volume Property

In WTE applications, use the volume property to control the volume of synthesized voice produced by the TTS engine. The values for this property are specified in the form of percentages, as listed in Table 10-3.

The default value of volume property is set to 100 percent by the TTS engine.

The pitch Property

The pitch CSS property is used to define the level of the average pitch of synthesized voice produced by the TTS engine in hertz (Hz). The default value of the pitch of the Microsoft TTS engine is 170 Hz.

The speak-header cell Property

If you are including tables in your WTE application, you can use the speak-header cell property to define the procedure of handling the headers cell in a table when it is rendered by the TTS engine. The two possible values are "always" and "once." If the value is set to always, the TTS engine speaks the header cell contents before rendering every cell. If the value is set to once, the TTS engine speaks the header cell once until a data cell is associated with a new header cell as compared to the previous data cell.

Value	Description
block	Defines an element as a block by inserting a line break before and after the element.
inline	Defines an element as an <inline> element.
list-item	Defines an element as a list item and works much the same as the block property. It also adds a list item marker to the element.
none	Specifies that an element and its child elements should not be displayed.

Table 10-2   *Values of the display Property*

Value	Description
0%	Specifies silence, and the user isn't able to hear anything from the server
25%	Specifies one-fourth of the maximum volume
50%	Specifies half the maximum volume
75%	Specifies three-fourths of the maximum volume
100%	Specifies the maximum possible volume

Table 10-3   *Values of the volume Property*

The speech-rate Property

In WTE applications, the speech-rate property is used to control the rate of spoken output in the form of words per minute. The default value for the Microsoft TTS engine is 169 words per minute.

Summary

This chapter presented the Web Telephony Engine, the latest technology from Microsoft for creating full-fledged, autonomous voice applications that can be accessed from both voice browsers as well as conventional browsers. The chapter began with an outline of the general features and overview of WTE. Subsequently, we explained the process of installing and configuring WTE. We showed you the various call handling features of applications built with WTE, and the role of TAPI in this regard. Following this, you learned about the prompts in WTE and the different modes of collecting user input. The discussion turned to the techniques of navigating in WTE applications, with emphasis on how you might use HTML elements and their extensions for this purpose. Following this, we discussed the implementation of certain common features of WTE-based applications, such as check boxes, list boxes, labels, and frames. Towards the end of the chapter, we showed you the workings of event handlers and detailed most of the major events individually.

Now that you've read this chapter, you should have enough know-how to develop effective dual-access voice applications on your own.

Introduction to IP Telephony

IN THIS CHAPTER:

IP Telephony

Standards for IP Telephony

TAPI Programming Interfaces

The H.323 Lines Video Streaming Project

Summary

❝Mr. Watson, come here. I want to see you." These words, spoken by Graham Bell over the first phone line over a century ago, changed the very concept of communication, marking the beginning of what is known as *telephony*. Starting with a dedicated wire line carrying voice signals between the source and the destination, the telephony system, within a few months, was transformed into the centralized switching model that is still in use today. In this model, to establish a telephony link between two cities or two states or even two countries, all that is needed is to connect a few centralized switching systems with one another.

Ever since Mr. Bell spoke those fateful words, as you know, the communication industry has continued to scale new heights. Today, the pace of its progress is stupendous, and the communication revolution has a bearing on almost every facet of our lives. Today's telephony system, a combination of software/hardware elements, represents a quantum leap over the legacy telephony system represented by the centralized switching model. It has evolved into an altogether distinct phenomenon called *Internet Protocol telephony* (or IP telephony for short). This chapter is dedicated to helping you understand what IP telephony is all about.

IP Telephony

IP telephony is an offshoot of the revolutionary phase in the evolution of modern communication heralded by the Internet. The origin of the Internet may be traced back to attempts made by the U.S. Defense Department to establish some sort of connection among its randomly distributed computers. The Internet, at the time of its inception, was a wide area network (WAN) connecting computers spread all over America. In the early '70s when Ray Tomlinson created the first e-mail system for this network, he didn't know that he had triggered a process that would soon endow the Internet with universal popularity. As the Internet gained in popularity, new techniques to lower the maintenance cost of the existing infrastructure and to make it more efficient were contrived. As a result, every contemporary industry could avail the Internet to automate its functionality at least partially.

Due to the increasing use of computers in the industry and the services sectors, enormous amounts of data have been entered into the storage media of computers and supercomputers in the last two decades. This in turn has led to the emergence of yet another revolutionary development, called IP telephony, that effects a merger of telephony and IP-based computer networks. The possibility of accessing the enormous amounts of data stored in computers all over the world through a simple medium like a telephone was good news even for under-developed nations which, being unable to afford computers in large numbers, were left behind in the IT race. However, a few problems kept developers from merging the two networks for quite some time. Let's take a look at what these problems were.

Differences between IP-based Networks and Telephony Networks

The people who designed the first computer networking systems did not anticipate that someday their systems would be required to make use of telephony networks. Consequently, these networks received and sent information in the form of data packets, unlike telephony networks, which use analog signals. Physically, these two systems were entirely different.

Such dissimilarities between the two networks had to be tackled before a useful combination of the two could be developed. We discuss these dissimilarities in the next sections and explain how they were overcome.

Signal Difference

The most primary prerequisite for introducing telephony to IP-based computer networks was the conversion of the signals these two systems operate on. This task was, and still is, accomplished by devices called *modems*, with which most of us are quite familiar. Modems contain *digital signal processors* (DSPs), and as digital signals are modulated and demodulated into analog signals, DSPs carry out a lot of signal processing.

Protocol difference

Protocols constitute another major difference between telephony and computer networks. The way IP networks function is quite different from the way telephony networks function. For instance, in a PSTN, for every call, a circuit is created between the caller and the called party. This circuit does not break until the caller hangs up. Obviously, this isn't a very efficient way of establishing calls in terms of economic utilization of available bandwidth. In contrast to this, in IP networks data is transferred in the form of packets, and the same circuit is used to carry voice packets from different subscribers. To overcome this difference in protocols and also take into account some other call-processing protocols requires a gateway.

The functions of a *gateway* include translating the call-processing protocols as well as managing the disparity in speech coding between the IP and PSTN networks. Therefore, these gateways are termed *IP-PSTN gateways*. Figure 11-1 schematically illustrates the gateway architecture.

Realizing the great potential of merging computer networks and telephony systems in communication applications, many companies came up with devices and even programming interfaces to overcome the differences between these networks. These devices have been successful to a great extent in harnessing the exciting possibilities of mixing computer networks and telephony systems. Let's now take a look at some of the central features of this merger.

Advantages of IP Telephony

So far, we have discussed different networks that are used for different services: the telephone network, such as PSTNs for making voice calls and sending fax messages; the Internet for data services such as e-mail, file transfer, and web services; cellular mobile networks for making voice calls while on the move; and so on. Apart from these networks, some companies have set up their own networks for audio and video transfer. All these networks have different hardware/software requirements and different maintenance structures. In addition, these have limited use unless they are interlinked or integrated.

However, IP telephony brought about a communication revolution by facilitating the transfer of voice, video, and data through a single network using a common transport medium—IP. This has led to the evolution of a new concept—*convergence* of technologies, which means rendering several technologies intercompatible.

With this development, an entirely new set of applications was at our disposal—video conferencing, real-time document collaboration, distance learning/training, telecommuting,

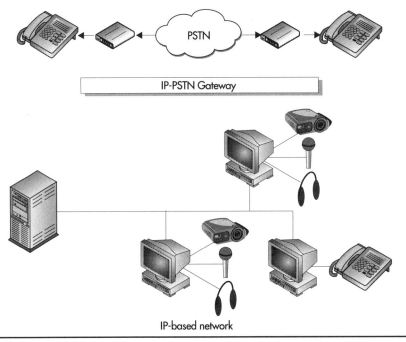

Figure 11-1   *An IP-PSTN gateway*

video mail, and video on demand, to name a few. In terms of economics, IP telephony has no matching competitor. By offering a common transport for a variety of communications, it considerably lowered the costs of maintaining and managing discrete networks, also cutting costs on fronts such as client support while making them more efficient.

For IP telephony to be successful, it was essential to evolve some standards for transfer and processing of data among systems supporting different hardware. Such standards would govern the data transfer over a variety of communication media (for example, ADSL, ISDN, leased lines, coaxial cable, and twisted pair) and provide flexibility in physical media to systems using the technology.

Standards for IP Telephony

To facilitate convergence of different communication technologies, the International Telecommunications Union (ITU) came up with standards such as H.323, which in conjunction with standards like RTP (short for Real-Time Transfer Protocol, an Internet Engineering Task Force standard), countered LAN latency in IP networks and other similar problems. This ensured quality of service (QoS) in multimedia communication over connectionless networks as well as providing for services such as fast call settings, data support, and protection of audio/video streams.

Following is a discussion of some of the standards evolved for IP telephony.

H.323

H.323 is a set of recommendations defined by the ITU for multimedia communication for packet-based networks such as IP-based networks (including the Internet), Internet packet exchange (IPX) networks, local area networks (LANs), metropolitan area networks (MANs), and wide area networks (WANs). It contains standards for call setup and termination, security and authentication, and bandwidth management, as well as a few standard codecs for audio and video compression and decompression. The H.323 standard recommends the following command and control protocols:

▶ RAS to manage registration, admission, and status

▶ Q.931 to manage call setup and termination

▶ H.245 to negotiate channel usage and capabilities

▶ H.235 for security and authentication

RAS (which stands for Registration, Admission, and Status) governs the process of resolving an endpoint's alias addresses, discovering the gatekeeper, and controlling bandwidth operations between a gatekeeper and the endpoint. RAS, however, isn't used if gatekeepers are not present.

Q.931 is used to set up a connection between two terminals.

The H.245 control channel is responsible for handling control messages such as capability exchanges, commands, and indications that govern the operation of the H.323 terminal.

The H.235, another ITU Telecommunication Standardization Sector (ITU-T) recommendation, enacts and takes care of various security aspects of H.323 such as the authentication and integrity verification of H.323 messages. It guards data in H.323 communications by ensuring that it isn't altered in any way. This standard also verifies the identity of the user.

H.323 ensures that standard audio and video codecs are supported. For data sharing, it enforces the T.120 standard (a standard for data transfer). The H.323 standard is network, platform, and application independent; consequently, all H.323-compliant terminals can interoperate with one another.

In essence, H.323 standardizes call-control and multimedia-bandwidth management for point-to-point and multipoint conferences.

H.323 defines four major components for an H.323-based communication system that provides point-to-point and point-to-multicast communication services. Following is a brief description of these components.

Terminals

Terminals are the client endpoints on the network. They could be a PC or a stand-alone device running an H.323 stack and multimedia applications. All terminals must support voice communications; video and data support is optional.

Gateways

A gateway is essentially a protocol converter and connects two discrete networks. Gateways bridge H.323 conferences to other networks such as a PSTN by translating protocols for call setup/release and communication protocols, and converting multimedia formats to ensure compatibility with the networks connected by the gateway. Gateways are not required if other networks or non–H.323-compliant terminals are not needed to be connected to an H.323 network.

Gatekeepers

Gatekeepers, though not indispensable elements of an H.323 conference, perform tasks such as address translation and bandwidth management. They resolve LAN aliases to IP addresses and perform address lookups. Gatekeepers help economize on the bandwidth available for the connection by limiting the number of H.323 calls.

Multipoint Control Units

As long as a connection exists between two terminals, they are in conversation. The moment a third joins, the interaction becomes a conference, and with this, H.323 seeks to avail the services of a Multipoint Conference Server (MCS), commonly known as an H.323 Multipoint Control Unit (MCU). The main element of any H.323 MCU is the Multipoint Controller (MC) and the optional Multipoint Processor (MP). The main job of MC is to work out a framework that ensures a set of average and common media processing capabilities among all the terminals involved. It never involves itself in the processing of media streams, leaving that to the MPs. MPs and MCs can coexist in a single unit or can be part of other H.323 components.

RSVP

The Resource Reservation Protocol (RSVP), an IETF standard, is tailored to facilitate resource reservations as networks of varying topologies and media connected through routers communicate with each other. RSVP propagates QoS requirements for a particular media broadcast through all the paths between the sender and all the possible receivers. The receivers respond back, giving reserve messages describing the bandwidth characteristics of the data they propose to receive from the sender. As these messages pass through the intermediate routers, based on the bandwidth available for these resources, the routers decide whether to accept the proposed reservation of resources or not. If one router decides to commit the resources, these reserve messages are passed to the next router on the way to the sender.

If you wanted to put these standards to the test, you could use an IP-based network to make and receive calls and see all these standards in action. (In fact, this is what we do later in this chapter, in the section "The H.323 Lines Video Streaming Project.") To get two terminals to connect on H.323 lines and see what happens during a call session, the call maker and receiver terminals both have to be H.323 compliant. Therefore, you could use Windows 2000 Professional terminals, which are H.323 compliant, in a LAN environment with a Windows 2000 Server, as we do in our example project later in the chapter. Next, you would need to determine if you have any telephony interfaces to enable applications to access all the telephony resources available on a computer. The media or data on a call must also be available to applications in a standard manner. Various programming interfaces allow you to access the features of IP telephony. You would probably prefer a programming interface that does your job without your having to care much about the intricacies of the architecture. Let's take a look at some of the programming interfaces available in the market, considering the one by Microsoft in detail.

TAPI Programming Interfaces

Anticipating the enormous popularity of IP telephony, some companies came up with easy-to-use telephony programming interfaces to facilitate application development in less time and with less effort. Among these, some such as those developed by Dialogic (now a part of Intel) and Parity Software stood to gain wide popularity. Dialogic provides a set of APIs and a development platform, whereas Parity Software has developed a set of proprietary ActiveX Controls. Those who seek to use COM prefer Microsoft's Telephony Application Programming Interface (TAPI), which in its third version has been presented as a suite of COM Interfaces, giving you the opportunity to develop applications in any language under the Microsoft domain. Moreover, this interface cuts down drastically on client-server communication in Remote Procedure Call (RPC) protocol, thereby simplifying the process of developing a telephony application for the Windows environment. Of course, for employing this interface, you need to have some degree of command over the concepts of COM. If you want to know about COM before getting involved with TAPI, you may want to refer to *Inside COM* (Microsoft Press). In the meantime, we next delve into more detail about TAPI 3.0.

TAPI 3.0

TAPI 3.0 outlines simple, generic methods in user mode for making connections between two or more computers and accessing any media streams involved in these connections. It works out a common interface between communication architectures that are physically and logically distinct, and enables the user to exercise control over data and media exchange. Microsoft TAPI in its third version is composed of the following four components:

- ▶ TAPI 3.0 COM interfaces
- ▶ TAPI server
- ▶ Telephony service providers (TSPs)
- ▶ Media service providers (MSPs)

TAPI 3.0, unlike its ancestor TAPI 2.1, is completely COM based. In place of APIs, we have a COM interface for every set of interrelated operations. Operations such as initializing a TAPI session, shutting down a TAPI session, enumerating different lines for a TAPI session, and other similar functionalities pertaining to a TAPI session have been abstracted as methods of a single interface. The same trend goes for all other interrelated functionalities.

The TAPI server can be seen as the repository of general telephony information; it has the static role of being the hub of all TAPI activities. Application-specific tasks such as accessing a device installed on a computer are performed by using this server as a bridge.

Interfaces serve as a bridge between communication devices and TAPI applications, and are made into dynamic link libraries. The TAPI server receives the commands meant to be exchanged with the device from the TAPI application and passes them over to the telephony service providers (TSP), which handle these commands, known as *control commands*. TSPs offers you close control on the call session and the telephony devices installed on a particular system.

Much like a TSP, which can be perceived as an abstraction for call control, a media service provider (MSP) supplies high-level control over media involved in calls. An MSP always works in conjunction with a TSP. MSPs implement a set of interfaces to expose protocol-specific mechanisms to TSPs or applications. Sometimes MSPs also implement vendor-specific interfaces and aggregate them into standard TAPI objects such as Call, CallHub, and so on exposed to an application so it can exercise control over device-specific features. This gives TAPI applications real-time control over media streams. DirectShow APIs present a very efficient way of harnessing and governing media streams that MSPs make use of. Although TSPs supervise the call activities, MSPs implement DirectShow interfaces for any media capability the telephony service in question has, to provide access to and control over media streams associated with a call.

Drawing on the resources of the four components we've discussed, TAPI simulates call making and receiving procedures on computer networks. It further distributes the workload by implementing a COM interface for each set of related functionalities.

Next, we explain how TAPI controls calls and media involved in calls.

Call Control in TAPI

Receiving a call or placing a call is done through a simple set of instructions. Let's see what these instructions are before delving into the details of the call control procedure of TAPI 3.0.

1. Initialize the TAPI session (similar to initializing a COM session).

2. Enumerate all telephony lines available on the computer, such as network cards, modems, ISDN lines, and so on.

3. Enumerate the supported dialing processes of each telephony line—for instance, specifying the phone number, IP address, and so on.

4. Choose a line based on queries for support for appropriate media (audio, video) and address types.

5. Initiate the dialing process or specify interest in waiting for a call on that line, registering your application's notification receiver for that line. TAPI will notify your application of any new call on that line.

6. Select appropriate terminals for giving inputs and receiving outputs for the call.

7. Place the call or imitate the call-receiving confirmation that is normally done by lifting the receiver.

8. Select appropriate terminals on the Call object.

9. Call the Connect method of the Call object to place the call.

TAPI has smartly combined these nine steps in five COM objects:

▶   TAPI

▶   Address

▶   Terminal

▶   Call

▶   CallHub

We begin with initializing the TAPI session by making an instance of the TAPI object and calling its Initialize method, a process very much like calling the CoInitialize() function to initialize the COM environment. This TAPI object represents all the telephony resources available on a system.

An Address object can be perceived as a telephony line available on any computer. Address objects can be used to query for media and for procuring other support for a line. An application can use this object to wait for a call or to make a call on a particular line.

Terminal objects basically represent the input or output endpoints for a call, such as a telephone, microphones, speakers, or even a file, which implies that they could be anything that is capable of providing inputs or receiving outputs.

A connection between the local address and one or more of the other addresses is represented by the Call object. The Call object exposes methods for achieving call control. It also facilitates querying underlying media streams.

The CallHub object contains methods to delve into an ongoing call, gathering information regarding the participants and governing them (subject to the credentials of a particular user).

A CallHub object is created as soon as a call is received through TAPI. It can't be created by applications. The CallHub is essentially a representation of a group of calls where each member of the call can be singled out for performing tasks specific to that member by retrieving the Call object for that call member.

We now consider how TAPI allows you to have control over the media stream involved in any call.

Media Streaming Model in TAPI

In any ongoing call session, data that is exchanged after the handshaking process is the media for that communication session. TAPI 3.0, through MSPs, exposes the media streams associated with a call and allows applications to exercise detailed control over the media streams.

For this function, TAPI makes use of another set of interfaces called DirectShow interfaces. These interfaces spare the programmer the trouble of writing device driver–level codes because the streaming architecture of these interfaces themselves provides access to Windows Device Driver Model.

TAPI thus makes it possible to gain access to media streams and direct them through different hardware components without having to go into intricate details of device driver programming.

DirectShow's design ensures that applications are isolated from the intricacies of media data transfer, hardware and media format differences, and so on. DirectShow employs a modular approach using an array of pluggable operating system components called *filters,* arranged in a configuration called a *filter graph.* A filter graph governs the connection of the filters and keeps watch over the flow of the stream's data through these filters. Each filter offers its capabilities through its *pins,* which are simply a set of special interfaces that can consume streaming data such as digital audio. So all you need to do is to build and manipulate filter graphs by adding or removing filters, connect these filters, negotiate their capabilities by scrutinizing their pins, and use them to access or control media streams or even employ them as bridges across different participants of a call, as shown in Figure 11-2.

DirectShow also ensures QoS in media transfer by exposing filters for RTP that, after studying the bandwidth needs of codecs associated with a particular media stream, negotiate

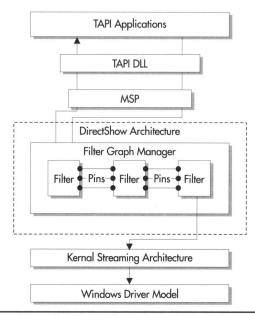

Figure 11-2   *MSP-DirectShow collaboration for media stream control*

the bandwidth needs with the network capabilities in order to guarantee appropriate point-to-point QoS in media transfer.

With this, you have gathered enough knowledge to be able to develop a simple caller and call receiver application. In the upcoming section, you see how to make a caller application that will use H.323 lines to make a call and also formulate a receiver program to receive the call. One welcome bit of news is that Windows 2000 terminals come with two service providers—the H.323 TSP and the H.323 MSP. H.323 TSP, besides implementing support for different address formats such as IP addresses, computer names, e-mail addresses, and so on, performs IP name resolution for us. H.323 MSP builds DirectShow filter graphs to support multimedia over the connection. Thus, TAPI 3.0 serves our purpose quite well. We use Microsoft TAPI 3.0 to develop an IP telephony application in the next section.

The H.323 Lines Video Streaming Project

For this project, our aim is to develop two applications: a call dialer, or caller, and a call receiver—each endowed with some media capabilities. Before we get into the programming details, we first plan how we would like these applications to function, as discussed next.

The Flow of Applications

Here's what we propose to accomplish through these two applications. The call receiver application starts and initializes a TAPI session on a Windows 2000 system in a LAN environment, visually represented in Figure 11-3. Our application enumerates all the TAPI addresses available on the system and registers itself to receive incoming calls on the address that supports both audio and video—the H.323 lines in this case.

On a different Windows 2000 system in the same network, with a video-capturing device (a web cam or a video camera) installed on it, the caller application starts a TAPI session of its own. Figure 11-4 shows both applications.

As shown in Figure 11-5, using the caller application, the user selects the address type that H.323 TSP supports (IP address, machine name, and so on) and makes the call specifying the destination address.

The H.323 TSP resolves the destination address and notifies the call receiver application of the caller application's intention to establish a connection, as shown in Figure 11-6. The call receiver receives the notification and establishes the connection.

At this point, the H.323 MSPs at both ends build DirectShow filter graphs and set up a video stream between the two systems.

We want our applications to work as we've just described. Now we actually develop the applications. Let's christen the caller application VideoSource and the call receiver application VideoSink and get started.

Figure 11-3   *Call receiver application on a Windows 2000 system*

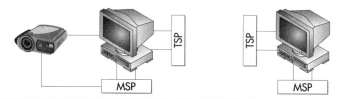

Figure 11-4   *Call receiving application still waiting for calls while caller application on another Window 2000 system instantiates*

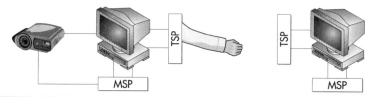

Figure 11-5   *The caller application dials on an IP address.*

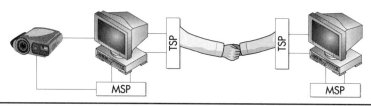

Figure 11-6   *The call receiver receives the call and renders the video stream associated with it.*

The VideoSource and VideoSink Applications

You need to have Microsoft Platform SDK (http://msdn.microsoft.com/) installed on your system to get the header files and libraries for basic functionalities. We have developed these applications in VC++ and have used MFC for developing the user interface of the applications. Let's take a look at the code we would use for these applications, starting with VideoSource (Listing 11-1).

Listing 11-1:   *Source Code for VideoSourceDlg.cpp*

```
// VideoSourceDlg.cpp : implementation file
//
#include "stdafx.h"
#include "VideoSource.h"
#include "VideoSourceDlg.h"
#ifdef _DEBUG
#define new DEBUG_NEW
#undef THIS_FILE
static char THIS_FILE[] = __FILE__;
#endif
#define ENABLE(x)                    ::EnableWindow(GetDlgItem(x)->m_hWnd,TRUE);
#define DISABLE(x)                   ::EnableWindow(GetDlgItem(x)-
m_hWnd,FALSE);
#define SETSTATUSDATA(x)       SetDlgItemText(IDC_STATUS_BAR,x);
/////////////////////////////////////////////////////////////////////////
// CVideoSourceDlg dialog
CVideoSourceDlg::CVideoSourceDlg(CWnd* pParent /*=NULL*/)
     : CDialog(CVideoSourceDlg::IDD, pParent)
{
     //{{AFX_DATA_INIT(CVideoSourceDlg)
     //}}AFX_DATA_INIT
     // Note that LoadIcon does not require a subsequent DestroyIcon in Win32
     m_hIcon = AfxGetApp()->LoadIcon(IDR_MAINFRAME);
     m_pTAPI = NULL;
     m_pAddress = NULL;
     m_pBCall = NULL;
}
void CVideoSourceDlg::DoDataExchange(CDataExchange* pDX)
{
     CDialog::DoDataExchange(pDX);
     //{{AFX_DATA_MAP(CVideoSourceDlg)
     DDX_Control(pDX, IDC_ADDRESS_TYPES_AVAILABLE, m_ctrlAddressesAvailable);
     //}}AFX_DATA_MAP
}
BEGIN_MESSAGE_MAP(CVideoSourceDlg, CDialog)
     //{{AFX_MSG_MAP(CVideoSourceDlg)
     ON_WM_SYSCOMMAND()
     ON_WM_PAINT()
```

```
        ON_WM_QUERYDRAGICON()
        ON_BN_CLICKED(IDC_DIAL, OnDial)
        ON_WM_DESTROY()
        ON_BN_CLICKED(IDC_DISCONNECT, OnDisconnect)
        //}}AFX_MSG_MAP
END_MESSAGE_MAP()
//////////////////////////////////////////////////////////////////////////
// CVideoSourceDlg message handlers
BOOL CVideoSourceDlg::OnInitDialog()
{
        CDialog::OnInitDialog();
        SetIcon(m_hIcon, TRUE);                    // Set big icon
        SetIcon(m_hIcon, FALSE);            // Set small icon
        PrepareToMakeCalls();
      ENABLE(IDC_DIAL);
      DISABLE(IDC_DISCONNECT);
      PopulateAddressComboBox();
        return TRUE;  // return TRUE  unless you set the focus to a control
}
void CVideoSourceDlg::OnPaint()
{
        if(IsIconic())
        {
                CPaintDC dc(this); // device context for painting
                SendMessage(WM_ICONERASEBKGND, (WPARAM) dc.GetSafeHdc(), 0);
        // Center icon in client rectangle
                int cxIcon = GetSystemMetrics(SM_CXICON);
                int cyIcon = GetSystemMetrics(SM_CYICON);
                CRect rect;
                GetClientRect(&rect);
                int x = (rect.Width() - cxIcon + 1) / 2;
                int y = (rect.Height() - cyIcon + 1) / 2;
                // Draw the icon
                dc.DrawIcon(x, y, m_hIcon);
}
        else
        {
                CDialog::OnPaint();
        }
}
HCURSOR CVideoSourceDlg::OnQueryDragIcon()
{
        return (HCURSOR) m_hIcon;
}
void CVideoSourceDlg::OnDial()
{
    HRESULT hr = S_OK;
      DWORD      dwAddressType;
      CString szAddressToCall;
    BSTR    bstrAddressToCall;
      dwAddressType =
```

```
m_ctrlAddressesAvailable.GetItemData(m_ctrlAddressesAvailable.GetCurSel());
GetDlgItemText(IDC_ADDRESS,szAddressToCall);
    hr = GetAddressThatSupportsAudio(dwAddressType);
    if(S_OK != hr)
  {
        SETSTATUSDATA("Couldn't find a TAPI address for making calls.");
        return;
    }
    long lMediaTypes = TAPIMEDIATYPE_AUDIO;
    if(IsMediaTypeSupported(m_pAddress, TAPIMEDIATYPE_VIDEO))
        lMediaTypes |= TAPIMEDIATYPE_VIDEO;
    bstrAddressToCall = szAddressToCall.AllocSysString();
    hr = m_pAddress->CreateCall( bstrAddressToCall,
                                 dwAddressType,
                       lMediaTypes,
                                &m_pBCall);
    SysFreeString ( bstrAddressToCall );
    if(S_OK != hr)
  {
        SETSTATUSDATA("Could not create a call.");
        return ;
    }
    ITStreamControl * pStreamControl;
    hr = m_pBCall->QueryInterface(__uuidof(ITStreamControl),
                                  (void **) &pStreamControl);
    if(SUCCEEDED(hr))
    {
        IEnumStream * pEnumStreams;
        hr = pStreamControl->EnumerateStreams(&pEnumStreams);
        pStreamControl->Release();
        if(SUCCEEDED(hr))
        {
            ITStream * pStream;
            while ( S_OK == pEnumStreams->Next(1, &pStream, NULL) )
            {
                ITTerminal * pTerminal;
                hr = CreateTerminal(pStream,&pTerminal);
                if(SUCCEEDED(hr))
                {
                    hr = pStream->SelectTerminal(pTerminal);
                    pTerminal->Release();
                }
                pStream->Release();
            }
            pEnumStreams->Release();
        }
    }
    hr = m_pBCall->Connect(VARIANT_FALSE);
    if(S_OK != hr)
    {
```

```
        m_pBCall->Release();
         m_pBCall = NULL;
         SETSTATUSDATA("Could not connect the call.");
         return;
    }
      SETSTATUSDATA("Call Connected.");
    ENABLE(IDC_DISCONNECT);
    DISABLE(IDC_DIAL);
}
HRESULT CVideoSourceDlg::CreateTerminal(ITStream * pStream,ITTerminal **
ppTerminal)
{
    HRESULT            hr;
    long               lMediaType;
    TERMINAL_DIRECTION dir;
    hr = pStream->get_MediaType( &lMediaType );
    if(S_OK != hr) return hr;
    hr = pStream->get_Direction( &dir );
    if(S_OK != hr) return hr;
    if((lMediaType == TAPIMEDIATYPE_VIDEO) && (dir == TD_RENDER))
    {
            HRESULT hr;
            BSTR    bstrCLSID_VideoWindowTerm;
            CString szTerminalClassID("{F7438990-D6EB-11d0-82A6-00AA00B5CA1B}");
        bstrCLSID_VideoWindowTerm = szTerminalClassID.AllocSysString();
            if(bstrCLSID_VideoWindowTerm == NULL)
                   hr = E_OUTOFMEMORY;
            else
            {
                    ITTerminalSupport * pTerminalSupport;
                    hr = m_pAddress->QueryInterface(__uuidof(ITTerminalSupport),
     (void**)&pTerminalSupport);
        if(S_OK == hr)
                       {
                           pTerminalSupport->
CreateTerminal(bstrCLSID_VideoWindowTerm, TAPIMEDIATYPE_VIDEO,TD_RENDER,
ppTerminal);
        pTerminalSupport->Release();
                       }
                }
            return hr;
    }
    ITTerminalSupport * pTerminalSupport;
    hr = m_pAddress->QueryInterface( __uuidof(ITTerminalSupport),
                                    (void **)&pTerminalSupport);
    if(SUCCEEDED(hr))
    {
        hr = pTerminalSupport->GetDefaultStaticTerminal(lMediaType,
                                                        dir,
                                                        ppTerminal);
        pTerminalSupport->Release();
```

```
    }
    return hr;
}
HRESULT CVideoSourceDlg::PrepareToMakeCalls()
{
    HRESULT     hr;
    hr = CoCreateInstance(__uuidof(TAPI),
                          NULL,
                          CLSCTX_INPROC_SERVER,
                          __uuidof(ITTAPI),
                          (LPVOID *)&m_pTAPI
                          );
    if(S_OK != hr) return hr;
    hr = m_pTAPI->Initialize();
    if(S_OK != hr)
    {
        SETSTATUSDATA("TAPI failed to initialize");
        m_pTAPI->Release();
        m_pTAPI = NULL;
        return hr;
    }
      SETSTATUSDATA("TAPI Initialized.");
    return S_OK;
}
void CVideoSourceDlg::PopulateAddressComboBox()
{
    int i = m_ctrlAddressesAvailable.AddString("Conference Name");
    m_ctrlAddressesAvailable.SetItemData(i,LINEADDRESSTYPE_SDP);
    i = m_ctrlAddressesAvailable.AddString("Email Name");
m_ctrlAddressesAvailable.SetItemData(i,LINEADDRESSTYPE_EMAILNAME);
    i = m_ctrlAddressesAvailable.AddString("Machine Name");
m_ctrlAddressesAvailable.SetItemData(i,LINEADDRESSTYPE_DOMAINNAME);
    i = m_ctrlAddressesAvailable.AddString("Phone Number");
    m_ctrlAddressesAvailable.SetItemData(i,LINEADDRESSTYPE_PHONENUMBER);
    i = m_ctrlAddressesAvailable.AddString("IP Address");
    m_ctrlAddressesAvailable.SetItemData(i,LINEADDRESSTYPE_IPADDRESS);
m_ctrlAddressesAvailable.SetCurSel(i);
    m_ctrlAddressesAvailable.SetFocus();
}
HRESULT CVideoSourceDlg::GetAddressThatSupportsAudio(DWORD dwAddressType)
{
    HRESULT                 hr = S_OK;
    BOOL                    bFoundAddress = FALSE;
    IEnumAddress               *pEnumAddress;
    ITAddress                   *pAddress;
    ITAddressCapabilities    *pAddressCaps;
    long                    lType = 0;
    if(NULL != m_pAddress)
    {
        m_pAddress->Release();
```

```
                m_pAddress = NULL;
        }
        hr = m_pTAPI->EnumerateAddresses( &pEnumAddress );
        if(S_OK != hr) return hr;
        while ( !bFoundAddress )
        {
            hr = pEnumAddress->Next( 1, &pAddress, NULL );
            if(S_OK != hr) break;
            hr = pAddress->QueryInterface(__uuidof(ITAddressCapabilities),
    (void**)&pAddressCaps);
            if(SUCCEEDED(hr))
            {
                hr = pAddressCaps->get_AddressCapability( AC_ADDRESSTYPES, &lType );
                pAddressCaps->Release();
                if(SUCCEEDED(hr))
                {
                    if(dwAddressType & lType)
                    {
                        if(IsMediaTypeSupported(pAddress,TAPIMEDIATYPE_AUDIO))
            {
                            m_pAddress = pAddress;
                            bFoundAddress = TRUE;
                            break;
                        }
                    }
                }
            }
            pAddress->Release();
        }
        pEnumAddress->Release();
        if(!bFoundAddress) return E_FAIL;
        return S_OK;
}
BOOL CVideoSourceDlg::IsMediaTypeSupported(ITAddress * pAddress,long lMediaType)
{
        VARIANT_BOOL      bSupport = VARIANT_FALSE;
        ITMediaSupport      *pMediaSupport;
        if(SUCCEEDED(pAddress->QueryInterface(__uuidof(ITMediaSupport),
(void **)&pMediaSupport)))
        {
            pMediaSupport->QueryMediaType(lMediaType,&bSupport);
            pMediaSupport->Release();
        }
        return (bSupport == VARIANT_TRUE);
}
void CVideoSourceDlg::OnDestroy()
{
        CDialog::OnDestroy();
        if(NULL != m_pBCall)
        {
```

```
                m_pBCall->Release();
                m_pBCall = NULL;
        }
          if(NULL != m_pAddress)
        {
                m_pAddress->Release();
                m_pAddress = NULL;
        }
        if(NULL != m_pTAPI)
        {
            m_pTAPI->Shutdown();
            m_pTAPI->Release();
            m_pTAPI = NULL;
        }
}
void CVideoSourceDlg::OnDisconnect()
{
    HRESULT         hr = S_OK;
    if(NULL != m_pBCall)
    {
        hr = m_pBCall->Disconnect( DC_NORMAL );
        m_pBCall->Release();
        m_pBCall = NULL;
    }
if(S_OK == hr)
        {
                ENABLE(IDC_DIAL);
                DISABLE(IDC_DISCONNECT);
        }
        else
        SETSTATUSDATA("The call failed to disconnect");
        SETSTATUSDATA("Call Disconnected.    TAPI Initialized.");
}
```

Source Code Explanation for VideoSourceDlg.cpp

The code begins with the inclusion of various header files. As soon as the application gets instantiated properly, the function PrepareToMakeCalls gets a call; this in turn instantiates a TAPI object and calls the Initialize method of the ITTAPI interface of this object to start a TAPI session. We don't provide for receiving TAPI event notification in our application, as it would not serve any purpose in particular. Our application tries to dial a certain address (addresses are the entities that are capable of making or receiving calls) and on successful connection, it sets up a video stream between itself and the connected computer. Nowhere in the life cycle of this application does it actually need any notification from the call receiver application.

Now, as the user chooses a particular address type, specifies the address, and clicks the Dial button, the function OnDial(), the BN_CLICKED event handler for this button, calls the GetAddressThatSupportsAudio function of the main dialog class to check whether the

selected address supports the required media capabilities. This function calls the
EnumerateAddresses method of the ITTAPI interface, which returns a pointer to
the IEnumAddress interface that can be used to enumerate all the addresses available
on the system.

```
hr = m_pTAPI->EnumerateAddresses(&pEnumAddress);
.
.
hr = pEnumAddress->Next(1,&pAddress,NULL);
```

These addresses are then examined for their support for a particular address type. We call
the get_AddressCapability method on the ITAddressCapabilities interface that has been
queried out of the Address object to determine whether it supports the address type selected
by the user.

```
hr = pAddress->QueryInterface(__uuidof(ITAddressCapabilities),
  (void**)&pAddressCaps);
.
.
hr = pAddressCaps->get_AddressCapability( AC_ADDRESSTYPES, &lType );
pAddressCaps->Release();
.
.
if(dwAddressType & lType)
{
if(IsMediaTypeSupported(pAddress,TAPIMEDIATYPE_AUDIO))
```

These addresses are now scrutinized for their media-handling capabilities. The function
IsMediaTypeSupported of the main dialog class queries the ITMediaSupport interface out of
the Address objects and calls its QueryMediaType method to determine whether it supports a
media type.

```
VARIANT_BOOL      bSupport = VARIANT_FALSE;
ITMediaSupport      *pMediaSupport;
if(SUCCEEDED(pAddress->QueryInterface(__uuidof(ITMediaSupport),
(void **)&pMediaSupport)))
{
        pMediaSupport->QueryMediaType(lMediaType,&bSupport);
```

If the address type selected by the user supports audio, it is checked for its video
capabilities by calling IsMediaTypeSupported again. If it supports the video media type,
the CreateCall method is called on the Address object identifying this address, specifying the
address type and the destination address as its parameters. This function returns a pointer
to the object's ITBasicCallControl interface, which can be used to make calls later on.

Following this, we call QueryInterface on this pointer to get a pointer to the ITStreamControl interface of the Call object.

```
ITStreamControl * pStreamControl;
hr = m_pBCall->QueryInterface(__uuidof(ITStreamControl),
                    (void **) &pStreamControl);
```

We can use this pointer to enumerate the available media streams by calling the EnumerateStreams method on it. This method returns a pointer to the IEnumStream interface, which has, in turn, a method called Next; this method, on being called, subsequently keeps providing pointers to the IStream interface.

```
IEnumStream * pEnumStreams;
.
.
.
hr = pStreamControl->EnumerateStreams(&pEnumStreams);
.
.
.
ITStream * pStream;
while( S_OK == pEnumStreams->Next(1, &pStream, NULL) )
```

We can use these pointers to determine the type of underlying streams and their directions—which essentially are the directions of the media streams corresponding to the local system—by calling the get_MediaType and get_Direction methods.

```
hr = pStream->get_MediaType( &lMediaType );
.
.
.
hr = pStream->get_Direction( &dir );
```

If the direction is TD_RENDER (which signifies that the terminal is not the source but some transient object, a video window in this case) and the media type is TAPIMEDIATYPE_VIDEO, we go on to create a video renderer terminal. We query for the ITTerminalSupport interface on the Address object, presenting the address to which this stream belongs. Then we call the CreateTerminal method of this interface to create the terminal.

```
pTerminalSupport->CreateTerminal(bstrCLSID_VideoWindowTerm,
TAPIMEDIATYPE_VIDEO,
TD_RENDER,
ppTerminal);
```

For the rest of the streams, we call the GetDefaultStaticTerminal method of this interface to get the default terminals associated with each of the streams.

Default terminals in this case are the default devices associated with the streams. Thus, they may be called *static terminals*. Because the video window is not a device, the video renderer terminal created earlier is a dynamic terminal.

```
hr = pTerminalSupport->GetDefaultStaticTerminal(lMediaType,
                                                 dir,
                                                 ppTerminal);

pTerminalSupport->Release();
```

All these terminals are selected on the stream calling SelectTerminal on the IStream interface. Next, we call the Connect method on the pointer of the ITBasicCallControl interface of the Call object that we received by calling CreateCall on the Address object. We pass VARIANT_FALSE as the only parameter to this function to specify that we want the call to be asynchronous, that is, we want it to return whether it connects or not. If the connection is made successfully, the streaming would start automatically.

Listing 11-2 presents the code we use for the call receiver application.

Listing 11-2: *VideoSinkDlg.cpp*

```cpp
// VideoSinkDlg.cpp : implementation file
//
#include "stdafx.h"
#include "VideoSink.h"
#include "VideoSinkDlg.h"
#ifdef _DEBUG
#define new DEBUG_NEW
#undef THIS_FILE
static char THIS_FILE[] = __FILE__;
#endif
#define ENABLE(x)                   ::EnableWindow(GetDlgItem(x)->m_hWnd,TRUE);
#define DISABLE(x)                ::EnableWindow(GetDlgItem(x)->m_hWnd,FALSE);
#define SETSTATUSDATA(x)        SetDlgItemText( IDC_STATUS_BAR,x);
//////////////////////////////////////////////////////////////////////////
// CVideoSinkDlg dialog
RECT lastRect;
const int U_MARGIN = 80;
const int PADDING = 10;
class CTAPINotifications : public ITTAPIEventNotification
{
private:
      CVideoSinkDlg *pVideoSinkDlg;
      LONG dwRefCount;
public:
      HRESULT STDMETHODCALLTYPE Event(TAPI_EVENT event,IDispatch * pEvent)
      {
            pEvent->AddRef();
            pVideoSinkDlg->TAPIEvent(event,pEvent);
            return S_OK;
```

```
      }
      CTAPINotifications(CVideoSinkDlg* pDlg)
      {
            pVideoSinkDlg = pDlg;
            dwRefCount = 1;
      }
      HRESULT STDMETHODCALLTYPE QueryInterface(REFIID riid,void **ppv)
      {
            *ppv = NULL;
            if(riid == __uuidof(ITTAPIEventNotification) || riid == IID_IUnknown)
                  *ppv = this;
            else
                  return E_NOINTERFACE;
            AddRef();
            return NOERROR;
      }
      ULONG STDMETHODCALLTYPE Release()
      {
            ULONG l = InterlockedDecrement(&dwRefCount);
            if(l == 0)
                  delete this;
            return l;
      }
      ULONG STDMETHODCALLTYPE AddRef()
      {
            ULONG l = InterlockedIncrement(&dwRefCount);
            return l;
      }
};
CVideoSinkDlg::CVideoSinkDlg(CWnd* pParent /*=NULL*/)
      : CDialog(CVideoSinkDlg::IDD, pParent)
{
      //{{AFX_DATA_INIT(CVideoSinkDlg)
      //}}AFX_DATA_INIT
      // Note that LoadIcon does not require a subsequent DestroyIcon in Win32
      m_hIcon = AfxGetApp()->LoadIcon(IDR_MAINFRAME);
      m_pTAPI             = NULL;
      m_pBCall            = NULL;
      m_pVideoWindow      = NULL;
}
void CVideoSinkDlg::DoDataExchange(CDataExchange* pDX)
{
      CDialog::DoDataExchange(pDX);
      //{{AFX_DATA_MAP(CVideoSinkDlg)
      //}}AFX_DATA_MAP
}
BEGIN_MESSAGE_MAP(CVideoSinkDlg, CDialog)
      //{{AFX_MSG_MAP(CVideoSinkDlg)
      ON_WM_PAINT()
      ON_WM_QUERYDRAGICON()
```

```
        ON_BN_CLICKED(IDC_ANSWER, OnAnswer)
        ON_WM_DESTROY()
        ON_WM_SIZING()
        ON_WM_ACTIVATE()
        ON_WM_MOVE()
        ON_WM_SYSCOMMAND()
        ON_BN_CLICKED(IDC_DISCONNECT, OnDisconnect)
        //}}AFX_MSG_MAP
END_MESSAGE_MAP()
////////////////////////////////////////////////////////////////////////////
// CVideoSinkDlg message handlers
BOOL CVideoSinkDlg::OnInitDialog()
{
        CDialog::OnInitDialog();
        SetIcon(m_hIcon, TRUE);                    // Set big icon
        SetIcon(m_hIcon, FALSE);               // Set small icon
        DISABLE(IDC_ANSWER);
        DISABLE(IDC_DISCONNECT);
      SETSTATUSDATA("Waiting for call...");
        PrepareToListenForCalls();
        return TRUE;  // return TRUE  unless you set the focus to a control
}
void CVideoSinkDlg::OnPaint()
{
        if(IsIconic())
        {
                CPaintDC dc(this); // device context for painting
        SendMessage(WM_ICONERASEBKGND, (WPARAM) dc.GetSafeHdc(), 0);
                int cxIcon = GetSystemMetrics(SM_CXICON);
                int cyIcon = GetSystemMetrics(SM_CYICON);
                CRect rect;
                GetClientRect(&rect);
                int x = (rect.Width() - cxIcon + 1) / 2;
                int y = (rect.Height() - cyIcon + 1) / 2;
                dc.DrawIcon(x, y, m_hIcon);
        }
        else
        {
                CDialog::OnPaint();
        }
}
HCURSOR CVideoSinkDlg::OnQueryDragIcon()
{
        return (HCURSOR) m_hIcon;
}
void CVideoSinkDlg::OnAnswer()
{
    SETSTATUSDATA("Answering the call...");
    HRESULT            hr;
    ITCallInfo      *pCallInfo;
```

```
    ITAddress        *pAddress;
    if(NULL == m_pBCall) return;
    hr = m_pBCall->QueryInterface(__uuidof(ITCallInfo),(void**)&pCallInfo);
if(S_OK != hr)
    {
        m_pBCall->Release();
        m_pBCall = NULL;
        return ;
    }
    hr = pCallInfo->get_Address(&pAddress);
    pCallInfo->Release();
    if(S_OK != hr)
    {
        m_pBCall->Release();
        m_pBCall = NULL;
        return;
    }
    ITStreamControl * pStreamControl;
    hr = m_pBCall->QueryInterface(__uuidof(ITStreamControl),(void **)
&pStreamControl);
    if(S_OK == hr)
    {
        IEnumStream * pEnumStreams;
        hr = pStreamControl->EnumerateStreams(&pEnumStreams);
        pStreamControl->Release();
        if(S_OK == hr)
        {
            ITStream * pStream;
            while(S_OK == pEnumStreams->Next(1, &pStream, NULL))
            {
                ITTerminal * pTerminal;
                hr = CreateTerminal(pAddress,pStream,&pTerminal);
            if(S_OK == hr)
                {
                    hr = pStream->SelectTerminal(pTerminal);
                pTerminal->Release();
            }
                pStream->Release();
            }
            pEnumStreams->Release();
        }
    }
    pAddress->Release();
    hr = m_pBCall->Answer();
      if(S_OK == hr)
    {
        SETSTATUSDATA("Call Connected");
            ENABLE( IDC_DISCONNECT);
            DISABLE( IDC_ANSWER );
    }
```

```
    else
    {
        SETSTATUSDATA("Waiting for call...");
            DISABLE( IDC_ANSWER );
        AfxMessageBox("Answer failed");
    }
}
HRESULT CVideoSinkDlg::PrepareToListenForCalls()
{
CoCreateInstance(__uuidof(TAPI),NULL,CLSCTX_INPROC_SERVER,
__uuidof(ITTAPI),reinterpret_cast<void**>(&m_pTAPI));
    m_pTAPI->Initialize();
    CTAPINotifications *m_pTAPIEventNotification = new CTAPINotifications(this);
    IConnectionPointContainer    *pCPC;
    IConnectionPoint             *pCP;

    HRESULT hr = m_pTAPI->QueryInterface(__uuidof(IConnectionPointContainer)
,(void **)&pCPC);
    if(S_OK != hr) return hr;
    hr = pCPC->FindConnectionPoint(__uuidof(ITTAPIEventNotification),&pCP);
    pCPC->Release();
    if(S_OK != hr) return hr;
    hr = pCP->Advise(m_pTAPIEventNotification,&m_dwCookie);
    pCP->Release();
    m_pTAPIEventNotification->Release();
    m_pTAPI->put_EventFilter(TE_CALLNOTIFICATION | TE_CALLSTATE | TE_CALLMEDIA);
IEnumAddress *      pEnumAddress;
    ITAddress *         pAddress;
    hr = m_pTAPI->EnumerateAddresses(&pEnumAddress);
    if(S_OK != hr)
{
    SETSTATUSDATA("Couldn't not find any address to expect the calls on.");
return hr;
    }
    while(TRUE)
    {
        hr = pEnumAddress->Next(1,&pAddress,NULL);
        if(S_OK != hr) break;
            long lMediaTypes = TAPIMEDIATYPE_AUDIO;
            VARIANT_BOOL    bSupport = VARIANT_FALSE;
            ITMediaSupport * pMediaSupport;
            if(S_OK == pAddress->QueryInterface(__uuidof(ITMediaSupport),(void
**)&pMediaSupport))
        {
            pMediaSupport->QueryMediaType(TAPIMEDIATYPE_AUDIO,&bSupport);
            pMediaSupport->Release();
        }
        if(bSupport)
        {
            VARIANT_BOOL    bSupport = VARIANT_FALSE;
```

```
            ITMediaSupport * pMediaSupport;
                 if(S_OK == pAddress->
QueryInterface(__uuidof(ITMediaSupport),(void **)&pMediaSupport))
     {
                 pMediaSupport->QueryMediaType(TAPIMEDIATYPE_VIDEO,&bSupport);
pMediaSupport->Release();
                 }
            if(bSupport)
                     lMediaTypes |= TAPIMEDIATYPE_VIDEO;
                 HRESULT  hr;
                 long      lRegister;
                 hr = m_pTAPI->
RegisterCallNotifications(pAddress,VARIANT_TRUE,VARIANT_TRUE,
lMediaTypes,0,&lRegister);
        }
        pAddress->Release();
    }
    pEnumAddress->Release();
    if( S_OK != hr )
    {
        m_pTAPI->Release();
        m_pTAPI = NULL;
         return hr;
    }
      return hr;
}
HRESULT CVideoSinkDlg::CreateTerminal(
ITAddress    * pAddress,ITStream * pStream,ITTerminal ** ppTerminal)
{
    HRESULT           hr;
    long              lMediaType;
    TERMINAL_DIRECTION dir;
    hr = pStream->get_MediaType(&lMediaType);
    if(S_OK != hr) return hr;
    hr = pStream->get_Direction( &dir );
    if(S_OK != hr) return hr;
    if((lMediaType == TAPIMEDIATYPE_VIDEO) && (dir == TD_RENDER))
    {
            HRESULT hr;
            BSTR    bstrCLSID_VideoWindowTerm;
            CString szTerminalClassID("{F7438990-D6EB-11d0-82A6-00AA00B5CA1B}");
            bstrCLSID_VideoWindowTerm = szTerminalClassID.AllocSysString();
            if(bstrCLSID_VideoWindowTerm == NULL)
                 hr = E_OUTOFMEMORY;
        else
            {
                 ITTerminalSupport * pTerminalSupport;
                 hr = pAddress->QueryInterface(
__uuidof(ITTerminalSupport),(void **)&pTerminalSupport);
                 if(S_OK == hr)
```

```
                {
                        pTerminalSupport->
CreateTerminal(bstrCLSID_VideoWindowTerm,TAPIMEDIATYPE_VIDEO,
TD_RENDER,ppTerminal);
                        pTerminalSupport->Release();
                }
        }
        return hr;
}
    ITTerminalSupport * pTerminalSupport;
    hr = pAddress->QueryInterface(__uuidof(ITTerminalSupport),
(void **)&pTerminalSupport);
    if(S_OK == hr)
    {
        hr = pTerminalSupport->
GetDefaultStaticTerminal(lMediaType,dir,ppTerminal);
        pTerminalSupport->Release();
    }
    return hr;
}
HRESULT CVideoSinkDlg::TAPIEvent(TAPI_EVENT event, IDispatch *pEvent)
{
    HRESULT hr;
    switch(event)
    {
        case TE_CALLNOTIFICATION:
         {
            ITCallNotificationEvent          * pNotify;
            hr = pEvent->QueryInterface(__uuidof(ITCallNotificationEvent),
(void **)&pNotify );
            if(S_OK != hr)
                AfxMessageBox("Incoming call, but failed to get the interface");
            else
            {
                CALL_PRIVILEGE         cp;
                ITCallInfo            *pCall;
                hr = pNotify->get_Call( &pCall );
                pNotify->Release();
                if(S_OK == hr)
                {
                    hr = pCall->get_Privilege( &cp );
                    if((S_OK != hr) || (CP_OWNER != cp))
                    {
                        pCall->Release();
                        pEvent->Release();
                        return S_OK;
                    }
                    hr = pCall->
QueryInterface(__uuidof(ITBasicCallControl),(void**)&m_pBCall );
                    pCall->Release();
```

```
                    if(S_OK == hr)
                    {
                                ENABLE( IDC_ANSWER);
                DISABLE( IDC_DISCONNECT);
                    SETSTATUSDATA("Incoming Owner Call");
                    }
                }
            }
        break;
    }
    case TE_CALLSTATE:
    {
        CALL_STATE          cs;
        ITCallStateEvent * pCallStateEvent;
        hr = pEvent->QueryInterface( __uuidof(ITCallStateEvent),
(void **)&pCallStateEvent );
        if(S_OK != hr) break;
        hr = pCallStateEvent->get_State( &cs );
        pCallStateEvent->Release();
        if(S_OK != hr) break;
        if(CS_OFFERING == cs)
        {
            SETSTATUSDATA("Click the Answer button.");
        }
        else if(CS_DISCONNECTED == cs)
        {
            if(NULL != m_pBCall)
            {
                m_pBCall->Release();
                m_pBCall = NULL;
            }
                ENABLE( IDOK);
            DISABLE( IDC_DISCONNECT        );
            SetDlgItemText(IDC_STATUS,"Waiting for a call...");
        }
        break;
    }
    case TE_CALLMEDIA:
    {
        CALL_MEDIA_EVENT        cme;
        ITCallMediaEvent        *pCallMediaEvent;
        hr = pEvent->QueryInterface( __uuidof(ITCallMediaEvent),
(void **)&pCallMediaEvent );
        if(S_OK != hr) break;
        hr = pCallMediaEvent->get_Event( &cme );
        if(S_OK == hr)
        {
            switch (cme)
            {
            case CME_STREAM_NOT_USED:
```

```
                    case CME_STREAM_INACTIVE:
                    case CME_NEW_STREAM:
                        break;
                     case CME_STREAM_FAIL:
                        AfxMessageBox("Call media event: stream failed");
                        break;
                      case CME_TERMINAL_FAIL:
                        AfxMessageBox("Call media event: terminal failed");
            break;
                    case CME_STREAM_ACTIVE:
                        {
                                HRESULT hr;
                                ITTerminal * pTerminal;
                                ITStream * pStream;
                                    hr = pCallMediaEvent->get_Stream( &pStream );
if((S_OK != hr) || (pStream == NULL)) break;
                                long lMediaType;
                                hr = pStream->get_MediaType(&lMediaType);
                    if(S_OK != hr) break;
                                if(lMediaType != TAPIMEDIATYPE_VIDEO) break;
                                TERMINAL_DIRECTION td;
                                IEnumTerminal * pEnumTerminal;
hr = pStream->EnumerateTerminals( &pEnumTerminal );
                                pStream->Release();
                    if(S_OK != hr) break;
                                while(S_OK == pEnumTerminal->
Next(1,&pTerminal,NULL))
                                {
                                if(S_OK == pTerminal->get_Direction(&td))
        {
                                        if(td == TD_RENDER)
                                        {
                                            pEnumTerminal->Release();
                                            hr = S_OK;
                                            break;
                                        }
                                }
                                pTerminal->Release();
                                }
                                if(S_OK == hr)
                    {
                                        hr = pTerminal->
QueryInterface( __uuidof(IVideoWindow), (void**)&m_pVideoWindow );
                        pTerminal->Release();
                                    if(S_OK == hr)
                    {
                                SetUpVideoWindow();
                                        m_pVideoWindow->Release();
                    }
                    }
```

```
                                else
                                        pEnumTerminal->Release();
                                break;
                        }
                    }
                }
                pCallMediaEvent->Release();
                break;
            }
        }
    pEvent->Release();
    return S_OK;
}
void CVideoSinkDlg::SetUpVideoWindow()
{
    RECT rc;
    GetClientRect(&rc);
    m_pVideoWindow->put_Owner((LONG_PTR)m_hWnd);
    m_pVideoWindow->put_WindowStyle(WS_CHILDWINDOW | WS_BORDER);
    m_pVideoWindow->SetWindowPosition( PADDING, U_MARGIN + PADDING,
    (rc.right-(rc.left+PADDING+PADDING)),
                (rc.bottom-(rc.top + U_MARGIN +PADDING+PADDING)) );
 m_pVideoWindow->put_Visible( VARIANT_TRUE );
}
void CVideoSinkDlg::OnDestroy()
{
    CDialog::OnDestroy();
    if(NULL != m_pVideoWindow)
{
    m_pVideoWindow->Release();
            m_pVideoWindow = NULL;
        }
    if(NULL != m_pBCall)
    {
        m_pBCall->Disconnect(DC_NORMAL);
        m_pBCall->Release();
        m_pBCall = NULL;
    }
    if(NULL != m_pTAPI)
    {
        m_pTAPI->Shutdown();
        m_pTAPI->Release();
            m_pTAPI = NULL;
    }
}
void CVideoSinkDlg::OnSizing(UINT fwSide, LPRECT pRect)
{
    if(!(fwSide == WMSZ_BOTTOMRIGHT || fwSide == WMSZ_RIGHT
|| fwSide == WMSZ_BOTTOM))
    {
```

```
                if((pRect->right - pRect->left) < 353)
                        pRect->left = lastRect.left;
                if((pRect->bottom - pRect->top) < 375)
                        pRect->top = lastRect.top;
        }
        else
        {
                if((pRect->right - pRect->left) < 353)
                        pRect->right = pRect->left + 353;
                if((pRect->bottom - pRect->top) < 375)
                        pRect->bottom = pRect->top + 375;
        }
        CDialog::OnSizing(fwSide, pRect);
        if(m_pVideoWindow != NULL)
{
                RECT rc;
                GetClientRect(&rc);
                m_pVideoWindow->SetWindowPosition( PADDING, U_MARGIN + PADDING,
                    (rc.right-(rc.left+PADDING+PADDING)),
                            (rc.bottom-(rc.top + U_MARGIN +PADDING+PADDING)) );
m_pVideoWindow->put_Visible( VARIANT_TRUE );
        }
}
void CVideoSinkDlg::OnActivate(UINT nState, CWnd* pWndOther, BOOL bMinimized)
{
        CDialog::OnActivate(nState, pWndOther, bMinimized);
        GetWindowRect(&lastRect);
}
void CVideoSinkDlg::OnMove(int x, int y)
{
        CDialog::OnMove(x, y);
        GetWindowRect(&lastRect);
}
void CVideoSinkDlg::OnDisconnect()
{
        SETSTATUSDATA("Disconnecting the Call...");
        HRESULT          hr = S_FALSE;
     if(NULL != m_pBCall)
        hr = m_pBCall->Disconnect(DC_NORMAL);
     if (S_OK != hr)
            AfxMessageBox("Disconnect failed");
}
```

Source Code Explanation for VideoSinkDlg.cpp

The code for VideoSink begins with the inclusion of various header files followed by various preprocessor declarations and function macro declarations for enabling and disabling buttons and for updating the status panel. The lines of code that immediately follow declare a global variable and various constant declarations to help place and resize the video window.

```
RECT lastRect;
const int U_MARGIN = 80;
const int PADDING = 10;
```

We implement ITTAPIEventNotification here, which is an outgoing interface that is supposed to be implemented in all applications that need to intercept various TAPI events in the course of a call session. TAPI calls the Event method of ITTAPIEventNotification in response to events related to call states, media status, and so on.

In addition to the IUnknown methods that we implement because the ITTAPIEventNotification interface is derived from IUnknown, we implement the Event method of this interface. The implementation of the Event method has code lines that call AddRef on the IDispatch object associated with the events that are passed to this method, to make the method stay and keep it from being disposed. After this, we call the TAPIEvent function of the main dialog class, which is implemented to intercept the TAPI events to various call and media statuses.

```
pEvent->AddRef();
pVideoSinkDlg->TAPIEvent(event,pEvent);
```

To enable our application to listen to incoming calls, we make a call to PrepareToListenForCalls of the main dialog class. Furthermore, to make the application start looking for incoming calls as soon as it gets instantiated, we make a call to PrepareToListenForCalls function in OnInitDialog function, which is the event handler of the WM_INITDIALOG message for the main dialog window.

In the PrepareToListenForCalls function, we instantiate the TAPI object and call the Initialize method of its ITTAPI interface to initialize a TAPI session.

```
CoCreateInstance(__uuidof(TAPI),NULL,CLSCTX_INPROC_SERVER,
__uuidof(ITTAPI),reinterpret_cast<void**>(&m_pTAPI));
    m_pTAPI->Initialize();
```

We then follow the standard connection-point procedure to set a connection between the connection point implemented by the TAPI object and the application's sink, which in our case is the object of the CTAPINotifications class. To get all the required TAPI notifications in our application, we need to tell TAPI the types of events we are interested in.

```
m_pTAPI->put_EventFilter(TE_CALLNOTIFICATION | TE_CALLSTATE | TE_CALLMEDIA);
```

The put_EventFilter method, as the name suggests, specifies the event types we would like to have notifications for. A call to this method is mandatory to enable your application to receive any event notification in your application.

Now we have to search for resources available on the system that are capable of making or receiving calls. For this, we may call EnumerateAddresses on the TAPI object, which returns a pointer to IEnumAddress. This interface can be used to enumerate the Address objects for all the resources available on the system.

```
hr = m_pTAPI->EnumerateAddresses(&pEnumAddress);
.
.
.
hr = pEnumAddress->Next(1,&pAddress,NULL);
```

These addresses can be scrutinized for their media capabilities by querying for the ITMediaSupport object and calling the QueryMediaType method of this object.

```
long lMediaTypes = TAPIMEDIATYPE_AUDIO;
VARIANT_BOOL     bSupport = VARIANT_FALSE;
ITMediaSupport * pMediaSupport;
if(S_OK == pAddress->QueryInterface(__uuidof(ITMediaSupport),
(void **)&pMediaSupport))
            {
                pMediaSupport->QueryMediaType(TAPIMEDIATYPE_AUDIO,&bSupport);
                pMediaSupport->Release();
            }
```

We query all the addresses and register our application by calling the RegisterCallNotifications method of the TAPI object, to receive new call notifications on the address that supports both audio and video. We call this method with VARIANT_TRUE as its third argument to signify that we want owner privileges on the incoming calls to be able to answer the calls later on.

```
hr = m_pTAPI->RegisterCallNotifications(
pAddress,VARIANT_TRUE,VARIANT_TRUE,lMediaTypes,0,&lRegister);
```

With this, we have finished the work of setting our application to listen to incoming calls. Now we wait until we receive the TE_CALLNOTIFICATION notification. This notification implies that a new communication session has arrived at the address we registered to receive calls on, which means that a new Call object has been created. To access this Call object, first we query the ITCallNotificationEvent interface from the object associated with this notification and then the query ITCallInfo interface of the Call object from this interface.

```
        case TE_CALLNOTIFICATION:
        {
            ITCallNotificationEvent          * pNotify;
            hr =
pEvent->QueryInterface(__uuidof(ITCallNotificationEvent),
(void **)&pNotify );
                ITCallInfo             *pCall;
                hr = pNotify->get_Call( &pCall );
                pNotify->Release();
```

Now let's check whether we possess the owner privileges for this call.

```
if(S_OK == hr)
{
    hr = pCall->get_Privilege( &cp );
    if((S_OK != hr) || (CP_OWNER != cp))
    {
        pCall->Release();
        pEvent->Release();
        return S_OK;
    }
}
```

If we have owner privileges, we query the ITBasicCallControl interface from the ITCallInfo interface for answering the call.

```
                    hr = pCall->QueryInterface(
__uuidof(ITBasicCallControl),(void**)&m_pBCall );
```

The TE_CALLNOTIFICATION is followed by the TE_CALLSTATE notification. On receiving this notification, we query the ITCallStateEvent interface and call its get_State method to determine the state of the new call.

```
    case TE_CALLSTATE:
    {
        CALL_STATE          cs;
        ITCallStateEvent * pCallStateEvent;
        hr = pEvent->QueryInterface( __uuidof(ITCallStateEvent),
(void **)&pCallStateEvent );
        hr = pCallStateEvent->get_State( &cs );
```

If the state is CS_OFFERING, it signifies that the new call is being handed to the application and that this call can be answered if the application possesses owner privileges on this call. In this case, we prompt the user to answer the call.

```
if(CS_OFFERING == cs)
{
SETSTATUSDATA("Click the Answer button.");
```

Now let's see what happens when the user clicks the Answer button. The OnAnswer function of the main dialog class first retrieves the Address object on which this call has arrived. It does that by querying ITCallInfo of the Call object, on which it calls the get_Address method to get the pointer to the ITAddress interface of the Address object.

```
ITCallInfo      *pCallInfo;
ITAddress       *pAddress;
    .
    .
```

```
hr = m_pBCall->QueryInterface(__uuidof(ITCallInfo),(void**)&pCallInfo);
.
hr = pCallInfo->get_Address(&pAddress);
```

This function next queries the ITStreamControl interface and enumerates the available media streams by calling the EnumerateStreams method on it.

All the streams will be checked for their directions and the type of media they are carrying. For the stream with the direction TD_RENDER and media type TAPIMEDIATYPE_VIDEO, we create a video-rendered terminal and select it for the stream. For the rest of the streams, we select the default static terminals, as we did earlier for the VideoSource application. The terminals are selected on the streams by calling SelectTerminal on the IStream interface. Now we may call the Answer method on the pointer of the ITBasicCallControl interface of the Call object that we received with the TE_CALLNOTIFICATION notification.

```
hr = m_pBCall->Answer();
```

With this the call gets connected and the application has to wait to receive notifications pertaining to media-related activities on the call. The rest of the work is done only after receiving the TE_CALLMEDIA notification. We query ITCallMediaEvent and call its get_Event method to determine the type of media event that occurred.

```
hr = pEvent->QueryInterface( __uuidof(ITCallMediaEvent),
(void **)&pCallMediaEvent );
.
.
hr = pCallMediaEvent->get_Event( &cme );
{
//If it happens to be CME_STREAM_ACTIVE we'd call its get_Stream method to obtain
//ITStream interface pointer.
case CME_STREAM_ACTIVE:
{
hr = pCallMediaEvent->get_Stream( &pStream );
```

We call get_MediaType method on this pointer to get the type of media this stream is carrying. Before moving ahead, we must make sure that the media stream is of type TAPIMEDIATYPE_VIDEO.

```
hr = pStream->get_MediaType(&lMediaType);
```

We now enumerate all the terminals on this stream by calling the EnumerateTerminals method on this pointer and finding the terminal with a media stream that has TD_RENDER as its direction.

```
.
.
if(lMediaType != TAPIMEDIATYPE_VIDEO) break;
TERMINAL_DIRECTION td;
IEnumTerminal * pEnumTerminal;
```

```
hr = pStream->EnumerateTerminals( &pEnumTerminal );
.
.
if(td == TD_RENDER)
{
pEnumTerminal->Release();
hr = S_OK;
```

For this terminal, we query the IVideoWindow interface.

```
hr = pTerminal->QueryInterface( __uuidof(IVideoWindow),
(void**)&m_pVideoWindow );
```

We call various methods for specifying its parent window and setting its position on the parent window before calling its put_Visible method so as to make it visible.

```
m_pVideoWindow->put_Visible( VARIANT_TRUE );
```

Executing the Program

If you want to execute VideoSource and VideoSink, open the project files of the software in the VC++ environment and build the programs. Next, ship one of the programs to a different Windows 2000 machine on your LAN environment. Start VideoSink and VideoSource applications on two different machines. (The system on which VideoSource application is running must have a camera installed on it.) The VideoSource application must display the status "TAPI Initialized," as shown in Figure 11-7.

The VideoSink application must display the status "Waiting for call," as shown in Figure 11-8.

In the VideoSource application, choose IP Address in the Address Types list and enter the IP address of the machine where the VideoSink application is running. Next, click the Dial button. The VideoSource application displays the status "Call Connected," as shown in Figure 11-9.

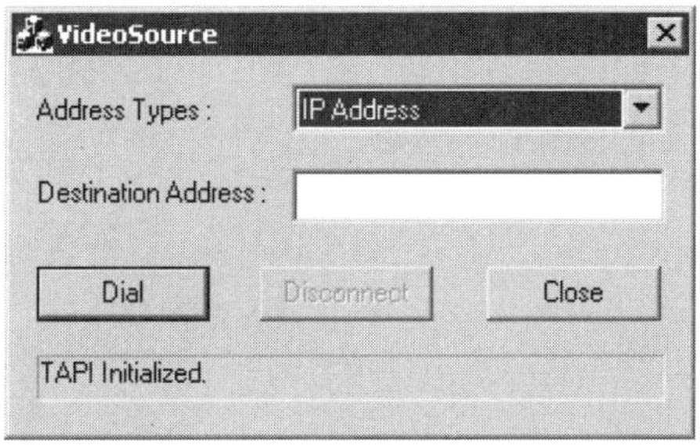

Figure 11-7   *VideoSource application*

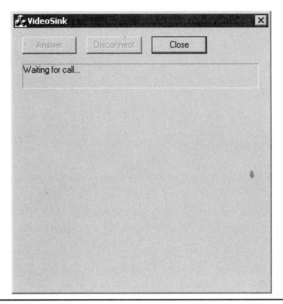

Figure 11-8   *VideoSink application*

The VideoSource application should show the status "Click the Answer button," which signifies that a new call has arrived at its end. The Answer button is enabled too, as shown in Figure 11-10.

Click the Answer button to receive the call. The resulting output is shown in Figure 11-11.

The status should now be "Call Connected" and a video panel should appear in the window running the video that is being captured at VideoSource's end. At this point, the Disconnect button is enabled, giving the user the choice to disconnect the call at any moment provided it doesn't get disconnected from the VideoSource's end earlier.

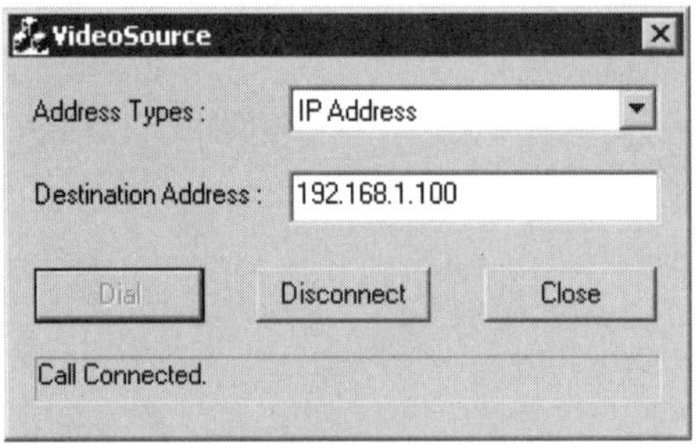

Figure 11-9   *VideoSource application dialing an IP address*

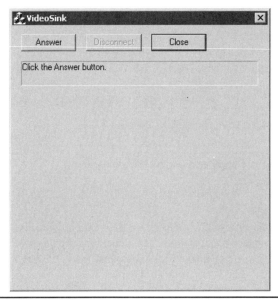

Figure 11-10   *VideoSink application gets the notification of the call.*

Figure 11-11   *VideoSink application answers the call and a video stream is set up between the two applications.*

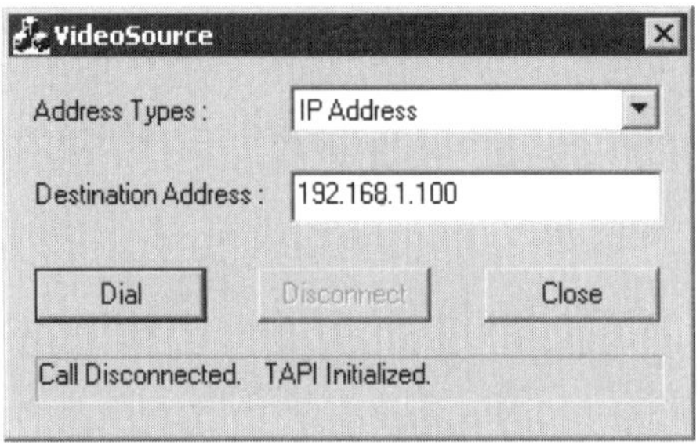

Figure 11-12 *VideoSource application disconnecting the call*

The ongoing call session can now be brought to an end by clicking the Disconnect button of either of the two applications. Remember that disconnecting the call from VideoSink's end will not notify VideoSource of the disengagement, as we have not implemented any notification receiver for the VideoSource application. Because we have implemented the notification receiver interface for the VideoSink application, disconnecting the call from VideoSource will certainly give VideoSink a notification, and VideoSink will release the video panel it created and resume waiting for calls once again. VideoSource, on the other hand, would show the status "Call Disconnected. TAPI Initialized." to indicate that although the ongoing call has been disconnected, TAPI is still ready to allow users to make calls, as shown in Figure 11-12 above.

Summary

This chapter endeavored to take you a step closer to being a part of the revolution known as IP telephony. We discussed how computer and telephony networks walking hand in hand opened myriad avenues for a new array of applications and services in the field of communication. You saw how various organizations realized the potential of this merger, and strove to implement various standards and regulations to make these two networks work together harmoniously. We also discussed a modest application of this merger of technologies, which has great prospects for popular use in the future.

CHAPTER 2

Developing a Voice-based Shopping Mall with ASP

I n this chapter, we develop a voice-based shopping mall application using Active Server Pages (ASP) and VoiceXML. This application is designed to provide the facility of a web-based shopping mall over the telephony network. Users can buy various goods by accessing the application using the telephony device and selecting from a variety of categories. This case study will help you to understand how ASP pages are used in VoiceXML-based applications for such complex processes as dynamic generation of VoiceXML forms and menus.

Working Scheme of the Application

Let's outline the working scheme of the application we intend to develop. In this application, the user first logs on to the system by submitting a user ID and password. On the basis of this information, the system authenticates the user. If the user's credentials are verified successfully, the application starts by prompting available options to the user and waits for the user to respond.

In the next phase, the user receives a list of categories and upon selection of a particular category from the list, the user is prompted with the items available under that category. At this stage, the user can either purchase the item or revoke the order. In the former case, the order is to be confirmed by the user, after which the records are updated. In the latter case, the application is terminated.

The complete process is represented in the flowchart in Figure 12-1.

Building the Home Page

Preparing the home page is the first step towards developing any VoiceXML-based application. As soon as the user accesses the application, the home page provides two choices: either logging on to the system to proceed further or terminating the session by choosing the exit option.

Listing 12-1 shows the source code for shopping.asp, which works as the home page of our application.

Listing 12-1: *Source Code for shopping.asp*

```
<%@ Language=VBScript %>
<%
     Response.ContentType = "text/xml"
          Response.Write("<?xml version= ""1.0""?>")
%>
   <vxml version="1.0">
     <link next="http://localhost/shopping.asp">
          <grammar type="application/x-gsl">
          shopping
          </grammar>
     </link>
     <menu>
```

```
<prompt>Welcome to the Voice Store</prompt>
        <prompt>Please say or press any one of the following:<enumerate/> </prompt>
        <choice dtmf="1" next="http://localhost/login.asp">login</choice>
        <choice dtmf="2" next="#exit">exit</choice>
        <help>
                To start this application again say shopping.
    </help>
        <noinput>I didn't hear anything, please say login <enumerate/></noinput>
        <nomatch> I didn't get that, please say or press again<enumerate/></nomatch>
        <catch event="nomatch noinput" count="4">
                    <prompt>You have exceeded the limits allowed for retries.
System will now stop the application.
</prompt>
                    <throw event="telephone.disconnect.hangup"/>
        </catch>
        </menu>
        <form id="exit">
            <block>
            <prompt>
                Thanks for visiting the Voice Store
            </prompt>
</block>
        </form>
 </vxml>
```

As you can see in Listing 12-1, in the very beginning of the code we have set the content type for the VoiceXML document using the Response.ContentType method:

```
<%@ Language=VBScript %>
<%
    Response.ContentType = "text/xml"
    Response.Write("<?xml version= ""1.0""?>")
%>
```

After the VoiceXML and XML version declarations, we define a <link> element for the home page. This is necessary because the home page is made to work as the root-level document for the entire application so that users can access its content from anywhere in the application by just saying the hot word "shopping."

```
<link next="http://localhost/shopping.asp">
    <grammar type="application/x-gsl">
            shopping
    </grammar>
</link>
<menu>
```

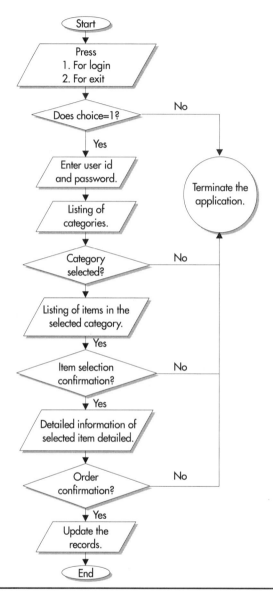

Figure 12-1   *Flowchart of Voice Store application*

Figure 12-2 shows the output of shopping.asp.

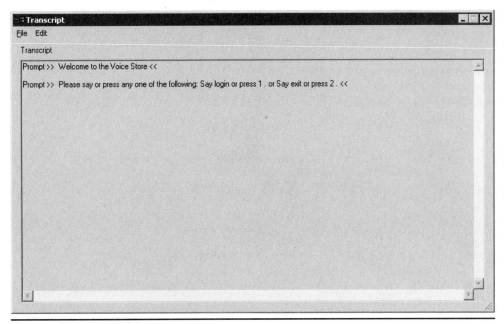

Figure 12-2   *Output of shopping.asp*

Preparing the Login Section

If the user selects the login option in the home page, the control is transferred to the login.asp file, which handles the login section of the application. The login section accepts the user id and password in the form of numbers and transfers this information to the server. Listing 12-2 shows the code for the login.asp file.

Listing 12-2:   *Source Code for login.asp*

```
<%@ Language=VBScript %>
<%
            Response.ContentType = "text/vxml"
            Response.Write("<?xml version= ""1.0""?>")
%>
<vxml version="1.0" application = "http://localhost/shopping.asp" >
    <var name="userid"/>
    <var name="pass"/>
<form id="user">
      <field name="userid" type="digits">
        <prompt>Please enter your user id</prompt>
```

```
            <filled>
                <assign name="document.userid" expr="userid"/>
                <goto next="#pass"/>
            </filled>
        </field>
</form>
<form id="pass">
    <field name="pass" type="digits">
            <prompt> Please enter your password </prompt>
        <filled>
                        <assign name="document.pass" expr="pass"/>
            <goto next="#password"/>
                </filled>
    </field>
</form>
<form id="password">
 <block>
    <var name="loginname"  expr="document.userid"/>
    <var name="password" expr="document.pass"/>
    <submit next="http://localhost/browse.asp" method="get" namelist="loginname
password "/>
 </block>
</form>
 </vxml>
```

Figure 12-3 shows the output for this code.

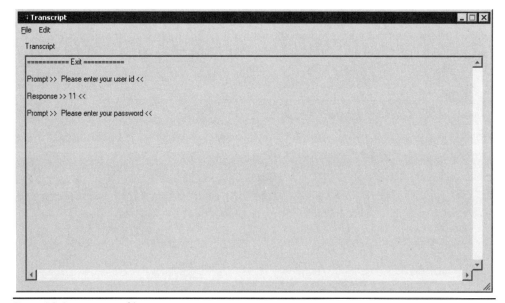

Figure 12-3   *Output of login.asp*

User Authentication and Building the Category Section

This section consists of two parts: the first one for the user authentication process and the second for controlling further proceedings once the user is successfully authenticated. The file named browse.asp, shown in Listing 12-3, contains the code for both processes.

Listing 12-3: *Source Code for browse.asp*

```
<%@LANGUAGE=VBSCRIPT %>
<%
dim uname,pwd
uname = trim(Request.QueryString("loginname"))
pwd = trim(Request.QueryString("password"))
Response.ContentType = "text/xml"
Response.Write("<?xml version= ""1.0""?>")
%>
<vxml version="1.0">
<form>
<block>
<%
     Dim con, rs, rs1
     set con = Server.CreateObject("ADODB.Connection")
     con.open ("shop")
     set rs = con.Execute("SELECT userid, name, address  FROM customer WHERE
userid =" & uname & "")
          if rs(0) > 0 then
               set rs1 = con.Execute("SELECT Count(password) FROM customer
WHERE userid =" & uname & " AND  password =" & pwd & "")
                    if rs1(0) > 0 then
               Response.Write("<goto next=""#browse""/>")
                    else
                    Response.Write("<prompt>Invalid password, please log
in again</prompt>")
                         Response.Write("
<goto next=""http://localhost/login.asp""/>")
                    End if
          else
               Response.Write("<prompt>Invalid user name, please log
in again</prompt>")
                    Response.Write("<goto next=""http://localhost/login.asp""/>")
          End If
%>
</block>
</form>
<menu id="browse">
<%
          Response.Write("<prompt> Welcome " & rs("name") & " </prompt>")
%>
```

```
    <prompt>Please say or press any one of the
following categories:<enumerate/> </prompt>
     <%
     set rs = con.Execute("SELECT DISTINCT(category) FROM item ")
     dim number
     number = 1
     Do Until rs.EOF
     Response.Write("<choice dtmf="""& (number) & """ next=""#" & rs("category")
 & """ >  " & rs("category") & " </choice>")
     rs.MoveNext
     number=number+1
     Loop
     Response.Write("<choice dtmf="""& (number) & "
"" next=""http://localhost/shopping.asp#exit"">exit</choice>")
     rs.movefirst
     %>
     <help>
           Please choose one of the available categories.
   </help>
     <noinput>I didn't hear anything please say or press
again <enumerate/></noinput>
     <nomatch> I didn't get that, please say or press
 again<enumerate/></nomatch>
<catch event="nomatch noinput" count="4">
                <prompt>You have exceeded the limits allowed for retries. System
 will now stop the application.</prompt>
                <throw event="telephone.disconnect.hangup"/>
     </catch>
     </menu>
 <%
     set rs = con.Execute("SELECT DISTINCT(category) FROM item ")
     Do Until rs.EOF
          Response.Write("<form id=""  " & rs("category") & " "">")
          Response.Write("<block>")
          Response.Write("<var name = ""cat"" expr = ""'" & rs("category")
& "'"  />")
          Response.Write("<var name = ""uname"" expr = """ & (uname) & """  />")
          Response.Write("<submit next=""http://localhost/
items.asp"" method=""get"" namelist=""cat uname ""/>" )
          Response.Write("</block>")
          Response.Write("</form>")
     rs.MoveNext
     Loop
     rs.close
     %>
</vxml>
```

As evident from the code, in the first part, we authenticate the user on the basis of the information received from login.asp. We store this information and then start the <vxml> coding, as shown in the code snippet that follows:

```
dim uname,pwd
uname = trim(Request.QueryString("loginname"))
pwd = trim(Request.QueryString("password"))
Response.ContentType = "text/xml"
Response.Write("<?xml version= ""1.0""?>")
%>
<vxml version="1.0">
<form>
<block>
```

In the next step, we authenticate the user by opening a database connection and selecting
the user id and password from the customer table on the basis of the information we have in the
variables. We first verify the validity of the user id. If the user id provided by the user is
found in our database, we move on to selecting the password from the customer table and
checking its validity. If either of these entries is invalid, the user receives the relevant error
message and the home page of the application is loaded again.

If the password provided by the user is found to be associated with the user id provided,
we move on to the next stage of the application, which is building the category information.
Otherwise, an error message is prompted to the user and the home page of the application is
loaded again. The code snippet for this task is shown here:

```
<%
    Dim con, rs, rs1
    set con = Server.CreateObject("ADODB.Connection")
    con.open ("shop")
    set rs = con.Execute("SELECT userid, name, address  FROM customer WHERE
userid =" & uname & "")
            if rs(0) > 0 then
                    set rs1 = con.Execute("SELECT Count(password) FROM customer
WHERE userid =" & uname & " AND  password =" & pwd & "")
                        if rs1(0) > 0 then
                                Response.Write("<goto next=""#browse""/>")
                        else
                                Response.Write("<prompt>Invalid password, please log
in again</prompt>")
                        Response.Write("<goto
next=""http://localhost/login.asp""/>")
                        End if
            else
                    Response.Write("<prompt>Invalid user name, please log in
again</prompt>")
                    Response.Write("<goto next=""http://localhost/login.asp""/>")
End If
%>
```

After the authentication process, we prompt the user with all the categories available
in our database. The user can select any one of the categories to listen to the list of items
available for that category.

For prompting all the available categories, we include a select query, which will select all the available categories in the item table. To block repetition, we use the DISTINCT keyword in the query. After selecting the records from the table, we specify a looping condition for building a menu-based interface for prompting the categories.

Every <choice> element in the menu we generate dynamically points to a form in the document. These forms are also generated dynamically on the basis of the information regarding the categories that we retrieve from the database. The code snippet shown here is for generating the forms dynamically:

```
<%
    set rs = con.Execute("SELECT DISTINCT(category) FROM item ")
    Do Until rs.EOF
        Response.Write("<form id=""  " & rs("category") & " "">")
        Response.Write("<block>")
        Response.Write("<var name = ""cat"" expr = ""
'" & rs("category") & "'"  />")
        Response.Write("<var name = ""uname"" expr = """ & (uname) & """  />")
        Response.Write("<submit next=""http://localhost/
items.asp"" method=""get"" namelist=""cat uname ""/>" )
        Response.Write("</block>")
        Response.Write("</form>")
    rs.MoveNext
    Loop
    rs.close
    %>
```

As seen in the preceding code, the ID attribute of forms contains a dynamic value retrieved from the database. When the user selects a category from the menu, the relevant form is called for processing. In the form, we declare two VoiceXML variables named "uname" and "cat" and assign them the value for the selected category and the user id, respectively.

In the next step, we call the file named items.asp for building the list of items available in the selected category. For this task, we use the <submit> element and pass the values of "uname" and "cat" to items.asp by using the namelist attribute.

Listing 12-4 shows the VoiceXML output generated by browse.asp on execution.

Listing 12-4: *Output of browse.asp*

```
<?xml version = "1.0"?>
<vxml version = "1.0">
    <form>
        <block>
            <goto next = "#browse" />
        </block>
    </form>
    <menu id = "browse">
        <prompt>
            Welcome Charul Shukla
```

```
            </prompt>
            <prompt>
                    Please say or press any one of the following categories:
                    <enumerate />
            </prompt>
            <choice dtmf = "1" next = "#computers">
                    computers
            </choice>
            <choice dtmf = "2" next = "#food">
                    food
            </choice>
            <choice dtmf = "3" next = "http://localhost/shopping.asp#exit">
                    exit
            </choice>
            <help>
                    Please choose one of the available categories.
            </help>
            <noinput>
                    I didn't hear anything, please say or type again
                    <enumerate />
            </noinput>
            <nomatch>
                    I didn't get that, please say or type again
                    <enumerate />
            </nomatch>
            <catch count = "4" event = "nomatch noinput">
                    <prompt>
                            You have exceeded the limits allowed for
retries. System will now stop the application.
                    </prompt>
                    <throw event = "telephone.disconnect.hangup" />
            </catch>
        </menu>
        <form id = "computers">
            <block>
                    <var expr = "'computers'" name = "cat" />
                    <var expr = "11" name = "uname" />
                    <submit next = "http://localhost/
items.asp" method = "get" namelist = "cat uname" />
            </block>
        </form>
        <form id = "food">
            <block>
                    <var expr = "'food'" name = "cat" />
                    <var expr = "11" name = "uname" />
                    <submit next = "http://localhost/items.asp" method = "get"
namelist = "cat uname" />
            </block>
        </form>
</vxml>
```

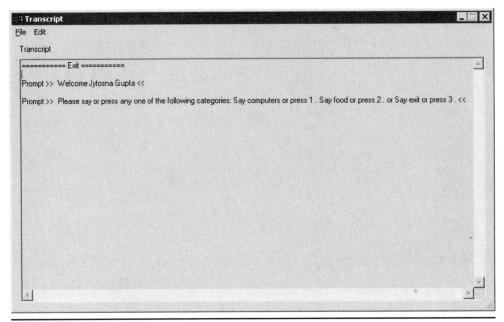

Figure 12-4   *Output of browse.asp*

Figure 12-4 shows the output generated by browse.asp in a simulator.

Building the Items List

In this section, we examine how the list of items in the category selected by the user is built by retrieving the items list from the database. The file named items.asp is responsible for controlling this process. Listing 12-5 shows the source code of items.

Listing 12-5:   *Source Code for items.asp*

```
<%@LANGUAGE=VBSCRIPT %>
<%
dim choose,username
choose = trim(Request.QueryString("cat"))
username = trim(Request.QueryString("uname"))
Response.ContentType = "text/xml"
Response.Write("<?xml version= ""1.0""?>")
%>
<vxml version="1.0">
<menu id="listing">
<%
```

```
Response.Write("<prompt>Please say or press any one of the following items
 available under the " & choose &" category <enumerate/> </prompt>")
Dim con, rs
      set con = Server.CreateObject("ADODB.Connection")
      con.open ("shop")
      set rs = con.Execute("SELECT name FROM item WHERE category='" & choose & "'
 AND availables='yes'")
      dim number
      number = 1
      Do Until rs.EOF
      Response.Write("<choice dtmf="""& (number) & """
next=""#" & rs("name") & """ >  " & rs("name") & " </choice>")
      rs.MoveNext
      number=number+1
      Loop
      Response.Write("<choice dtmf="""& (number) & """
next=""http://localhost/shopping.asp#exit"">exit</choice>")
      rs.movefirst
      %>
</menu >
       <%
      set rs = con.Execute("SELECT name,price FROM item
WHERE category='" & choose & "'AND availables='yes'")
      Do Until rs.EOF
            Response.Write("<form id=""  " & rs("name") & " "">")
Response.Write("<field name = ""select"" type = ""boolean"">")
            Response.Write("<prompt>You have selected
" & rs("name") & " </prompt>")
            Response.Write("<prompt>This is priced
" & rs("price") & " dollars </prompt>")
            Response.Write("<prompt>To purchase this item say yes,
otherwise say no</prompt>")
            Response.Write("<filled>")
                        Response.Write("<if cond=""select==true"">")
                        Response.Write("<var name = ""item""
expr = ""'" & rs("name") & "'""  />")
                        Response.Write("<var name = ""uname""
expr = """ & (username) & """  />")
                        Response.Write("<submit
next=""http://localhost/confirm.asp""
method=""get"" namelist="" item uname""/>" )
                        Response.Write("<else/>")
                        Response.Write("
<submit next=""http://localhost/shopping.asp#exit"" />" )
            Response.Write("</if >")
            Response.Write("</filled>")
            Response.Write("</field>")
      Response.Write("</form>")
      rs.MoveNext
      Loop
```

```
      rs.close
      %>
</vxml>
```

In this code, we first store the information received from the query string in the variables for later use. Following this, we start the VoiceXML coding for building the interface. For listing the available items, we use a menu-based interface, because such an interface is convenient for users of the application.

For generating the list of items, we select all the items available in the category selected by the user and then specify a looping condition to build a series of <choice> elements for all the items. The code snippet for this task is as follows:

```
<%
Response.Write("<prompt>Please say or press any one
of the following items available under
the " & choose &" category <enumerate/> </prompt>")
      Dim con, rs
      set con = Server.CreateObject("ADODB.Connection")
      con.open ("shop")
      set rs = con.Execute("SELECT name FROM item
WHERE category='" & choose & "' AND availables='yes'")
      dim number
      number = 1
      Do Until rs.EOF
      Response.Write("<choice dtmf="""& (number) & """
next=""#" & rs("name") & """ >  " & rs("name") & " </choice>")
      rs.MoveNext
      number=number+1
      Loop
      Response.Write("<choice dtmf="""& (number) & """
next=""http://localhost/shopping.asp#exit"">
exit</choice>")
      rs.movefirst
      %>
```

In the next phase, we build forms dynamically for all the available items. Here, we inform the user of the item selected as well as its price for the user to confirm the purchase. In these forms, we prompt the user and also declare some VoiceXML variables for holding different values such as the price of the item.

If the user says "yes" to confirm the purchase of the selected item, we check this condition by using the script and then transfer the control to the next file, named confirm.asp, to take the order from the user for further processing. The code responsible for this task is shown in the code snippet that follows:

```
<%
set rs = con.Execute("SELECT name,price FROM item
```

```
WHERE category='" & choose & "'AND availables='yes'")
     Do Until rs.EOF
            Response.Write("<form id=""  " & rs("name") & " "">")
Response.Write("<field name = ""select"" type = ""boolean"">")
     Response.Write("<prompt>You have selected " & rs("name") & " </prompt>")
            Response.Write("<prompt>This is priced
" & rs("price") & " dollars </prompt>")
            Response.Write("<prompt>To purchase this item say yes, otherwise say
 no</prompt>")
            Response.Write("<filled>")
                        Response.Write("<if cond=""select==true"">")
                        Response.Write("<var name = ""item""
expr = """'" & rs("name") & "'"" />")
                        Response.Write("<var name = ""uname""
expr = """ & (username) & """ />")
                        Response.Write("<submit
next=""http://localhost/confirm.asp"" method=""get""
namelist="" item uname""/>" )
                   Response.Write("<else/>")
                        Response.Write("
<submit next=""http://localhost/shopping.asp#exit"" />" )`
                        Response.Write("</if >")
            Response.Write("</filled>")
     Response.Write("</field>")
            Response.Write("</form>")
     rs.MoveNext
     Loop
     rs.close
     %>
```

The VoiceXML generated by items.asp is shown in Listing 12-6.

Listing 12-6:   *Output of items.asp*

```
<?xml version = "1.0"?>
<vxml version = "1.0">
     <menu id = "listing">
          <prompt>
                    Please say or press any one of the
following items available under the food category
                    <enumerate />
          </prompt>
          <choice dtmf = "1" next = "#milk">
                milk
          </choice>
          <choice dtmf = "2" next = "#butter">
                butter
          </choice>
```

```
            <choice dtmf = "3" next = "#eggs">
                    eggs
            </choice>
            <choice dtmf = "4" next = "http://localhost/shopping.asp#exit">
                    exit
            </choice>
    </menu>
    <form id = "milk">
            <field name = "select" type = "boolean">
                    <prompt>
                            You have selected milk
                    </prompt>
                    <prompt>
                            This is priced 10 dollars
                    </prompt>
                    <prompt>
                            To Purchase this item say yes, otherwise no
                    </prompt>
                    <filled>
                            <if cond = "select==true">
                                    <var expr = "'milk'" name = "item" />
                                    <var expr = "11" name = "uname" />
                                    <submit next = "http://localhost/confirm.asp"
method = "get" namelist = "item uname" />
                                    <else />
                                    <submit next = "http://localhost/shopping.asp#exit"
/>
                            </if>
                    </filled>
            </field>
    </form>
    <form id = "butter">
            <field name = "select" type = "boolean">
                    <prompt>
                            You have selected butter
                    </prompt>
                    <prompt>
                            This is priced 20 dollars
                    </prompt>
                    <prompt>
                            To purchase this item say yes, otherwise say no
                    </prompt>
                    <filled>
                            <if cond = "select==true">
                                    <var expr = "'butter'" name = "item" />
                                    <var expr = "11" name = "uname" />
                                    <submit next = "http://localhost/confirm.asp" method
= "get" namelist = "item uname" />
                                    <else />
                                    <submit next = "http://localhost/shopping.asp#exit">
```

```
        </if>
                </filled>
            </field>
    </form>
    <form id = "eggs">
            <field name = "select" type = "boolean">
                <prompt>
                        You have selected eggs
                </prompt>
                <prompt>
                        This is priced 8 dollars
                </prompt>
                <prompt>
                        To purchase this item say yes, otherwise say no
                </prompt>
                <filled>
                    <if cond = "select==true">
                            <var expr = "'eggs'" name = "item" />
                            <var expr = "11" name = "uname" />
                            <submit next = "http://localhost/confirm.asp"
method = "get" namelist = "item uname" />
                            <else />
                            <submit next = "http://localhost/
shopping.asp#exit" />
                    </if>
                </filled>
            </field>
    </form>
</vxml>
```

Figure 12-5 shows the output generated by items.asp when executed on a simulator.

Collecting the Order from the User

In this stage of the application, we collect the order for the item selected by the user in terms of quantities, and after this we inform the user of the total cost for the purchase and query the user to confirm the order. The file named confirm.asp contains the code for this task.

Listing 12-7 shows the entire source code of confirm.asp.

Listing 12-7: *Source Code for confirm.asp*

```
<%@LANGUAGE=VBSCRIPT %>
<%
dim selitem,username
selitem = trim(Request.QueryString("item"))
username = trim(Request.QueryString("uname"))
Response.ContentType = "text/xml"
```

```
Response.Write("<?xml version= ""1.0""?>")
%>
<vxml version="1.0">
<var name="number"/>
<var name="price"/>
<script>
<![CDATA[
function multiply(n)
{
return number * n;
}
]]>
</script>
        <%
      Dim con, rs, rs1
      Dim price, quantity,ctdate
      ctdate= now()
      set con = Server.CreateObject("ADODB.Connection")
      con.open ("shop")
      set rs = con.Execute("SELECT name,price FROM item
WHERE name='" & selitem & "'AND availables='yes'")
            Response.Write("<form id=""  " & rs("name") & " "">")
Response.Write("<field name = ""confirm"" type =""number"">")
                      Response.Write("<prompt>Please say the
quantity of " & (selitem) & "  </prompt>")
                            Response.Write("<filled>")
                                Response.Write("
<assign name = ""document.number"" expr = ""confirm""  />")
                  Response.Write("<assign name = ""document.price""
expr = "" " & rs("price") &" ""  />")
                                Response.Write("<submit
next=""#final"" method= ""get"" namelist=""number price""/>" )
                  Response.Write("</filled>")
            Response.Write("</field>")
            Response.Write("</form>")
      rs.close
      %>
       <%
            set rs = con.Execute("SELECT name, address  FROM customer
WHERE userid= " & username & "")
      Response.Write("<form id=""  final "">")
                        Response.Write("<field name = ""select"" type =
""boolean"">")
                  Response.Write("<prompt>You have ordered <value
expr=""number""/> quantities of  " & (selitem) & " </prompt>")
                        Response.Write("<prompt>The total cost
is<value expr
 = ""multiply(price)"" /> </prompt>")
                        Response.Write("<prompt>The order will be
shipped to the following address: </prompt>")
```

```
                    Response.Write("<prompt> " & rs("name") & " " &
rs("address") & " " & username &" </prompt>")
            Response.Write("<prompt> Say yes to confirm the
order, otherwise say no</prompt>")
            Response.Write("<filled>")
                    Response.Write("<if cond=""select==true"">")
                    Response.Write("<var name = ""uname""
expr = """ & (username) & """  />")
                        Response.Write("<var name = ""date""
expr = ""'" & (ctdate) & "'""  />")
                    Response.Write("<var name = ""item""
expr = ""'" & (selitem) & "'""  />")
                Response.Write("<submit next=""http://localhost/
order.asp"" method=""get""
namelist="" uname date item number price""/>" )
       Response.Write("<else/>")
                    Response.Write("<submit
next=""http://localhost/shopping.asp#exit"" />" )
            Response.Write("</if >")
            Response.Write("</filled>")
       Response.Write("</field>")
            Response.Write("</form>")
       %>
</vxml>
```

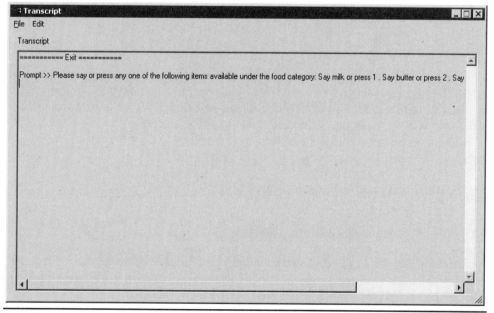

Figure 12-5   *Output of items.asp*

In the first few lines of code, we access the information the query string holds and store this information in two variables named "uname" and "selitem" for later use.

Following this, we build a VoiceXML form for collecting the quantity of the item required by the user. Once this information is received, we store the quantity and the price, respectively, in the two variables "number" and "price." The code snippet for achieving this task is as follows:

```
    <%
Dim con, rs, rs1
Dim price, quantity,ctdate
ctdate= now()
set con = Server.CreateObject("ADODB.Connection")
con.open ("shop")
set rs = con.Execute("SELECT name,price FROM item
WHERE name='" & selitem & "'AND availables='yes'")
    Response.Write("<form id=""  " & rs("name") & " "">")
                Response.Write("<field name = ""confirm"" type =""number"">")
                    Response.Write("<prompt>Please say the
quantity of " & (selitem) & "   </prompt>")
                            Response.Write("<filled>")
                                    Response.Write("<assign
name = ""document.number"" expr = ""confirm""  />")
        Response.Write("<assign name = ""document.price""
expr = "" " & rs("price") &" ""  />")
                            Response.Write("<submit
next=""#final"" method= ""get"" namelist=""number price""/>" )
        Response.Write("</filled>")
                Response.Write("</field>")
    Response.Write("</form>")
rs.close
    %>
```

After collecting all the required information from the user, we call the next form, named "final." In this form, we first retrieve the user's name and address from the customer table on the basis of the user id furnished. We also compute the total cost for the order by using the script written in the beginning of the document.

After retrieving the records from the database, we present to the user detailed information regarding the order. This information includes the following items:

▶ Quantity and name of the ordered item

▶ Total cost of order

▶ Address of delivery based on our database

After informing the user of these details, we query the user to confirm the order. If the user confirms the order by saying "yes," we store all available information in different variables and call the next file named order.asp to pass all the information to it.

If the user discards the order, we simply terminate the application. The VoiceXML output generated by confirm.asp is shown in Listing 12-8.

Listing 12-8:   *Output of confirm.asp*

```
<?xml version = "1.0"?>
<vxml version = "1.0">
      <var name = "number" />
      <var name = "price" />
      <script>
            <![CDATA[
function multiply(n)
{
return number * n;
}
]]>
      </script>
      <form id = "milk">
            <field name = "confirm" type = "number">
                  <prompt>
                        Please say the quantity of milk
                  </prompt>
                  <filled>
                        <assign expr = "confirm" name = "document.number" />
                        <assign expr = " 10 " name = "document.price" />
                        <submit next = "#final" method = "get" namelist = "number
price" />
                  </filled>
            </field>
      </form>
      <form id = "final">
            <field name = "select" type = "boolean">
                  <prompt>
                        You have ordered
                        <value expr = "number" />
                        quantities of  milk
                  </prompt>
                  <prompt>
                        The total cost is
                        <value expr = "multiply(price)" />
                  </prompt>
                  <prompt>
                        The order will be shipped to the following address:
                  </prompt>
                  <prompt>
                        Jytosna Gupta 19 A , ansari road 22
                  </prompt>
```

```
                    <prompt>
                        Say yes to confirm the order, otherwise say no
                    </prompt>
                    <filled>
                        <if cond = "select==true">
                            <var expr = "22" name = "uname" />
                            <var expr = "'5/7/2002 2:53:23 PM'" name = "date" />
                            <var expr = "'milk'" name = "item" />
                            <submit next = "http://localhost/order.asp" method =
"get" namelist = "uname date item number price" />
                            <else />
                            <submit next = "http://localhost/shopping.asp#exit"
/>
                        </if>
                    </filled>
                </field>
        </form>
</vxml>
```

Figure 12-6 shows the output of confirm.asp in a simulated environment.

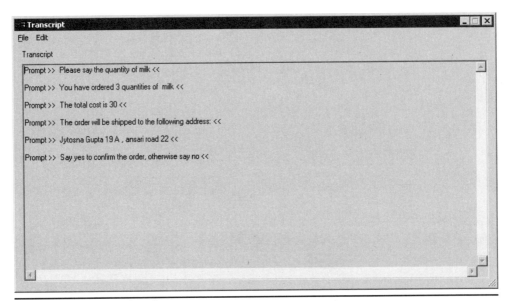

Figure 12-6   *Output of confirm.asp*

Updating Records and Terminating the Application

The code for order.asp, shown in Listing 12-9, represents the final stage of our application. Here, we update our records by inserting the transaction records into the database and then terminate the application.

Listing 12-9: *Source Code for order.asp*

```
<%@LANGUAGE=VBSCRIPT %>
<%
dim item,uname, ctdate, number,price,cost
uname = trim(Request.QueryString("uname"))
ctdate = trim(Request.QueryString("date"))
item = trim(Request.QueryString("item"))
number = trim(Request.QueryString("number"))
price = trim(Request.QueryString("price"))
Response.ContentType = "text/xml"
Response.Write("<?xml version= ""1.0""?>")
%>
<vxml version="1.0">
        <%
         cost = price * number
      Dim con, rs
      set con = Server.CreateObject("ADODB.Connection")
      con.open ("shop")
      Response.Write("<form id=""insert"">")
            Response.Write("<block>")
            Response.Write("<prompt>Updating records </prompt>")
      set rs= con.Execute("INSERT INTO orders (cost, item, quantity,
userid, orderdate) VALUES ('" & cost &"', '" & item &"',
 '" & number &"','" & uname &"','" & ctdate &"')")
            Response.Write("<submit next=""http://localhost/
shopping.asp#exit"" />" )
            Response.Write("</block>")
            Response.Write("</form>")
      %>
</vxml>
```

As evident from the code, we first store all the received information in the variables and then start building the VoiceXML code.

In the next phase, we include an SQL statement to insert all the available information in the orders table, as listed here:

► User ID

► Date of order

► Item

► Quantity

► Total cost of order

After inserting all the information in the table, we terminate the application and end the session with the user. The VoiceXML output of order.asp is shown in Listing 12-10.

Listing 12-10: *Output of order.asp*

```
<?xml version = "1.0"?>
<vxml version = "1.0">
      <form id = "insert">
            <block>
                  <prompt>
                        Updating records
                  </prompt>
                  <submit next = "http://localhost/shopping.asp#exit" />
            </block>
      </form>
</vxml>
```

Figure 12-7 shows the output generated by order.asp when executed in a simulator.

Summary

In this chapter, we developed a voice-based application that uses ASP. The application, called the Voice Store application, served to illustrate the use of ASP pages in complex procedures such as generating dynamic forms and menus in voice-based applications.

We first outlined the working scheme of the proposed application. Subsequently, we showed you the home page options. We then explained the workings of the login section and how the code meets our design goals. You saw the processes of user authentication and building the category section with details on how the code generates forms dynamically. After this, we discussed the next stage of the application, detailing the code for the tasks of building the items list and confirming the order. The chapter concluded with a brief account of how the application is terminated.

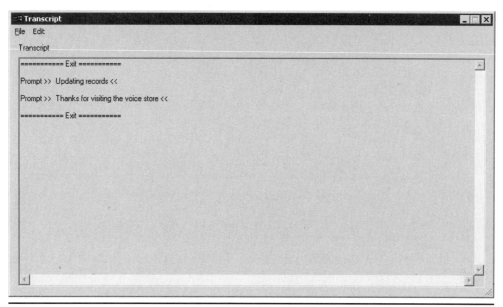

Figure 12-7   *Output of order.asp*

CHAPTER 3

Developing Voice Applications with SALT

I n this chapter, we present the details of one more technology for building voice applications: *Speech Application Language Tags* (SALT). The SALT Forum, the committee formed for evolving the technology, has just completed the formulation of the techniques involved in SALT, and the first working draft of the proposed technology was released in February 2002. Developers can use this technology to extend the capabilities of current web markup languages such as HTML and build complete voice-based applications. This chapter equips you with enough know-how of the techniques involved in SALT, based on the first working draft release, to provide you with a platform for developing applications using this technology.

Introduction to SALT

By now, the potential of web technology has been exploited almost fully, and the development of web-based applications has given way to enthusiastic, yet systematic efforts to evolve new media for communication in general and business communication in particular. For over two decades, extensive and easily accessible systems for customer support have come to be seen as a key component for successful business. In developing the infrastructure for customer support, companies and corporate groups mostly bank upon voice-based applications that use IVR systems. Ever since the IVR system was conceived, a growing number of companies are setting up their own IVRS systems for providing facilities such as customer support centers.

In this book, we have already discussed the suitability of VoiceXML for building large-scale, voice-based applications, as well as the possibilities offered by the Web Telephony Engine for building multifeatured voice applications. As already mentioned, VoiceXML was introduced by a committee formed by several major companies engaged in the field of information technology, and this committee, in association with the World Wide Web (W3C) consortium, brought about the standardization of the language. The Web Telephony Engine, on the other hand, evolved from a scheme of Microsoft's for integrating the various technologies launched by that company on a single platform. This tool can be run on the Windows platform to extend the various HTML elements so as to render them in audible format.

For building voice applications using VoiceXML, you need to learn a completely new set of languages such as VoiceXML, CCXML, and SSML. This proves to be a time-consuming task as far as legacy web developers are concerned. In 2001, several leading software and hardware companies such as Cisco, Intel, Microsoft, Comverse, SpeechWorks, and Philips organized a committee called the SALT Forum to formulate another language that could be used for developing multimodel voice-based applications by extending HTML and XHTML elements. This language was also intended to support various platforms and other markup languages such as SMIL for enabling the inclusion of enhanced features in voice applications. The committee succeeded in the venture, and this marked the beginning of a new era for voice application developers in that they could now develop applications using the language of their choice and were no longer restricted to using any single language.

In March 2002, the SALT Forum released the first working draft for SALT that presents a vivid and comprehensive outline of the features of the proposed language. SALT employs a set of XML-based basic elements that have attributes and some Document Object Model

(DOM) properties and methods. SALT is equally effective for building applications with the voice-only interface (telephony based) and those of the multimodel structure (that is, having both telephony and visual media interface) by extending the HTML and XHTML elements. In developing the specifications for SALT, the forum observed a set of basic designing principles, which are detailed in the following section.

Designing Principles of SALT

In developing the SALT language, the SALT Forum adhered to certain judiciously worked-out designing principles. That SALT realizes easy development of voice applications and supports a multimodel structure for developing applications may be attributed to these principles. The core designing principles observed while evolving SALT are as follows:

► SALT proposes to provide clean and easy integration with the existing web page-based visual applications so that web developers can continue to apply their skills and the content available on web sites continues to be of use.

► SALT does not extend any markup language directly; it provides a speech interface as a separate layer that is extensible across the markup languages. This serves to separate business logic from the speech interface.

► SALT proposes to provide powerful control over the dialog execution process by using DOM. As most web developers are already familiar with the concept of DOM, the development of voice applications with SALT should be easy for them.

► SALT intends to facilitate developing applications that can cater to a large number of devices by supporting the multimodel architecture. For example, a PC having the capabilities of a voice browser should be able to access the SALT application by using speech recognition and speech synthesis processes. At the same time, PDA devices with visual browsers should also be able to access SALT applications by rendering them visually.

► SALT applications address a wide range of clients including desktop PCs, mobile phones, ordinary telephones, and PDA devices.

Overview of SALT Elements

For developing applications, the SALT Forum introduces three main top-level elements, each containing some subelements. The three top-level elements in SALT are as follows:

► The <listen> element for speech input

► The <dtmf> element for DTMF-based input

► The <prompt> element for speech output

All the functionality related to speech input and output of an application is controlled by these elements, which are equipped with various attributes and properties for the purpose. In the next section, we discuss the speech input process in SALT.

Getting Speech Input in SALT

In SALT applications, the <listen> element is a top-level element used for the purpose of natural speech recognition. The <listen> element contains various sublevel elements, such as <grammar> and <bind>, that can be used to enhance the speech input collection capability of an application. This element also contains various methods for controlling the process of speech input collection efficiently. In the sections that follow, we discuss some of the sublevel elements of the <listen> element.

The <grammar> Element

The <grammar> element specifies a set of acceptable words and phrases while collecting input from the user. Documents can use either inline grammars or external grammars, which are referenced through the src attribute of the <grammar> element. While using inline grammars, you may employ any of the text-based grammar formats such as the W3C speech recognition grammar format.

To render SALT applications interoperable, the SALT Forum retains existing standards for various purposes, such as those for writing the grammars for applications. Similarly, one can use the speech recognition grammar format introduced by W3C in developing voice applications in SALT. The SALT browser is also capable of supporting any other grammar format. The attributes of the <grammar> element are described in Table 13-1.

The following code snippet shows the schema for defining external grammars in SALT applications.

```
<salt:grammar src="http://www.dreamtechsoftware.com/salt/grammars/
main.xml" type="application/srgs+xml" />
```

If you specify the src attribute while working with inline grammars, it will generate an invalid document error during execution. You can define the grammars inline in your SALT documents by using the schema shown in the following code snippet:

```
<salt:grammar xmlns="http://www.w3.org/2001/06/grammar">
<grammar>
<rule name="main">
<oneof>
<item> Toys </grxml:item>
<item> Food </grxml:item>
<item> Cloths </grxml:item>
</oneof>
</rule>
</grammar>
</salt:grammar>
```

Attribute	Description	Optional
name	Defines the name of a grammar in the form of a string. The name can be used for the activation and deactivation of the grammar in case there are multiple grammars within the same <listen> element.	Yes
src	Defines the URI of the grammar file in case external grammars are used.	Yes
type	Defines the MIME type of the grammar in case external grammars are used.	Yes
xmlns	Defines the namespace and the schema of the grammar format in the form of XML standard namespacing syntax. This attribute is used with inline grammars.	Yes
xml:lang	Defines the language type for which grammars are used, such as U.S. English if the user input is expected to be in U.S. English format.	Yes

Table 13-1   *Attributes of the <grammar> Element*

The <bind> Element

The <bind> element is a child-level element of the <listen> element. This element binds values collected as spoken input from a user to page elements, and then processes the spoken input to generate a result. This result comes in the form of an XML document, often containing a semantic markup language, such as Natural Language Semantic Markup Language (NLSML) for specifying the result of the recognition process, or an alternate scheme, such as the N-best recognition result scheme to grade or validate the result of the recognition process. It has been proposed that all SALT browsers support the NLSML format introduced by the W3C. The SALT browsers can also support other semantic markup languages for enhanced functionality.

The attributes of the <bind> element are described in Table 13-2.

Attribute	Description	Optional
targetelement	Defines the name of the target element to which the values collected from the user input are to be assigned.	No
targetattribute	Defines the name of the target attribute to which the values collected from the user input are to be assigned.	Yes
targetmethod	Defines the name of the method of the target element that will be called if the binding operation is executed.	Yes
value	Defines an XAPTH string that specifies the value to be assigned to targetelement or targetattribute.	No
test	Defines an XPATH string that specifies a condition the execution of the binding operation may be subject to.	Yes

Table 13-2   *Attributes of the <bind> Element*

Let's consider a series of code snippets that clarify the working of the <bind> element. In these examples, we assume that the user is interacting with a voice application for ordering food from a restaurant. The spoken input received from the user is shown here:

```
I'd like to have one classic pizza.
```

Upon receiving the spoken input from the user, the system parses the input and produces the result as an XML document in NLSML format, as shown in Listing 13-1.

Listing 13-1:   *Resulting NLSML Document*

```
<result grammar="http://www.dreamtechsoftware.com/salt/
examples/" xmlns:xf="http://www.w3.org/2000/xforms">
<interpretation confidence="0.3">
          <input mode="speech">
               I'd like to have one classic pizza.
          </input>
          <xf:instance>
               <foodshop>
               <order_qty confidence="0.47">one</order_qty>
               <item_category confidence="0.40">classic</item_category>
               <item_name confidence="0.42">pizza</item_name>
               </foodshop>
          </xf:instance>
     </interpretation>
</result>
```

Now the resulting XML document is used with the <bind> element to assign the values to the elements residing on the page. Listing 13-2 shows a SALT document that uses the <bind> element with the targetelement attribute for the binding operation.

Listing 13-2:   *SALT Document Containing the Binding Operation*

```
<xhtml xmlns:salt="urn:schemas.saltforum.org/2002/02/SALT">
     <form id="restaurant">
          <input name="quantity" type="text"/>
          <input name="category" type="text" />
          <input name="item" type="text" />
     </form>
<salt:listen id="foodorder">
     <salt:grammar src="http://www.dreamtechsoftware.com/salt/examples/
grammars/restaurant.xml" />
```

```
            <salt:bind targetelement="quantity" value="//order_qty" />
        <salt:bind targetelement="category" value="//item_category" />
        <salt:bind targetelement="item" value="//item_name" />
</salt:listen>
</xhtml>
```

You can also subject the binding process to some conditions. For example, you may specify that the binding operation be performed only when the confidence level of an Item category is greater than 0.45. The code in Listing 13-3 subjects the binding process to such a condition.

Listing 13-3:   *SALT Document Containing Conditional Binding Operation*

```
<xhtml xmlns:salt="urn:schemas.saltforum.org/2002/02/SALT">
     <form id="restaurant">
          <input name="quantity" type="text"/>
          <input name="category" type="text" />
          <input name="item" type="text" />
     </form>
<salt:listen id="foodorder">
     <salt:grammar src="http://www.dreamtechsoftware.com/salt/examples/
grammars/restaurant.xml" />
     <salt:bind targetelement="quantity" value="//order_qty" />
     <salt:bind targetelement="item"
value="//item_category" test="//item_category[@confidence &gt; 0.45]" />
     <salt:bind targetelement="item" value="//item_name" />
</salt:listen>
</xhtml>
```

The <bind> element is used for simple processing tasks. For performing complex tasks, the Document Object Model implemented by SALT browsers is preferable.

The <param> Element

The <param> element is used to pass information regarding the platform setting to the implementing platform as parameters. The <param> element contains the two attributes described here:

Attribute	Description	Optional
name	Defines the name of the parameter.	No
xmlns	Defines the namespace for the XML content residing in the parameter.	Yes

Using <listen> Attributes and Properties

SALT applications can also make use of the attributes and properties of the <listen> element. It is assumed that all SALT browsers should support the attributes of the <listen> element, which are described in Table 13-3.

You can also use the properties associated with the <listen> element, in building applications:

Property	Description	Type
recoresult	Holds the result of recognition. If nothing is recognized, the return is empty.	Read-only
text	Holds the string containing the text of words recognized by the recognition process.	Read-only
status	Contains the status code returned by the recognition platform.	Read-only

Events Supported by the <listen> Object

The <listen> DOM object also supports some events for handling the listening process efficiently. Table 13-4 describes all the events supported by the <listen> element.

Different Recognition Modes of the <listen> Element

SALT applications permit using the <listen> element in three modes for the purpose of speech recognition. The three modes listed here are explained in the sections that follow.

► Automatic mode

► Single mode

► Multiple mode

Attribute	Description	Optional
initialtimeout	Defines the time limit between the start of the recognition process and speech detection in milliseconds. If this attribute isn't specified, the system uses the default value.	Yes
babbletimeout	Defines the maximum time within which user utterance is to be obtained.	Yes
maxtimeout	Defines the timeout period between the start of the recognition process and return of results to the browser.	Yes
endsilence	Defines the time period of silence after which the results of recognition are returned to the browser.	Yes
reject	Defines the recognition rejection threshold. If the recognition level is below the value defined for the system, the system throws the onnoreco event.	Yes
xml:lang	Defines the language the system may assume for user speech while attempting to recognize it. If not specified, the system uses the default value.	Yes
mode	Defines the mode of listening operation. If not defined, the system uses the automatic mode.	Yes

Table 13-3   *Attributes of the <listen> Element*

Event	Description
onreco	Is fired after the system completes the recognition process successfully and the results are made available for the browser. This event enables programmatic analysis of recognition results.
onsilence	Is fired if the system isn't able to detect any speech within the time limit defined by the initialtimeout attribute.
onspeechdetected	Is fired upon detection of speech by the recognizer. The actual time for firing this event varies with different platforms. In some cases, it can be configured by using the <param> element.
onnoreco	Is fired when the recognizer isn't able to return the complete recognition result to the browser.
onaudiointerrupt	Is fired when the communication channel with the user is lost; for example, when the line with the user is disconnected. The execution of this event stops the recognition process and the recognition results collected thus far are returned to the browser.
onerror	Is fired if a serious error occurs during the recognition process.

Table 13-4   *Events Associated with the <listen> Object*

Automatic Mode

In SALT applications, *automatic mode* is preferred when client devices are telephony based or when speech recognition is hands free. In automatic mode, the system itself handles the execution and termination of the listening process. The application need not handle these events explicitly. The system will collect the spoken input, detect the completion of user speech by using the endsilence attribute, and stop the speech recognition process. The schema shown in the code snippet that follows defines automatic mode:

```
<listen mode="automatic" >
```

Single Mode

Single mode is used in situations where you need to control execution and stop the process explicitly within the application, as in a "push-to-talk" environment, for example. In single mode, the recognition result is returned only upon receiving an explicit stop call from the application. Single mode may be defined by using the schema shown in this code snippet:

```
<listen mode="single" >
```

Multiple Mode

In *multiple mode*, recognition results are returned to the browser in regular intervals of time. This mode suits such situations as when input is in the form of a dictation, with silence occurring between two phrases spoken by the user. The recognition process continues until the application generates an explicit stop call. Multiple mode may be defined by using the following schema:

```
<listen mode="multiple" >
```

Recording with the <listen> Element

In SALT applications, recording operations may be performed by using the <record> element as in VoiceXML applications. The <child> element of the <record> element performs recording operations. This element may be used with most of the attributes, properties, events, and methods associated with the <listen> element, as well as with some additional ones. You can include only one <record> element in a single <listen> element. The attributes of the <record> element are as follows:

Attribute	Description	Optional
type	Defines the type for saving the recorded audio. If not specified, the default format, Wave, is used. The availability of recording formats varies with different platforms.	Yes
beep	Indicates a Boolean value. If TRUE, the system will play a beep before the recording process begins. The default value is FALSE.	Yes

Some additional attributes have been included in the <bind> element that enhance the <record> element's capabilities:

Attribute	Description
recordlocation	Defines the URI of the location of the recorded audio.
recordtype	Defines the type of the record audio format.
recordduration	Defines the duration of the recorded audio in milliseconds.
recordsize	Defines the size of the recorded audio in bytes.

The properties listed here manage the result returned by the recording process:

Property	Description	Type
recordlocation	Contains the URI of the location of the recorded audio.	Read-only
recordtype	Contains the type of the record audio format.	Read-only
recordduration	Contains the length of the recorded audio in milliseconds.	Read-only
recordsize	Contains the size of the recorded audio in bytes.	Read-only

Using DTMF Input in SALT

In this section, we consider the next top-level element in SALT, the <dtmf> element, which is used to specify the possible DTMF inputs and how the application deals with them. The <dtmf> element also contains the <grammar> and the <bind> elements used with the <listen> element. In addition, the object model of the <dtmf> element exposes various properties and methods that it can use.

Using the <grammar> Element with <dtmf>

The <grammar> element used with DTMF-based input differs from its counterparts in speech grammars in one regard. In DTMF input grammars, this element contains the list of acceptable DTMF keys instead of words and phrases. The use of the xml:lang attribute serves no purpose in DTMF grammars, as they define the acceptable input as DTMF keys.

Using the < bind> Element with <dtmf>

The <bind> element is a child-level element of the <dtmf> element. This element binds the values collected as key presses from the user into page elements and processes the result of spoken input. This result is generated in the form of an XML document, which most often contains a semantic markup language for specifying the recognition result.

Using <dtmf> Attributes and Properties

You can also use attributes and properties with the <dtmf> element. Table 13-5 describes all the attributes that can be used with the <dtmf> element.

You can also use the following properties in association with the <dtmf> element:

Property	Description	Type
dtmfresult	Holds the DTMF values. The values are updated at the end of DTMF collection when the XML document containing the semantic markup is returned.	Read-only
text	Holds the string containing the list of keys pressed by the user during the recognition process. The values are appended to the string on every key press event.	Read-only
status	Contains the status code returned by the DTMF collector.	Read-only

In addition to these properties, the DTMF object also exposes some methods to control the processing. By using these methods, the browser is able to start, stop, and flush DTMF objects. All the following methods are exposed by the DTMF object:

Object	Description
start	Starts the DTMF collection.
stop	Stops the DTMF collection and returns the collection results to the browser.
flush	Flushes the DTMF buffer. If this method is called after the DTMF object is started, there is no effect.

Attribute	Description	Optional
initialtimeout	Defines the time limit between the start of recognition and speech detection in milliseconds. If this attribute isn't specified, the system uses the default value.	Yes
endsilence	Defines the period of silence after which the result of the recognition process is returned to the browser.	Yes
interdigittimeout	Defines the timeout period between the DTMF keystrokes in milliseconds. If the period exceeds the defined value, the system throws an onnoreco event.	Yes
flush	Indicates a Boolean value to determine whether to flush the DTMF buffer or not.	Yes

Table 13-5   *Attributes of the <dtmf> Element*

Events Supported by the DTMF Object

The <dtmf> DOM object also supports certain events for managing the DTMF collection process efficiently. Table 13-6 describes all the events supported by the <dtmf> element.

This completes our discussion on the speech input techniques used in SALT applications. We next move on to the speech output techniques in SALT. The third element among the top-level elements in SALT, <prompt>, is used for this purpose.

Event	Description
onkeypress	Is fired every time the user presses a DTMF key. The value of the DTMF key is appended in the text attribute of the <dtmf> element.
onreco	Is fired after the system completes the DTMF recognition process successfully. This event stops the execution of the DTMF object and updates the dtmfresult property with the results.
onsilence	Is fired if the system isn't able to detect any DTMF value within the time limit defined by the initialtimeout attribute, resulting in halting the execution of the DTMF object.
onnoreco	Is fired when a nonacceptable DTMF key is pressed, which violates the grammar rules, or when the limit defined by the interdigittimeout is exceeded. This event stops the execution of the DTMF object and updates the dtmfresult property with the result.
onaudiointerrupt	Is fired when the communication channel with the user is lost—for example, when the line with the user is disconnected. As the default action, this event stops the execution of the DTMF object, updates the dtmfresult property, and flushes the DTMF buffer.
onerror	Is fired if a serious error occurs during the DTMF recognition or collection process.

Table 13-6   *Events Associated with the <dtmf> Object*

Speech Output in SALT

Assuming you've read through the preceding chapters, you are already familiar with the <prompt> element of VoiceXML, which is used for handling speech output in VoiceXML applications. For SALT applications as well, the <prompt> element controls all tasks related to the speech output process. In SALT applications, prompts are queued and played by using the prompt queue object. The <prompt> element holds the following content:

▶ Inline or referenced text associated with the speech output information

▶ Variables, the values of which are retrieved at the time of rendering

▶ Reference to the audio files

Producing Simple Speech Output

The <prompt> element enables developers to include text in an application. This text can be transformed to an audible form at the time of rendering, as shown in the following code snippet.

```
<prompt id="main">
Welcome to the Voice Bank.
</prompt>
```

To improve the quality of speech output, SALT allows developers to use the elements of any speech synthesis markup language. However, as already mentioned, it has been proposed that all SALT browsers support the Synthesized Speech Markup Language (SSML) introduced by W3C. Developers can work with the elements of SSML, such as <prosodic>, to improve the quality of speech output.

Using the <content> Element with <prompt>

The <content> element may be used to include the reference of external contents in a document at the time of rendering the document. By using the <content> element as shown in the code snippet that follows, you can add references to external content such as dynamically generated text or links to audio files that reside on the server.

```
<prompt>
     Welcome to Voice Bank.
     <content href="http://www.dreamtechsoftware.com/salt/examples/
wave/mainmenu.wav" />
</prompt>
```

Attribute	Description	Optional
href	Defines the URI referencing the audio file or external content.	No
yype	Defines the MIME type for external content.	Yes

Using the <param> Element with <prompt>

The <param> element configures the additions or the nonstandard settings of the prompt engine. The <param> element works as a child element of the <prompt> element. Here are the two attributes you would use with <param>:

Attribute	Description	Optional
name	Defines the name of the parameter to be configured.	No
xmlns	Defines the namespace for the XML content residing in the parameter.	Yes

The <prompt> element also has some associated attributes and properties that provide for enhanced control over the behavior of the element. Table 13-7 describes the attributes of the <prompt> element.

The following properties are supported by the <prompt> element:

Property	Description	Type
bookmark	Contains the last bookmark encountered.	Read-only
status	Contains the status code returned by the speech platform.	Read-only

In addition to these properties, various methods of the prompt object can be used for controlling prompt queuing and starting. All the methods exposed by the prompt object are described here:

Method	Description
start	Queues the prompts in the prompt queue and starts the playback of prompts immediately.
queue	Queues the prompts in the prompt queue.

Attribute	Description	Optional
bargein	Indicates a Boolean type value for stopping the prompt playback when the user input is detected. If the value is TRUE, the playback of the prompt is stopped. When a DTMF input is received from the user, the prompt queue is flushed. If the value is FALSE, the detection of DTMF input has no effect on the prompt playback. If this attribute isn't specified, the default value, TRUE, is used.	Yes
prefetch	Indicates a Boolean type value. If the value is TRUE, the platform may fetch, if possible, external prompt content that is expected to be lengthy or requires large download time. The default value is FALSE.	Yes
xmlns	Defines the namespace and the schema of the inline prompt contents in the form of XML standard namespacing syntax.	Yes
xml:lang	Defines the language type for which grammars are used, such as U.S. English if the prompt content is expected to be in U.S. English format.	Yes

Table 13-7   *Attributes of the <prompt> Element*

Events Supported by the Prompt Object

The prompt object also supports some events for handling the process efficiently. These event handlers may be specified as attributes of the <prompt> element. Following are all the events supported by the prompt object:

Event	Description
onbookmark	Is fired when the system encounters a bookmark.
onbargein	Is fired when a DTMF input is received from the user while playing back the prompt.
oncomplete	Is fired when the playback of a prompt is completed successfully without any error.
onerror	Is fired if a serious error occurs during the prompt playback process.

Promptqueue Object

In SALT applications, the promptqueue object is a browser-level object that is responsible for controlling the playback operations of prompts. The sole property available with the promptqueue object is the status property, as described here:

Property	Description	Type
status	Contains the status code returned by the speech platform. The value 0 indicates successful completion of prompt playback, whereas a negative value indicates an error in the prompt playback process.	Read-only

The methods exposed by the promptqueue object are listed in Table 13-8.

Method	Description
start	Starts the playback of prompts queued in the prompt queue. After playing back the last available prompt, the application throws an onempty event to the promptqueue object.
pause	Pauses the current playback without clearing the audio buffer.
resume	Resumes the playback without flushing the audio buffer.
stop	Resumes the playback and flushes the entire audio buffer.
change	Changes the speed and volume of playback.

Table 13-8   *Methods Exposed by the Promptqueue Object*

The promptqueue object also supports some events for efficiently handling the processes associated with it. The events supported by the promptqueue object are as follows:

Event	Description
onempty	Is fired when the playback of all the queued prompts is over and the queue is empty.
onaudiointerrupt	Is fired when the communication channel with the user is lost, such as when the line with the user is disconnected. The execution of this event stops the current playback and flushes the prompt queue.
onerror	Is fired if a serious error occurs during the synthesis process, as a result of which the playback is stopped.

Summary

This chapter provided the technical details of Speech Application Language Tags (SALT), one of the latest technologies for building multifeatured voice applications by extending HTML and XHTML elements. We discussed SALT with reference to the first working draft of the technology released by the SALT Forum. We analyzed the main features of SALT beginning from the design guidelines adopted by developers for formulating a powerful language capable of creating multifeatured voice applications.

We looked at the three top-level SALT elements at length with emphasis on how these may be used for processing input- and output-related parameters. We showed you the various methods, events, and properties that can be associated with this element for managing spoken input and explained the three modes for this element. You learned about the second top-level element, <dtmf>, its subelements, and the properties, events, and methods associated with it and some of its uses. You also learned about the third top-level element, <prompt>, which is used for controlling output.

The coverage on SALT offered by this chapter will suffice to give you a clear understanding of this nascent technology, one that is bound to find immense favor with the developers of voice-based applications.

Index

Complete References

Herbert Schildt
0-07-213485-2

Jeffery R. Shapiro
0-07-213381-3

Chris H. Pappas & William
H. Murray, III
0-07-212958-1

Herbert Schildt
0-07-213084-9

Ron Ben-Natan & Ori Sasson
0-07-222394-4

Arthur Griffith
0-07-222405-3

For the answers to everything related to your technology, drill as deeply as you please into our Complete Reference series. Written by topical authorities, these comprehensive resources offer a full range of knowledge, including extensive product information, theory, step-by-step tutorials, sample projects, and helpful appendixes.

OSBORNE
www.osborne.com

For more information on these and other Osborne books, visit our Web site at www.osborne.com

INTERNATIONAL CONTACT INFORMATION

AUSTRALIA
McGraw-Hill Book Company Australia Pty. Ltd.
TEL +61-2-9417-9899
FAX +61-2-9417-5687
http://www.mcgraw-hill.com.au
books-it_sydney@mcgraw-hill.com

CANADA
McGraw-Hill Ryerson Ltd.
TEL +905-430-5000
FAX +905-430-5020
http://www.mcgrawhill.ca

GREECE, MIDDLE EAST,
NORTHERN AFRICA
McGraw-Hill Hellas
TEL +30-1-656-0990-3-4
FAX +30-1-654-5525

MEXICO (Also serving Latin America)
McGraw-Hill Interamericana Editores S.A. de C.V.
TEL +525-117-1583
FAX +525-117-1589
http://www.mcgraw-hill.com.mx
fernando_castellanos@mcgraw-hill.com

SINGAPORE (Serving Asia)
McGraw-Hill Book Company
TEL +65-863-1580
FAX +65-862-3354
http://www.mcgraw-hill.com.sg
mghasia@mcgraw-hill.com

SOUTH AFRICA
McGraw-Hill South Africa
TEL +27-11-622-7512
FAX +27-11-622-9045
robyn_swanepoel@mcgraw-hill.com

UNITED KINGDOM & EUROPE
(Excluding Southern Europe)
McGraw-Hill Education Europe
TEL +44-1-628-502500
FAX +44-1-628-770224
http://www.mcgraw-hill.co.uk
computing_neurope@mcgraw-hill.com

ALL OTHER INQUIRIES Contact:
Osborne/McGraw-Hill
TEL +1-510-549-6600
FAX +1-510-883-7600
http://www.osborne.com
omg_international@mcgraw-hill.com